ROMANS

An Interpretive Outline

ROMANS
An Interpretive Outline

A Study Manual of Romans, Including a
Series of Interpretive Notes and Charts
on the Major Doctrines of the Epistle

by

DAVID N. STEELE
CURTIS C. THOMAS

Authors of

The Five Points of Calvinism:
Defined, Defended, Documented

Preface by

GORDON H. CLARK, PH. D.
Professor and Chairman, Dept. of Philosophy,
Butler University

PRESBYTERIAN AND REFORMED PUBLISHING CO.
PHILLIPSBURG, NEW JERSEY

Copyright, 1963

By The Presbyterian and Reformed Publishing Co.

Philadelphia, Pa.

First Edition _____ 1963
Reprinted _____ 1967

Also translated and printed in Chinese in 1966 by
The Reformation Translation Fellowship

ISBN: 0-87552-443-5

Library of Congress Catalog Card Number 63-21694

Printed in the United States of America

Affectionately dedicated

to our wives

RUTH and BETTY

without whose help, encouragement,
and patience this work could not have
been written.

PERMISSION TO QUOTE

ACKNOWLEDGMENTS

We wish to express our thanks to Loraine Boettner, Gordon H. Clark, Floyd Hamilton, and J. G. Vos for their willingness to read the manuscript, for their many helpful suggestions, and most of all, for the encouragement which they extended to us to publish the work. We are especially grateful to Charles H. Craig, director of The Presbyterian and Reformed Publishing Company, for undertaking the task of publication. We also want to acknowledge our indebtedness to our many other friends who did so much to assist us in preparing this material.

ABBREVIATIONS

ANT   *The Amplified New Testament* (1958)

The words inserted within the square brackets [ ] found throughout this translation indicate clarifying words or comments not actually expressed in the immediate Greek text.

ASV   *American Standard Version (American Revised Version* of 1901*)*

BV   *The Berkeley Version of the Bible in Modern English* (1954-1959)

cf.   compare

e.g.   for example

fn.   footnote

f., ff.   following verse (s) or page (s)

Gr.   Greek

i.e.   that is

NEB   *New English Bible* (1961)

NT   New Testament

OT   Old Testament

RSV   *Revised Standard Version* (1946-1952)

viz.   namely

WT   *The New Testament in the Language of the People,* by Charles B. Williams (1937)

CONTENTS

PLAN OF THE STUDY

INTERPRETIVE OUTLINE OF ROMANS

PART ONE:

JUSTIFICATION BY FAITH AND ITS CONSEQUENCES   Chs. 1-8

ix

CONTENTS—(Continued)

List of Illustrations and Diagrams

PREFACE

This second half of the twentieth century is an age of depression—not financial depression, but spiritual depression. Ecclesiastically there is wide-spread apostacy. The great bulk of religious literature published by, recommended by, or circulated in the major denominations undermines or overtly attacks the truthfulness of God's Word, the Bible. This is easily accomplished, for spot checks indicate that most church members have very little Biblical knowledge to undermine and do not much care whether the Bible is true or not.

Outside the visible Church, and this comprises at least half of the population of the United States, there is not only towering indifference to divine truth, but there are also organized groups who try to eradicate all ideas of God from our national life. They aim to use the government to suppress Christianity.

On the other end of the spectrum are the small denominations and independent congregations which adhere to the Bible as their standard. They are not completely illiterate in Biblical matters as the others are; but their level of knowledge, most unfortunately, does not equal that of the immediate followers of Luther, Calvin, and Knox, nor of the Puritans of the seventeenth century. Of course there are exceptions to the general rule: some small groups concentrate earnestly on Bible study; but by and large there is more dilute milk for babes than the strong meat needed for Christian vigor. This is an age of religious depression and spiritual debility.

For a first step to remedy this situation, apart from an intensive study of John's Gospel, there is nothing so profitable as a series of sermons or class discussions on Paul's epistle to the Romans. If any minister wants to strengthen his people, he can hardly do better than to give them a massive dose of Romans.

Someone objects that Romans is too profound, too difficult, and horrors! too theological! But theology is precisely what the world needs, because the world needs God. The object studied by theology is God, just as the object studied by botany is plant life. Now, a study of God will understandably involve difficulties. But Romans was not too difficult or too theological for the Holy Spirit to inspire Paul to send it to the Christians in Rome. These Christians were often of the lower classes of Roman society. Some were slaves; perhaps some could neither read nor write; none had graduated from an American high school. But they could and they did study the letter Paul had sent them. In view of this, the modern American ought to discard his inferiority complex.

Yes, there are difficulties. Some passages, such as Romans 5:12-21, are very difficult. But for all of that, Paul organized his material so logically that any semi-intelligent high school graduate can easily carry the outline in his head. The twentieth century Christian therefore has no excuse, for Romans is God's message to all of us.

And it is just what this debilitated age needs. Each verse is a concentrated vitamin pill designed to cure modernistic rickets.

The present book has been put together with great care by its authors. No doubt there are mistakes in it; the authors do not claim to be inspired apostles; nonetheless, with conscientious attention to detail, both of form and content, they have spared neither time nor typewriter in producing a manuscript suited to our needs. It is not a bare outline, such as mine in *The Biblical Expositor;* nor is it the immortal 716 page commentary of Charles Hodge. It is neither too long nor too short; but is just what is needed for a series of sermons or for several months of lessons in a Bible class.

There is one more point to be made about the difficulty of learning the message of Romans. A medieval story tells of a burden which gives strength to the man who lifts it, so that the heavier the burden is, the easier it is to carry it. God has imposed the burden of his Word upon us. He did not send it to a hierarchy of professional priests who stand between us and himself. God addressed the Bible to the people. But with the burden the Lord also sends the Spirit of Truth to lead us into all truth. As we read the inspired message, we can and we ought to seek illumination from the Holy Ghost. He was its original author and he is willing to help us through its difficulties.

Blind unbelief is sure to err,
And scan his work in vain.
God is his own Interpreter,
And he will make it plain.

GORDON H. CLARK

PLAN OF THE STUDY

A. *The Importance of Romans*

No other portion of Holy Scripture so completely or systematically sets forth the great doctrinal structure of the Christian faith as does Paul's letter to the Romans. Luther, in his preface to the Roman letter, wrote: "This Epistle is the chief book of the New Testament, the purest gospel. It deserves not only to be known word for word by every Christian, but to be the subject of his meditation day by day, the daily bread of his soul . . . . The more time one spends in it, the more precious it becomes and the better it appears." He spoke of it as "a light and way into the whole Scriptures, . . ." Calvin said of it "when any one understands this Epistle, he has a passage opened to him to the understanding of the whole Scriptures." Coleridge pronounced Romans "the most profound work ever written!" Meyer considered it "the greatest and richest of all the apostolic works." Godet referred to it as "the cathedral of the Christian faith" and observed that "The Reformation was undoubtedly the work of the Epistle to the Romans, as well as of that to the Galatians; and the probability is that every great spiritual revival in the church will be connected as effect and cause with a deeper understanding of this book."

The letter has not only received such praise from the Reformers and theologians of the past but Christian scholars of the present day hold it in the same high regard. Gordon H. Clark recently wrote of Romans that it is "the most profound of all the epistles, and perhaps the most important book in the Bible . . . ." Hamilton, in his recent commentary on Romans, calls it "the greatest book in the Bible." James I. Packer of England states that "there is one book in the New Testament which links up with almost everything that the Bible contains: that is the Epistle to the Romans, . . . In Romans, Paul brings together and sets out in systematic relation all the great themes of the Bible—sin, law, judgment, faith, works, grace, justification, sanctification, election, the plan of salvation, the work of Christ, the work of the Spirit, the Christian hope, the nature and life of the Church, the place of Jew and Gentile in the purpose of God, the philosophy of Church and of world history, the meaning and message of the Old Testament, the duties of Christian citizenship, the principles of personal piety and ethics. From the vantage-point given by Romans, the whole landscape of the Bible is open to view, and the broad relation of the parts to the whole becomes plain. The study of Romans is the fittest starting-point for biblical interpretation and theology."[1]

---

[1] James I. Packer, *Fundamentalism and the Word of God*, p. 106f. Should the reader entertain any doubt as to the absolute reliability and authority of the Bible as the inspired, inerrant Word of God, we recommend that Packer's work be given careful study. Also in relation to the inspiration and authority of the Holy Scriptures see D. Martyn Lloyd-Jones, *Authority*; J. N. Geldenhuys, *Supreme Authority*; Bernard Ramm, *The Pattern of Religious Authority*; B. B. Warfield, *The Inspiration and Authority of the Bible*; Ned B. Stonehouse and Paul Woolley, eds., *The Infallible Word*; Edward J. Young, *Thy Word Is Truth*; Carl F. H. Henry, ed., *Revelation and the Bible*; F. F. Bruce, *Are the New Testament Documents Reliable?*.

1

Should the Spirit of God be pleased to reveal the contents of Romans to the church of the present generation, true revival would be upon us. God would once again be exalted as the all wise, all mighty Sovereign of heaven and earth—the Originator, Director, and End of all things, the One who alone should be feared, loved, adored, worshipped, and served. The saving work of Jesus Christ, God's eternal Son, would once again be proclaimed as the only hope of salvation for lost humanity. Sinful men would be taught to see themselves as they truly are—corrupt, depraved, helpless, without strength or hope apart from the mercy of God—mercy which He sovereignly extends to the undeserving objects of His free choice. If Romans were properly understood and faithfully taught by the ministers of today, it would revolutionize modern Christendom. It would bring the church back to sound Biblical theology and true spiritual service. It would revive right thinking and result in right living.

B. *The Purpose and Organization of the Material Contained in this Study*

1. The Purpose of the Outline and the Notes

Because of the great importance of Romans, this material has been prepared to aid and encourage its study. This is not a verse by verse commentary. It is an interpretive outline designed to show the structure and argument and to give the meaning of Romans in a clear, non-technical form. Several interpretive notes on important subjects have been inserted in the Outline at the points where it was felt they would be of the most value. They are set off from the main text of the Outline. The purpose of these notes is threefold: (1) to define terms, (2) to summarize under one heading subjects that recur in different parts of the letter, and (3) to give concise statements and brief explanations of some of the leading doctrines of Romans. They have been numbered for easy cross-reference. For example, instead of saying "See second paragraph of note on Justification," we have said "See Note 1, B, p. 25." Where it was felt advisable, charts have been included for the purpose of illustration.

The study has been approached from a positive point of view. The emphasis throughout has been to try to show what Paul actually taught, not to state and refute what we consider to be unsound interpretations. For further help on interpreting this epistle, see the annotated bibliography, pp. 191,192.

2. Suggested Helps for Studying Romans

a. For those who are unable to read Greek (the language in which Romans was originally written) a translation of the letter will have to be used for its study. Since all translations have their strengths, as well as their weaknesses, we suggest that several be used. The texts of both the *Revised Standard Version* and Charles B. Williams' translation (entitled *The New Testament in the Language of the People,* hereafter referred to as WT) are given side by side, throughout the Outline. Unless otherwise indicated, all quotations within the Outline itself are from the RSV. Our use of this version is not to be construed as a blanket endorsement, for it has some defects; especially is this true in the Old Testament. Where we felt that there was a serious inaccuracy in translation, in either the RSV or WT, we pointed this out and gave what we considered to be a more satisfactory rendering of the Greek, citing authorities for doing so. We included these two translations of Romans for we felt that basically each of them gives an accurate rendering of the Greek text in clear, idiomatic English, that will be easily grasped by the average reader. Then too, we felt that the differences in the style and the choice of words used by each of these versions to translate the same Greek word or phrase would complement each other and give the reader a better insight into Paul's meaning. For a much more literal rendering of the Greek text we suggest that the *American Standard Version* of 1901 be consulted.[2] We particularly recommend that the *Amplified New Testament* be used. The *Berkeley Version* and the *New English Bible* should also prove helpful.

b. *The letter itself should be read repeatedly.*[3] If you are a beginner in Romans, much of the letter may appear unintelligible the first few times you read it, but do not let this discourage you. *Keep reading and studying* —the seemingly vague passages will soon begin to open up and yield great rewards to the *diligent* student! It was for the purpose of encouraging extensive reading and studying of Romans itself that two translations of the letter were included side by side throughout the Outline. Make it a practice to read the passage being studied at least twice in each translation before consulting the analysis of that passage presented in the Outline. In Bible study there can be no substitute for the Biblical text itself—it is the inspired Word of God—by His grace endeavor to master it!

c. Study the letter section by section in connection with the Interpretive Outline. When Paul wrote Romans he did not divide it into chapters or verses. Our present division of chapters was made in the thirteenth

---

[2] A very valuable tool for the Bible student's library is *The Cross Reference Bible*, ed., Harold E. Monser, published by Baker Book House, Grand Rapids. The text used is the ASV of 1901; the work, which contains 2,420 pages, gives many variant readings and renderings of both the OT and NT texts with topical analysis and cross references. Another useful work for getting at the literal text for those unfamiliar with Greek is *The Interlinear Greek-English New Testament*, by Rev. A. Marshall, published by Samuel Bagster and Sons Limited, 4 New Bridge Street, London EC4 (1960).

[3] Individual copies of the *Revised Standard Version* of Romans may be obtained for three cents per copy from the American Bible Society, 450 Park Avenue, New York 22, New York. *Williams' Translation* of Romans may be purchased for fifteen cents per copy from Moody Press, 820 North LaSalle St., Chicago, Illinois. While studying Romans it would be an excellent practice to carry a pocket size copy of the letter with you and read it whenever possible.

century and our present division of verses was made in 1551. These divisions were made by uninspired men and are to be treated accordingly. For a better understanding of the structure and argument of Romans we recommend the letter be studied a section at a time as divided in the Interpretive Outline—not a chapter at a time. The advantages of this method will become evident as the study progresses. For example, study Section I, "Paul's Introduction to the Letter," 1:1-15, until it is felt that this section is fairly well understood, then move on to Section II, "The Theme," 1:16,17. Follow the same procedure until all the letter is covered. When the letter is completed then start over. It will be surprising how much more will be gained the second and third times through!

d. Work systematically. Set aside some definite time each day to be devoted to this study. Remember, there is no effortless way to learn anything. Therefore, the study should be approached with the intention of putting forth real mental effort. The beginner should expect to spend several months if he really intends to comprehend the material. But keep in mind Luther's words about the importance of this letter: "It deserves not only to be known word for word by every Christian, but to be the subject of his meditation day by day, the daily bread of his soul . . . . *The more time one spends in it, the more precious it becomes and the better it appears.*"

e. Approach Romans with a prayerful attitude. Only the Spirit, Who inspired this letter, can open our darkened minds to see and receive its message. Therefore, we should acknowledge our dependence on Him and constantly seek His help.

3. Reason for Including the Appendixes

The appendixes A, B, and C deal with subjects closely related to Romans but which would have interrupted the continuity of the thought if they had been included as notes in the Outline itself. Appendix D has been added to identify some of the leading doctrines of Romans with that system of theology known as Calvinism and to demonstrate that these doctrines are not only taught in Romans but throughout the Bible. It is suggested that after you have gone through Romans the first time that this appendix be given careful study.

C. *An Introduction to Romans*

1. The Writer of the Letter

Paul, the author of Romans, stands out among men just as this letter stands out among the other writings of the New Testament. His faith and endurance, his deep piety and compassion, his penetrating mind and unconquerable spirit are without equal. We have no record of anyone else so completely dedicated to the gospel of Christ; nor has any other of the Lord's servants contributed so richly to our understanding of the Christian faith.

Paul, whose Hebrew name was Saul, was born in Tarsus of Cilicia. He was brought up in the Hebrew tradition in the strict sect of the Pharisees. Educated in Jerusalem by the notable rabbi Gamaliel, he became a leader in his religion. This accounts for his zealous persecution of the followers of Jesus of Nazareth. They believed Jesus had been crucified and raised from the dead as God's Christ, but Paul believed Him to be an imposter and under God's curse. It was when Paul was on his way to Damascus to arrest Christians that the risen Lord appeared to him in person and saved him. He was appointed by the Lord to be an apostle to the Gentiles and spent the rest of his life preaching the gospel and establishing churches throughout the Roman empire.

2. Occasion and Purpose of the Letter

The letter was written from Corinth, probably in the year 57 or 58 A.D. For many years Paul had wanted to visit Rome and at last hoped to be able to do so on his way to Spain. The letter was apparently written to prepare the way for his anticipated visit.

The Roman church was made up of both Jews and Gentiles. It is quite evident that the saints in Rome were well grounded in the faith, for Paul commended them for their soundness in both doctrine and practice. The purpose of the letter, therefore, was preventive instead of corrective. His design was to set forth in clear and logical form the Christian system of doctrine and thus, to ward off any false teachings that might later arise.

3. A Brief Survey of the Letter

The letter naturally divides into three major parts. Part One deals with Justification by Faith and Its Consequences (chapters 1-8); Part Two deals with The Temporary Rejection of the Jews and the Inclusion of the Gentiles as God's People (chapters 9-11); and Part Three consists of Practical Exhortations and Personal Matters Directed to the Saints at Rome (chapters 12-16).

PART ONE

JUSTIFICATION BY FAITH AND ITS CONSEQUENCES

(chapters 1-8)

After introducing himself and stating the theme of the letter—the good news that righteousness is obtained through faith—Paul proceeds to establish the fact that all men are sinful and need righteousness. He shows that Jews and Gentiles alike are under the power of sin and, therefore, are unable to keep the law; consequently, they stand condemned before God and need some method of justification other than that based on personal obedience.

Paul then shows how Jesus Christ has done for sinful man what man could not do for himself; He worked out a perfect righteousness which is given (credited or imputed) to the sinner the moment he believes.

On the basis of Christ's righteousness, which is received by faith, the sinner is rendered acceptable to God and, therefore, is JUSTIFIED (acquitted—pronounced to be in right standing with God). The apostle then explains that being justified by faith, instead of causing one to live in sin, inevitably results in obedience to God. Only those who are not under law but under grace can find the motive to truly love God and to willingly serve Him. Next he turns his attention to the function of the law, showing that it reveals and condemns sin, but, just as it cannot justify the guilty, neither can it sanctify the believer. Sin remains in Christians as long as they remain in this world. Paul closes the section by showing that the believer, although plagued with sin and suffering while in this life, is nevertheless indwelt and aided by the Holy Spirit. He has been predestined to glory and is eternally secure "in Christ"— nothing in all creation can separate him from the love of God.

PART TWO

THE TEMPORARY REJECTION OF THE JEWS AND THE INCLUSION OF THE GENTILES AS GOD'S PEOPLE

(chapters 9-11)

The second major part of the letter deals with a problem which was quite perplexing in Paul's day—the unbelief of the nation Israel and the salvation of the Gentiles. The Jews were turning away from Jesus, but the Gentiles were turning to Him in faith and acknowledging Him as the Saviour—how could this be explained? If Jesus of Nazareth were the true Christ—the Son of God—why was the Jewish nation, God's covenant people, turning away from Him in unbelief? Paul solves the problem of the rejection of the Jews and the calling of the Gentiles by appealing to the principle of divine election, i.e., that God determines who will be shown mercy and saved and who will be rejected and left in their sins. Furthermore, the calling of the Gentiles and the rejection of the greater part of the Jews had been predicted by the prophets of old. After having established sovereign election as the eternal or ultimate reason as to why particular individuals are shown mercy and called by God, Paul then explains that the immediate cause of their being justified is the fact that they believe in Jesus Christ. Those who have faith in Christ are saved and those who do not are lost regardless of their race. In closing this section the apostle makes it clear that Israel's rejection is neither total (some Jews are being saved) nor final (God will at some future time show mercy to Israel as a nation).

PART THREE

PRACTICAL EXHORTATIONS AND PERSONAL MATTERS DIRECTED TO THE SAINTS AT ROME

(chapters 12-16)

Part three is primarily devoted to p r a c t i c a l instructions for believers. The apostle points out their duties to God and the Church, to fellow believers and the world, and to civil authorities. He encourages them to love one another and to live in light of the fact that their salvation is nearer than when they first believed. He then instructs them as to how they are to view matters of indifference (matters not in themselves sinful, but offensive to weak believers) by laying down several principles concerning Christian liberty and its use.

Paul explains his own feelings and relationship toward the saints at Rome and sends personal greetings to various individuals there. He solemnly warns them to have nothing to do with false doctrine or those who teach it, after which he conveys the greetings of his companions. The letter is concluded with a doxology in which the apostle gives praise to the eternal, all-wise God who has made known the gospel of Jesus Christ which is freely offered to all men—Jews and Gentiles alike.

4.   A Condensed Outline of the Letter

Some of the truths taught in Romans will be missed unless the structure of the letter is understood; for many of Paul's statements cannot be properly interpreted apart from an understanding of his overall argument. One of the basic rules for interpreting Scriptures (and particularly Romans) is to study each passage in its context. The Condensed Outline which follows is designed to help the reader do this.

The wording of the Condensed Outline is basically the same as that of the Interpretive Outline; the primary difference in the two is that the Condensed Outline contains only the major headings (Roman numerals I-XIII) and their A B C subpoints. The purpose for including this shorter outline is to make the basic structure of the letter more accessible for study.

PART ONE

JUSTIFICATION BY FAITH AND ITS CONSEQUENCES Chapters 1-8

I.   PAUL'S INTRODUCTION TO THE LETTER. 1:1-15

    A.   Paul identifies himself as an apostle set apart to preach the gospel of Jesus Christ. 1:1-7

B. He expresses his thankfulness to God for the saints at Rome and acknowledges his obligation and his eagerness to preach the gospel to all men. 1:8-15

II. THE THEME OF THE LETTER—THE GOSPEL, THE GOOD NEWS THAT TELLS OF THE RIGHTEOUSNESS OF GOD, WHICH HE FREELY GIVES "TO EVERY ONE WHO HAS FAITH" (to Jews and Gentiles alike). 1:16,17

Verses 16 and 17 contain the two leading doctrines of the Roman letter:

A. Salvation by faith alone.

B. The free offer of salvation to all men without distinction.

III. ALL MEN ARE UNDER THE POWER OF SIN AND CONSEQUENTLY ARE WITHOUT ANY RIGHTEOUSNESS OF THEIR OWN; THEREFORE, NO ONE WILL BE JUSTIFIED BY WORKS OF THE LAW FOR NO ONE HAS KEPT IT. 1:18—3:20

A. The Gentiles are sinful and are without personal righteousness. 1:18-32

B. The Jews are sinful and are without personal righteousness. 2:1—3:8

C. Summary and Conclusion—All are sinful and therefore no human being will be justified in God's sight by works of the law for no one has kept it. 3:9-20

IV. JUSTIFICATION BY FAITH ESTABLISHED—SINNERS ARE JUSTIFIED ON THE GROUND OF THE IMPUTED RIGHTEOUSNESS OF CHRIST, WHICH IS RECEIVED BY FAITH. 3:21—5:21

A. The gospel method of justification by faith explained. 3:21-31

B. The case of Abraham cited as an illustration and proof of the gospel method of justification by faith apart from works. 4:1-25

C. Some of the blessings resulting from justification by faith. 5:1-11

D. The gospel method of justification illustrated through a comparison of the saving work of Christ with the condemning work of Adam. 5:12-21

V. PAUL SHOWS HOW UNFOUNDED IS THE OBJECTION THAT BEING JUSTIFIED BY FAITH APART FROM PERSONAL MERIT LEADS ONE TO LIVE A LIFE OF SIN. ON THE

CONTRARY, GRACE IS THE SUPREME MOTIVE FOR OBEDI-
ENCE AND INEVITABLY RESULTS IN HOLY LIVING!   6:1—
7:6

A. Those who are justified by faith cannot continue to live in sin,
because, through their identification with Christ, they are
dead to sin.   6:1-11

B. Because those who are justified by faith are not under law
(i.e., saved by keeping its commandments) but under grace
(i.e., saved by the free mercy of God), they are, therefore,
called upon to yield themselves to God as His obedient slaves.
6:12—7:6

VI. THE FUNCTION OF THE LAW, BOTH BEFORE AND AFTER
JUSTIFICATION, IS TO REVEAL AND CONDEMN SIN; BUT
IT DOES NOT AND CANNOT PRODUCE HOLINESS.   7:7-25

A. Before Paul was converted (saved) the law made sin known
to him and thus caused him to realize that he was spiritually
dead.   7:7-13

B. After Paul was converted (saved) he delighted in the law of
God in his inmost self and served it with his mind but found
that sin still dwelt within him and caused him to do the very
evil which, as a believer, he had come to hate.   7:14-25

VII. THE JUSTIFIED, THOUGH PLAGUED WITH SIN AND AF-
FLICTIONS WHILE IN THIS WORLD, ARE NEVERTHELESS
SECURE "IN CHRIST"; TO ALL WHO ARE INDWELT BY THE
HOLY SPIRIT, SALVATION IS CERTAIN, FOR THE SPIRIT'S
WORK IN THEM IS PROOF OF THEIR HAVING BEEN PRE-
DESTINED TO ETERNAL GLORY—NOTHING CAN SEPARATE
THEM FROM GOD'S LOVE.   8:1-39

A. Through their identification with Christ, believers (though
sinful in themselves) have been freed from the law and therefore cannot be condemned.   Hence their salvation is certain.
8:1-4

B. Believers are indwelt by the Holy Spirit who has regenerated
them, who is sanctifying them, and who in the last day will
resurrect them.   8:5-11

C. Believers (through adoption) are, in their present state, the
children of God and, therefore, fellow heirs with Christ.   8:12-
17

D. Believers, though they must suffer various afflictions while
in this life, are sustained through them all by the encouragement and help that comes from God.   8:18-28

E. Believers are assured of final salvation, for they have been predestined to eternal glory. 8:29, 30

F. God is for believers, therefore, they are safe; He gave His own son to die for them and thereby to secure their justification and salvation. 8:31-34

G. God's love for His people is infinite and unchangeable, and nothing in all creation can separate believers from it. 8:35-39

PART TWO

THE REJECTION OF THE JEWS AND THE INCLUSION OF THE GENTILES AS GOD'S PEOPLE Chapters 9-11

VIII. THE ULTIMATE OR ETERNAL REASON FOR THE REJECTION OF THE GREATER PART OF ISRAEL AND THE CALLING OF THE GENTILES TO SALVATION IS GOD'S SOVEREIGN ELECTION. 9:1-29

A. Before entering into the discussion of the rejection of the Jews, Paul expresses his deep concern and love for them and his respect for their national privileges. 9:1-5

B. He next establishes the absolute right of God to do with His fallen, sinful creatures as He pleases and shows that God has selected from among the Jews and from among the Gentiles particular individuals to save while rejecting the rest. 9:6-24

C. The apostle then appeals to the Jewish Scriptures and shows that the salvation of the Gentiles and the rejection of the greater part of Israel had been predicted by the prophets. 9:25-29

IX. THE IMMEDIATE CAUSE OF ISRAEL'S REJECTION AND OF THE GENTILES' SALVATION WAS THE DIFFERENT MANNER IN WHICH THEY WERE RESPONDING TO THE GOSPEL (the good news that righteousness is obtained through faith in Jesus Christ). 9:30—10:21

A. The Gentiles were receiving God's free gift of righteousness by faith and were being justified, whereas, the Jews (ignorant of God's gift of righteousness) were trying to work out a righteousness of their own and were perishing. 9:30—10:4

B. The legal and gospel methods of justification are contrasted for the purpose of showing that the legal method is beyond the reach of sinful men, but that the gospel method is simple and easy and adapted to all men without distinction. 10:5-13

C. The gospel of Christ is not only adapted to all men but must be sent (preached) to all men if any are to be saved! 10:14-17

   D. The Old Testament prophets foretold of the universal spread of the gospel and of the inclusion of Gentiles as God's people as well as of the rejection of the gospel by Israel. 10:18-21

X. THE REJECTION OF THE JEWS, AS TO NUMBER, IS NOT TOTAL; AS TO TIME, IS NOT FINAL. 11:1-36

   A. The rejection of the Jews as to number is not total. 11:1-10

   B. The rejection of the Jews as to time is not final. 11:11-32

   C. Paul ascribes adoring praise to the all-wise and almighty Sovereign (whose resources, wisdom, decisions, and methods are beyond man's comprehension) who Himself is the Originator, Director, and End of all things! 11:33-36

PART THREE

PRACTICAL EXHORTATIONS AND PERSONAL MATTERS DIRECTED TO THE SAINTS AT ROME Chapters 12-16

XI. PRACTICAL EXHORTATIONS. 12:1—15:13
   A. Duties to God and to the Church. 12:1-8
   B. Duties to fellow believers and to the world. 12:9-21
   C. Duties to civil authorities. 13:1-7
   D. The duty to love one another; "love is the fulfilling of the law." 13:8-10
   E. All these duties should be viewed in light of the fact that salvation is nearer than when we first believed. 13:11-14
   F. Instructions concerning Christian liberty. 14:1—15:13

XII. PERSONAL MATTERS. 15:14—16:23
   A. Paul explains his own feelings and relationship toward the saints at Rome. 15:14-33
   B. He sends personal greetings to various individuals at Rome. 16:1-16
   C. The apostle warns the saints to have nothing to do with those who cause dissensions and difficulties by o p p o s i n g sound doctrine—such persons are false teachers; they are not true servants of Christ! 16:17-20
   D. He conveys the greetings of his companions to the Roman saints. 16:21-23

XIII. THE CONCLUDING DOXOLOGY. 16:25-27

Paul gives praise to the eternal, all-wise God who, through the prophetic Scriptures, has made known the gospel of Jesus Christ —the good news of salvation by faith freely offered to all men, Gentiles as well as Jews.

The Basic Structure of Romans

The letter consists of three major parts:

1. Chapters 1-8 set forth the doctrine of JUSTIFICATION BY FAITH AND ITS CONSEQUENCES.

2. Chapters 9-11 deal with the problem of the REJECTION OF THE JEWS and the INCLUSION OF THE GENTILES as God's people.

3. Chapters 12-16 consist of PRACTICAL EXHORTATIONS and PERSONAL MATTERS directed to the saints at Rome.

PART ONE

JUSTIFICATION BY FAITH AND ITS CONSEQUENCES Chs. 1-8

I. PAUL'S INTRODUCTION TO THE LETTER. 1:1-15

A. Paul (a special messenger of God) addresses himself to God's beloved in Rome. He had been "set apart" by God for the purpose of making known *the gospel*. Paul's message centered in Jesus Christ, who according to the flesh was descended from David but by His resurrection from the dead was proven to be the Son of God. (See I Cor. 15:3, 4.) 1:1-7

REVISED STANDARD VERSION 1:1-7	WILLIAMS' TRANSLATION 1:1-7
Paul, a servant^a of Jesus Christ, called to be an apostle, set apart for the gospel of God ²which he promised beforehand through his prophets in the holy scriptures, ³the gospel concerning his Son, who was descended from David according to the flesh ⁴and designated Son of God in power according to the Spirit of holiness by his resurrection from the dead, Jesus Christ our Lord, ⁵through whom we have received grace and apostleship to bring about obedience to the faith for the sake of his n a m e among all the nations, ⁶including yourselves who are called to belong to Jesus Christ; ⁷To all God's beloved in Rome, who are called to be saints: Grace to you and peace from God our Father and the Lord Jesus Christ.	Paul, a slave of Jesus Christ, called as an apostle, set apart to preach^a God's good news, ²which long ago He promised through His prophets in the holy Scriptures, ³about His Son, who on the physical^b side became a descendant of David, and on the holy spiritual side^c ⁴proved to be God's Son in power by the resurrection from the dead—I mean, Jesus Christ our Lord, ⁵through whom we have received God's favor and a commission as an apostle in His name to urge^d upon all the heathen obedience inspired by faith,^e ⁶among whom you too as called ones belong to Jesus Christ—⁷to all those in Rome who are God's loved ones, called to be His people:^f spiritual blessing^g and peace be yours from God our Father and from our Lord Jesus Christ.

ᵃ Or *slave*

ᵃ Implied.
ᵇ Lit., *according to the flesh.*
ᶜ Grk., *according to the spirit of holiness.*
ᵈ Implied.
ᵉ Subj. gen.
ᶠ Lit., *separate ones, saints.*
ᵍ Grk., *favor, grace.*

B. Paul expresses his thankfulness to God for them and reveals his desire to see them and to preach the gospel at Rome. He acknowledges his obligation and his eagerness to make known this good news to all men. 1:8-15

1:8-15 RSV	1:8-15 WT
⁸First, I thank my God through Jesus Christ for all of you, because your faith is proclaimed in all the world. ⁹For God is my witness, whom I serve with my spirit in the gospel of his Son,	⁸First, through Jesus Christ I thank my God for you all, because the report of your faith is spreading all over the world. ⁹Indeed, my witness is God, whom I serve in my spirit by telling^h the good news

ʰ Implied.

13

that without ceasing I mention you always in my prayers, [10]asking that somehow by God's will I may now at last succeed in coming to you. [11]For I long to see you, that I may impart to you some spiritual gift to strengthen you, [12]that is, that we may be mutually encouraged by each other's faith, both yours and mine. [13]I want you to know, brethren, that I have often intended to come to you (but thus far have been prevented), in order that I may reap some harvest among you as well as among the rest of the Gentiles. [14]I am under obligation both to Greeks and to barbarians, both to the wise and to the foolish: [15]so I am eager to preach the gospel to you also who are in Rome.

about His Son, that I never fail to mention[i] you every time I pray, [10]always entreating God that somehow by His will I may some day at last succeed in getting to see you.[j] [11]For I am longing to see you, to impart to you some spiritual gift, that you may be strengthened; [12]in other words, that we may be mutually encouraged, while I am with you, by one another's faith, yours and mine. [13]Furthermore, I want you to know, brothers, that I have often planned to come to see you (though until now I have been prevented), in order that I may gather some fruit[k] among you too, as I have among the rest of the heathen. [14]To Greeks and to all the other nations,[l] to cultured and to uncultured people alike, I owe a duty. [15]So, as far as I can, I am eager to preach the good news to you at Rome, too.

[i] Grk., *how ceaselessly I mention you,* etc.
[j] Lit., *prospered to come to you.*
[k] Meaning *spiritual results of his labors.*
[l] Lit., *the barbarians.*

II. THE THEME OF THE LETTER: THE GOSPEL, THE GOOD NEWS THAT TELLS OF THE RIGHTEOUSNESS OF GOD, WHICH HE FREELY GIVES "TO EVERY ONE WHO HAS FAITH" (to Jews and Gentiles alike). Paul was not ashamed of this message, for as he explains, it is the instrument God uses in saving sinners. (See Gal. 1:6-9.) 1:16,17

1:16,17 RSV

[16]For I am not ashamed of the gospel: it is the power of God for salvation to every one who has faith, to the Jew first and also to the Greek. [17]For in it the righteousness of God is revealed through faith for faith; as it is written, "He who through faith is righteous shall live."[b]

[b] Or *The righteous shall live by faith*

1:16,17 WT

[16]For I am not ashamed of the good news, for it is God's power for the salvation of everyone who trusts, of the Jew first and then of the Greek. [17]For in the good news[m] God's Way of man's right standing with Him[n] is uncovered, the Way of faith that leads to greater faith,[o] just as the Scripture says, "The upright man must live by faith."[p]

[m] Pro. in Grk.
[n] Grk., *God's righteousness,* technical phrase in Paul for *right standing with God,* or *God's way for man to be in right standing with Him.*
[o] Lit., *from faith to faith.*
[p] Hab. 2:4.

The two leading doctrines of Romans are stated in 1:16,17. It is as if these two verses were the "text" (the theme) and the remainder of the letter, the "sermon" (the explanation and proof of the theme). These two leading doctrines are:

A. Salvation by *faith alone*

The gospel reveals the "righteousness of God" (See Note 2,E, p. 33) which is given to all who believe. As will be shown later in great detail, sinners gain righteousness "through faith"—*not* by keeping God's law. By faith alone the unrighteous receive (i.e., are credited with) perfect righteousness. On the ground of this God-given righteousness they are *justified* (i.e., put in right standing with God and consequently declared acceptable to Him—acquitted from all guilt and condemnation, see Note 1,A, p. 24).

B. The free offer of salvation to *all men without distinction*

The offer of salvation on the sole condition of faith is made to *all men without distinction—Jews and Gentiles alike!* Many of the Jews believed that God would show mercy only to those who belonged to the nation Israel. If a Gentile wanted to be saved, the Jews thought that he had to submit to the law of Moses, be circumcised, and become a member of the Jewish nation; then God would save him. Paul shows that this is not the case. *All who believe the gospel,* regardless of their race, or regardless of any other consideration, *are promised salvation.*

It should be noted that the gospel which Paul preached was taught in the Old Testament. He quotes Habakkuk 2:4 to establish the doctrine of Justification by Faith which *is* the gospel and which *is* the theme of the Roman letter. The NEB translates the quotation from Habakkuk, in verse 17b, in the following way: "as Scripture says, 'he shall gain life who is justified through faith.' "

But before developing the theme of Justification by Faith Paul, from Ch. 1:18 through Ch. 3:20, establishes the fact that all men are sinful and shows that no one can possibly be justified on the basis of personal obedience to the law.

III. ALL MEN ARE UNDER THE POWER OF SIN AND CONSEQUENTLY ARE WITHOUT ANY RIGHTEOUSNESS OF THEIR OWN; THEREFORE, NO ONE CAN BE JUSTIFIED BY WORKS OF THE LAW FOR NO ONE HAS KEPT IT. 1:18—3:20

A. The Gentiles are sinful and are without personal righteousness. 1:18-32

Paul's design in this section (1:18-32) is to show that the Gentiles are sinful and without any personal righteousness. Because of their sinfulness, it is impossible for them to be justified (acquitted or put in right standing with God) on the ground of what they have done. When judged on the basis of their own works, they are unacceptable to God, they are condemned; for only on the basis of righteousness will God declare anyone acceptable to Himself. Since the Gentiles have no righteousness of their own, they cannot be justified—unless of course some provision were made whereby they could obtain the righteousness needed. Christ has provided the needed righteousness, but Paul does not explain this until he has first established the fact that men do need it—that they cannot be saved without it!

1. The Gentiles are shown to be justly exposed to God's wrath because, while possessing an adequate knowledge of God through the things created by Him, they did not honor or give thanks to Him. Suppressing the truth about Him, they turned to idols; they exchanged the glory of the immortal God for images—they worshipped and served gods of their own making rather than the God of heaven who had made them. 1:18-23

1:18-23 RSV

[18]For the wrath of God is revealed from heaven against all ungodliness and wickedness of men who by their wickedness suppress the truth. [19]For what can be known about God is plain to them, because God has shown it to them. [20]Ever since the creation of the world his invisible nature, namely, his eternal power and deity, has been clearly perceived in the things that have been made. So they are without excuse; [21]for although they knew God they did not honor him as God or give thanks to him, but they became futile in their thinking and their senseless minds were darkened. [22]Claiming to be wise, they became fools, [23]and exchanged the glory of the immortal God for images resembling mortal man or birds or animals or reptiles.

1:18-23 WT

[18]For God's anger from heaven is being uncovered against all the impiety and wickedness of the men who in their wickedness are suppressing the truth; [19]because what can be known of God is clear to their inner moral sense;[q] for in this way[r] God Himself has shown it to them. [20]For ever since the creation of the world, His invisible characteristics[s]—His eternal power and divine nature—have been made intelligible and clearly visible by His works. So they are without excuse, [21]because, although they once knew God, they did not honor Him as God, or give Him thanks, but became silly in their senseless speculations, and so their insensible hearts have been shrouded in darkness.[t] [22]Though claiming to be wise, they made fools of themselves, [23]and have transformed the splendor of the immortal God into images in the form of mortal man, birds, beasts, and reptiles.

[q] Lit., *within them.*
[r] Implied.
[s] Lit., *the invisible things of Him.*
[t] Lit., *were darkened.*

a. God has given mankind an adequate revelation of Himself (i.e., of His eternal power and deity—His invisible nature and attributes) through the things which He created. But men, because of their sinfulness, suppress the truth about Him. 1:18-20a

Hodge observes that "The knowledge of God does not mean simply a knowledge that there is a God, but as appears from what follows, a knowledge of his nature and attributes, his eternal power and Godhead, ver. 20, and his justice, ver. 32."[4] Cf., Acts 14:16,17.

---

[4] Charles Hodge, *Commentary on the Epistle to the Romans*, p. 36.

16

b. The heathen (Gentiles) are without excuse, for they deliberately gave up the knowledge of God and turned to idols. Notice the language of verse 25: "they exchanged the truth about God for a lie and worshipped and served the creature rather than the Creator, who is blessed forever!" 1:20b-23

Paul does not teach here that men have in creation a sufficient revelation of God to bring them to salvation (for he shows in Romans 10:14-17, that only by hearing about and believing in Jesus Christ as the risen Lord can men be saved—see Note 9, p. 84 and Note 10, p. 87). Yet, men do have a sufficient knowledge of God's existence and nature in the things He has made to render them responsible. They are obligated to honor and serve Him as God according to the knowledge they have. Their idolatry and their refusal to worship the true God is, therefore, inexcusable. (For Biblical references showing the effects of sin on human nature see the section on Total Inability in Part II of Appendix D on Calvinism, pp. 152-158.)

2. Because the Gentiles exchanged the truth about God for a lie and did not see fit to acknowledge Him, God gave them up to all kinds of sin. 1:24-31

1:24-31 RSV

[24]Therefore God gave them up in the lusts of their hearts to impurity, to the dishonoring of their bodies among themselves, [25]because they exchanged the truth about God for a lie and worshiped and served the creature rather than the Creator, who is blessed forever! Amen.
[26]For this reason God gave them up to dishonorable passions. Their women exchanged natural relations for unnatural, [27]and the men likewise gave up natural relations with women and were consumed with passion for one another. men committing shameless acts with men and receiving in their own persons the due penalty for their error.
[28]And since they did not see fit to acknowledge God, God gave them up to a base mind and to improper conduct. [29]They were filled with all manner of wickedness, evil, covetousness, malice. Full of envy, murder, strife, deceit, malignity,

1:24-31 WT

[24]So God has given them up to sexual impurity, in the evil trend of their heart's desires,[u] so that they degrade their own bodies with one another, [25]for they had utterly transformed the reality of God into what was unreal,[v] and worshiped and served the creature rather than the Creator, who is blessed forever! Amen. [26]This is why God has given them up to degrading passions. For their females[w] have exchanged their natural function for one that is unnatural, [27]and males too have forsaken the natural function of females and been consumed by flaming[x] passion for one another, males practicing shameful vice with other males, and continuing to suffer in their persons the inevitable penalty[y] for doing what is improper. [28]And so, as they did not approve of fully recognizing God any longer, God gave them up to minds that He did not approve,[z] to practices that were improper;[*] [29]be-

[u] Grk., *in their hearts' evil desires.*
[v] Lit., *the truth of God into what was false* (images).
[w] Only females, not women.
[x] Implied in strong term for *passion.*
[y] Lit., *penalty that was necessary.*
[z] Preserving Paul's fine play on words.
[*] *What does not belong to them;* hence contrary to nature.

they are gossips, [30]slanderers, haters of God, insolent, haughty, boastful, inventors of evil, disobedient to parents, [31]foolish, faithless, heartless, ruthless.

cause they overflow with every sort of evil-doing, wickedness, greed, and malice; they are full of envy, murder, quarreling, deceit, ill-will; [30]they are secret backbiters, open slanderers, hateful to God, insolent, haughty, boastful; inventors of new forms of evil, undutiful to parents, [31]conscience-less,† treacherous, with no human love or pity.

† Lit., *without intelligence* (moral).

As Hodge observes "God often punishes one sin by abandoning the sinner to the commission of others. Paul repeats this idea three times, verses 24, 26, 28. This judicial abandonment is consistent with the holiness of God and the free agency of man. God does not impel or entice to evil. He ceases to restrain. He says of the sinner, Let him alone, vers. 24-28."[5]

3. The Gentiles do not commit these sins ignorantly; they know (are fully aware of) God's decree that those who do such things deserve to die. Yet they not only commit these sins but approve of those who practice them. 1:32

1:32 RSV

[32]Though they know God's decree that those who do such things deserve to die, they not only do them but approve those who practice them.

1:32 WT

[32]Although they know full well God's sentence that those who practice such things deserve to die, yet they not only practice them but even applaud others who do them.

The knowledge that such things are sinful is written on man's heart. See the comments in the Outline on 2:12-16, and Note 5,B,1, p. 53.

B. The Jews are sinful and are without personal righteousness. 2:1—3:8

The Jews had come to the false conclusion that because God had in the past shown special favor to their race they would, therefore, be exempt from condemnation. They had come to believe that mere physical connection with the nation Israel (being Abraham's descendants) meant salvation. (See Luke 3:7-9; John 8:31-47. See also the Outline on Romans 9:1-13.) In this section Paul shows that the Jews (like the Gentiles) are sinful and therefore equally exposed to God's wrath.

1. God's judgment will be based on the principle of justice and will be the same for all men, Jews and Gentiles alike. 2:1-16

The Jews, in passing judgment on the Gentiles, condemned themselves for they were guilty of the very same sins.

---

[5] Hodge, *Romans*, p. 45.

a. God will judge men according to what they have done—according to their works. 2:1-11

2:1-11 RSV

Therefore you have no excuse, O man, whoever you are, when you judge another; for in passing judgment upon him you condemn yourself, because you, the judge, are doing the very same things. ²We know that the judgment of God rightly falls upon those who do such things. ³Do you suppose, O man, that when you judge those who do such things and yet do them yourself, you will escape the judgment of God? ⁴Or do you presume upon the riches of his kindness and forbearance and patience? Do you not know that God's kindness is meant to lead you to repentance? ⁵But by your hard and impenitent heart you are storing up wrath for yourself on the day of wrath when God's righteous judgment will be revealed. ⁶For he will render to every man according to his works: ⁷to those who by patience in well-doing seek for glory and honor and immortality, he will give eternal life; ⁸but for those who are factious and do not obey the truth, but obey wickedness, there will be wrath and fury. ⁹There will be tribulation and distress for every human being who does evil, the Jew first and also the Greek, ¹⁰but glory and honor and peace for every one who does good, the Jew first and also the Greek. ¹¹For God shows no partiality.

2:1-11 WT

Therefore, you have no excuse, whoever you are, who pose as a judge of others, for when you pass judgment on another, you condemn yourself, for you who pose as a judge are practicing the very same sins[a] yourself. ²Now we know that God's judgment justly[b] falls on those who practice such sins as these. ³And you, who pose as a judge of those who practice such sins and yet continue doing the same yourself, do you for once[c] suppose that you are going to escape the judgment of God? ⁴Do you think so little of the riches of God's kindness, forbearance, and patience, not conscious that His kindness is meant[d] to lead you to repentance? ⁵But in your stubbornness and impenitence of heart you are storing up wrath for yourself on the day of wrath, when the justice of God's judgments will be uncovered.[e] ⁶For when He finally judges,[f] He will pay everyone with exactness for what he has done, ⁷eternal life to those who patiently continue doing good and striving for glory, honor, and immortality; ⁸but wrath and fury, crushing suffering and awful anguish, to the self-willed who are always resisting the right and yielding to the wrong,[g] ⁹to every human soul who practices doing evil, the Jew first and then the Greek. ¹⁰But glory, honor, and peace will come to everyone who practices doing good, the Jew first and then the Greek; ¹¹for there is no partiality in God's dealings.

---

[a] Lit., *the same things*.
[b] Grk., *God's judgment is in accordance with truth* (reality).
[c] Aor. pres.
[d] Implied in gen. pres.
[e] Lit., *at the uncovering of God's just judgments*.
[f] Clause implied from context.
[g] *Aleetheia* here means *right*, not *truth*.

(1)   To those who by patience in well-doing seek for glory and honor and immortality, God will give eternal life. 2:6,7

(2)   But for those who are factious (self-willed) and do not obey the truth, but obey wickedness, there will be wrath and fury. 2:8

(3)   God will show no racial partiality in judging sin. Every man will be judged according to what he has done; if he has done good, he will be saved; if he has done evil, he will be lost; regardless of whether he is a Jew or Gentile. 2:1-5, 9-11

Although it may seem that Paul is teaching salvation by works in 2:1-11, this is not the case. He shows in 3:9-20 (see Outline) that no one will be saved by "doing good"—that is, on the ground of his own works—because no one has kept the law; no one has done good. All that is said here is that *if* anyone *does good* (conforms completely to the law's demands) he will be saved. See Note 1, p. 24.

b. God will judge men according to the light they have enjoyed —according to the law they have lived under. 2:12-16

2:12-16 RSV

[12]All who have sinned without the law will also perish without the law, and all who have sinned under the law will be judged by the law. [13]For it is not the hearers of the law who are righteous before God, but the doers of the law who will be justified. [14]When Gentiles who have not the law do by nature what the law requires, they are a law to themselves, even though they do not have the law. [15]They show that what the law requires is written on their hearts, while their conscience also bears witness and their conflicting thoughts accuse or perhaps excuse them [16]on that day when, according to my gospel, God judges the secrets of men by Christ Jesus.

2:12-16 WT

[12]All who sin without having the law will also perish apart from the law, and all who sin under the law will be judged by the law. [13]For merely hearing the law read[h] does not make men upright with God; but men who practice the law will be recognized as upright. [14]Indeed, when heathen people who have no law instinctively do what the law demands,[i] although they have no law they are a law to themselves, [15]for they show that the deeds the law demands are written on their hearts, because their consciences will testify for them, and their inner[j] thoughts will either accuse or defend them, [16]on the day when God through Jesus Christ, in accordance with the good news I preach, will judge the secrets people have kept.

[h] Lit., *hearers.*
[i] Grk., *the things of the law.*
[j] Lit., *thoughts in them.*

(1)   The Gentiles will be judged according to the law written on man's heart—the law of nature or conscience.

At creation God's law was written on man's heart in a clear and legible form, but when Adam sinned this law was defaced and marred. Man's conscience became seared, his understanding was darkened. He no longer had the spiritual sight with which to read this law clearly. The Gentiles, who have no other revelation of God's will (other than the marred law written on the heart) will not be as strictly judged as will be the Jews who were given a much clearer revelation of God's will in the law of Moses. But the Gentiles will be judged and *if they have sinned, they will perish* (2:12a)! If they have done what is right, they will be saved (2:14-16). See Note 5,B,1,2 and C,1, pp. 53,54.

(2)   The Jews will be judged not only by the law written on man's heart but also according to the law of Moses—the written law revealed in the Old Testament Scriptures.   Just possessing the written law does not mean salvation for the Jews *unless* they keep it.   (To be a "doer of the law" (2:13) means to keep it at every point—completely, absolutely!   See James 2:10,11; Gal. 3:10; Rom. 10:5.)   Since the Jews had a much clearer revelation of God's law than did the Gentiles, they will be judged in a much stricter manner—they will be "judged by the law" (2:12b, 13).   If any keep it, they will be justified (see Note 1, p. 24).   Paul is not saying that anyone *can* (is able to) *keep* the law— he is only showing what would happen *if* they did keep it.   See Note 5, pp. 53-55.

2.   When tested by the written law of Moses, the Jews are shown to be as justly and certainly exposed to condemnation as are the Gentiles. 2:17-24

2:17-24   RSV

[17]But if you call yourself a Jew and rely upon the law and boast of your relation to God [18]and know his will and approve what is excellent, because you are instructed in the law, [19]and if you are sure that you are a guide to the blind, a light to those who are in darkness, [20]a corrector of the foolish, a teacher of children, having in the law the embodiment of knowledge and truth—[21]you then who teach others, will you not teach yourself? While you preach against stealing, do you steal? [22]You who say that one must not commit adultery, do you commit adultery? You who abhor idols, do you rob temples? [23]You who boast in the law, do you dishonor God by breaking the law? [24]For, as it is written, "The name of God is blasphemed among the Gentiles because of you."

2:17-24   WT

[17]Now if you call yourself a Jew, and rely on law, and boast about God, [18]and understand His will, and by being instructed in the law can know the things that excel,[k] [19]and if you are sure that you are a guide to the blind, a light to those in darkness, [20]a tutor of the foolish, a teacher of the young, since you have a knowledge of the truth as formulated in the law—[l] [21]you who teach others, do you not teach yourself too? You who preach that men should not steal, do you steal yourself? [22]You who warn men to stop committing adultery, do you practice it yourself? You who shrink in horror[m] from idols, do you rob their temples? [23]You who boast about the law, do you by breaking it dishonor God? [24]For, as the Scripture says, the name of God is abused among the heathen because of you.[n]

---

[k] This tr. suits context better than *what is right.*
[l] Lit., *form of knowledge and truth.*
[m] Lit., *feels phys. repulsion.*
[n] Isa. 52:5, but not lit. quotation.

The Jews gloried in the fact that the written law had been given to them, but they dishonored God by breaking it and thus proved that they (like the Gentiles) were sinful and without righteousness.

3.   The value of circumcision explained.   2:25-29

2:25-29   RSV

[25]Circumcision indeed is of value if you obey the law; but if you break the law, your circumcision becomes uncircumcision.

2:25-29   WT

[25]Now circumcision benefits you only if you practice the law; but if you break the law, your circumcision is no better

26So, if a man who is uncircumcised keeps the precepts of the law, will not his uncircumcision be regarded as circumcision? 27Then those who are physically uncircumcised but keep the law will condemn you who have the written code and circumcision but break the law. 28For he is not a real Jew who is one outwardly, nor is true circumcision something external and physical. 29He is a Jew who is one inwardly, and real circumcision is a matter of the heart, spiritual and not literal. His praise is not from men but from God.

than uncircumcision.[o] 26So if the uncircumcised heathen man observes the just demands of the law, will he not be counted as though he were a Jew?[p] 27And shall not the heathen man who is physically uncircumcised, and yet observes the law, condemn you who have the letter of the law and are physically circumcised, and yet break the law? 28For the real Jew is not the man who is a Jew on the outside, and real circumcision is not outward physical circumcision. 29The real Jew is the man who is a Jew on the inside, and real circumcision is heart-circumcision, a spiritual, not a literal, affair. This man's praise[q] originates, not with men, but with God.

[o] Lit., *has become uncircumcision.*
[p] Abstract for concrete terms.
[q] A play on meaning of Heb. word for *Jew, a praised one.*

Paul shows that the mere external rite of circumcision will not exempt the Jews from condemnation—it has value only if those who are circumcised obey the law, which the Jews had failed to do. On the other hand, *IF* a Gentile should keep the law, his lack of physical circumcision would not keep him from reaping the blessings the law promised. It is not the outward physical state of man that God judges—He looks upon the heart and judges man's inward spiritual condition.

4. Jewish objections anticipated and refuted. 3:1-8

3:1-8 RSV

Then what advantage has the Jew? Or what is the value of circumcision? 2Much in every way. To begin with, the Jews are entrusted with the oracles of God. 3What if some were unfaithful? Does their faithlessness nullify the faithfulness of God? 4By no means! Let God be true though every man be false, as it is written,

"That thou mayest be justified in thy words,
and prevail when thou art judged."

5But if our wickedness serves to show the justice of God, what shall we say? That God is unjust to inflict wrath on us? (I speak in a human way.) 6By no means! For then how could God judge the world? 7But if through my falsehood God's truthfulness abounds to his

3:1-8 WT

What special privilege,[a] then, has a Jew?[b] Or, what benefit does circumcision[b] confer? 2They are great from every point of view. In the first place, the Jews are entrusted with the utterances of God. 3What then, if some of them have proved unfaithful? Can their unfaithfulness make null and void God's faithfulness? 4Not at all.[c] Let God prove true, though every man be false! As the Scripture says,

"That you may prove yourself upright in words you speak,
And win your case when you go into court."[d]

5But if our wrongdoing brings to light the uprightness of God, what shall we infer? Is it wrong (I am using everyday human terms) for God to inflict

[a] Lit., *superfluity.*
[b] Subj. gen.
[c] Lit., *let it not be.*
[d] Ps. 51:4; 116:11

glory, why am I still being condemned as a sinner? ⁸And why not do evil that good may come?—as some people slanderously charge us with saying. Their condemnation is just.

punishment? ⁶Not at all! If that were so, how could He judge the world? ⁷But, as you say, if the truthfulness of God has redounded to His glory because of my falsehood, why am I still condemned as a sinner? ⁸Why should we not say, as people abusively say of us, and charge us with actually saying, "Let us do evil that good may come from it"? Their condemnation is just.

Briefly, the argument runs like this: (1) *First Objection:* In view of what has been said, what advantage then is there in being a Jew and receiving circumcision? *Answer:* Much in every way. In the first place, the Jews had the word of God (the Old Testament), 3:1,2. (2) *Second Objection:* Has not God promised to be the God of the Jews? He cannot be unfaithful by punishing them, can He? *Answer:* God remains faithful regardless of what the Jews bring upon themselves by their own unfaithfulness, 3:3,4. (3) *Third Objection:* God would be unjust to punish the Jews for their wickedness since it commends His justice. *Answer:* If this principle were true, God could not punish anyone, Jew or Gentile; and also, such a principle would lead to the absurdity that it is right to do evil that good may come, 3:5-8.

C.   Summary and Conclusion.   3:9-20

Summary: *All men,* Jews and Gentiles alike, *are under the power of sin* and have failed to keep God's law; consequently, *there is not one righteous person.* 3:9-18

3:9-18 RSV

⁹What then? Are we Jews any better off?ᶜ No, not at all; for Iᵈ have already charged that all men, both Jews and Greeks, are under the power of sin, ¹⁰as it is written:
"None is righteous, no, not one;
¹¹no one understands, no one seeks for God.
¹²All have turned aside, together they have gone wrong;
no one does good, not even one."
¹³"Their throat is an open grave,
they use their tongues to deceive."
"The venom of asps is under their lips."
¹⁴"Their mouth is full of curses and bitterness."
¹⁵"Their feet are swift to shed blood,
¹⁶in their paths are ruin and misery,
¹⁷and the way of peace they do not know."

ᶜ Or *at any disadvantage?*
ᵈGreek *we*

3:9-18 WT

⁹What is our conclusion then? Is it that we Jews are better than they? Not at all! For we have already charged that Jews and Greeks alike are all under the sway of sin, ¹⁰as the Scriptures say:
"Not a single human creatureᵉ is upright,
¹¹No one understands, no one is searching for God;
¹²They all have turned aside, all have become corrupt,
No one does good, not even one!
¹³Their throats are just like open graves,
With their tongues they have spoken treachery;
The poison of asps is under their lips,
¹⁴Their mouths are full of bitter cursing.
¹⁵Their feet are swift for shedding blood,

ᵉ Grk., *not any flesh.*

23

[18]"There is no fear of God before their eyes."

[16]Ruin and wretchedness are on their paths,
[17]They do not know the way of peace.
[18]There is no reverence for God before their eyes."[f]

---

[f] Ps. 14:1-3; 5:9; 140:3; 10:7; 36:1; Isa. 59:7.

Conclusion: Since all men are sinful and have failed to keep God's law, *no one will be justified on the ground of his own works.* 3:19,20

3:19,20 RSV	3:19,20 WT
[19]Now we know that whatever the law says it speaks to those who are under the law, so that every mouth may be stopped, and the whole world may be held accountable to God. [20]For no human being will be justified in his sight by works of the law since through the law comes knowledge of sin.	[19]Now we know that everything the law says is spoken to those who are under its authority,[g] that every mouth may be stopped and the whole world be held responsible to God. [20]Because no human creature can be brought into right standing with God[h] by observing the law. For all the law can do is to make men conscious of sin.[i]

[g] Lit., *those in the law.*
[h] Grk., *will be justified.*
[i] *Through the law is the consciousness of sin.*

For additional Scriptural evidence relating to man's total spiritual inability to save himself or to prepare himself for salvation, see Part II of Appendix D, pp. 152-158. For the answer to the question as to how sinful men void of personal righteousness can be justified, see Note 1 below and the Outline of Romans on 3:21—5:21.

The Outline of Romans is continued on p. 25.

NOTE NO. 1 JUSTIFICATION

A. Justification is a legal sentence or declaration issued by God in which He pronounces the person in question free from any fault or guilt and acceptable in His sight. The person is declared to have met *all* the requirements of God's holy law and to possess a perfect righteousness. As Packer states, "The biblical meaning of 'justify' . . . is to pronounce, accept, and treat as just, i.e., as, on the one hand, not penally liable, and on the other, entitled to all the privileges due to those who have kept the law. It is thus a forensic term, denoting a judicial act of administering the law—in this case, by declaring a verdict of acquittal, and so excluding all possibility of condemnation. Justification thus settles the legal status of the person justified." [6] Upon examination, if a person is found to be guilty of any sin or lacking in righteousness in the least degree, he falls under the sentence of condemnation. Therefore,

---

[6] James I. Packer, "Just, Justify, Justification," *Baker's Dictionary of Theology,* p. 304.

only those who have *perfect* righteousness, either *personal* or *imputed* (i.e., credited to them), are justified. See Note 2,A, p. 29 for the meaning of imputed righteousness.

B.   There are two methods of justification set forth in the Scriptures. One is by WORKS, the other by FAITH.

1.   JUSTIFICATION BY WORKS — THE LEGAL METHOD
This method requires that men *perfectly obey God's law.* "For it is not the hearers of the law who are righteous before God, *but the doers of the law who will be justified*" (2:13). (The apostle is not saying in this verse that anyone *can* keep the law, but is saying that *if anyone does,* he will receive eternal life as his reward. Compare Matthew 19:16-22.) Paul makes it clear in 3:9-20 that *no one can fulfill the law's demands,* for all men are under the power of sin and without any righteousness whatsoever. Therefore he concludes that "*no human being will be justified in God's sight by works of the law*" (3:20). See Galatians 3:10-14. The law saves no one, it only makes sin known! See Note 5, p. 53.

2.   JUSTIFICATION BY FAITH — THE GOSPEL METHOD
The second method offered to men whereby they may be justified is through *faith.* This method is not developed in Romans until man's need of a method apart from obedience to the law (apart from personal merit or works) is thoroughly *established.* Starting at 3:21 and continuing through Chapter 10, Paul explains, illustrates and defends the doctrine of *Justification by Faith.* This is the burden of the Roman letter. See Note 2, p. 29 and Note 9, p. 84. See also Appendix A "James and Paul on Justification," p. 123ff.

The Outline of Romans is continued from p. 24.

IV. JUSTIFICATION BY FAITH ESTABLISHED—SINNERS ARE JUSTIFIED ON THE GROUND OF THE IMPUTED RIGHTEOUSNESS OF CHRIST, WHICH IS RECEIVED BY FAITH. 3:21—5:21

A.   The gospel method of Justification by Faith explained.   3:21-31

1.   The Old Testament Scriptures (the law and the prophets) testify to the fact that God gives righteousness to all who believe in Jesus Christ. (See Note 2, E, p. 33 for the meaning of "the righteousness of God.")   3:21,22

3:21,22 RSV	3:21,22 WT
[21]But now the righteousness of God has been manifested apart from law, although the law and the prophets bear witness to it, [22]the righteousness of God	[21]But now God's way of giving men right standing with Himself[1] has come to light; a way without connection with the law, and yet a way to which the law and

[1] Lit., *God's righteousness,* but here *God's way of giving men right standing with Himself.*

25

through faith in Jesus Christ for all who believe. For there is no distinction; the prophets testify. ²²God's own way of giving men right standing with Himself is through faith in Jesus Christ. It is for everybody who has faith, for no distinction at all is made.

2. All men (Jews and Gentiles alike) are sinful (as was shown above in 3:9-20) and cannot possibly be justified on the ground of their own personal righteousness or legal obedience. 3:23

3:23 RSV

²³since all have sinned and fall short of the glory of God,

3:23 WT

²³For everybody has sinned and everybody continues to come short of God's glory,

3. But sinners are justified (acquitted—put in right standing with God) by His grace (unmerited favor) as a gift. This method of justification has been made possible by the sacrificial death of Christ— the benefits of which are received by faith. 3:24

3:24 RSV

²⁴they are justified by his grace as a gift, through the redemption which is in Christ Jesus,

3:24 WT

²⁴but anybody may have right standing with God as a free gift of His undeserved favor, through the ransom provided in Christ Jesus.

4. The sacrificial death of Christ has satisfied the demands of justice; therefore God can righteously justify all who believe in Jesus Christ. Justice demands that sin be punished, and sin will be punished, either in the person of the unbelieving sinner or in the person of Jesus Christ, the believing sinner's substitute. 3:25,26

3:25,26 RSV

²⁵whom God put forward as an expiation by his blood, to be received by faith. This was to show God's righteousness, because in his divine forbearance he had ·passed over former sins; ²⁶it was to prove at the present time that he himself is righteous and that he justifies him who has faith in Jesus.

3:25,26 WT

²⁵For God once publicly offered Him in His death[k] as a sacrifice of reconciliation through faith, to demonstrate His own justice (for in His forbearance God had passed over men's former sins); ²⁶yes, to demonstrate His justice at the present time, to prove[l] that He is right Himself, and that He considers right with Himself the man who has faith in Jesus.

---

[k] Lit., in His blood (i.e., His death).
[l] Grk., in order to be right.

There are many Biblical scholars who contend that the Greek word, in vs. 25, rendered "expiation" by the RSV should be translated "propitiation." They point out that "expiation" is used to denote only the cancellation of sin, whereas "propitiation" denotes the turning away of the wrath of God; they hold that it is this latter idea which the Greek word properly conveys. This position is ably defended by Leon Morris in Chs. 4 and 5 of his work, The Apostolic Preaching of the Cross, published by Wm. B. Eerdmans Publishing Company, 1956. The BV renders the Greek word, " a reconciling sacrifice," the ASV, "a propitiation."

Paul is here explaining how God, being just, can justly declare a *guilty sinner* to be free from guilt. How can this be? "This seemingly impossible result was accomplished through the redemption that is in Christ Jesus. God sent Christ to die as a propitiatory sacrifice. To propitiate means to appease an injured party, to turn aside his wrath, to make him favorable to the offender. This is what Christ's blood accomplished. If it seemed unrighteous for God to acquit the guilty, Christ's death satisfied the requirements of righteousness, so that God could justify the sinner and at the same time remain just Himself. Christ's death, therefore, was a sacrifice to satisfy divine justice and as a consequence to reconcile us to God. Of course, not all sinners are acquitted. The benefit is restricted to those who have faith in Christ."[7]

5.   The results of the gospel method of justification. 3:27-31

3:27-31 RSV

[27]Then what becomes of our boasting? It is excluded. On what principle? On the principle of works? No, but on the principle of faith. [28]For we hold that a man is justified by faith apart from works of law. [29]Or is God the God of Jews only? Is he not the God of Gentiles also? Yes, of Gentiles also, [30]since God is one; and he will justify the circumcised on the ground of their faith and the uncircumcised because of their faith. [31]Do we then overthrow the law by this faith? By no means! On the contrary, we uphold the law.

3:27-31 WT

[27]So where has human boasting gone? It was completely shut out. On what principle?[m] On that of doing something? No, but on the principle of faith. [28]For we hold that a man is brought into right standing with God by faith, that observance of the law has no connection with it. [29]Or is He the God of Jews alone? Is He not the God of heathen peoples too? Of course, He is the God of heathen peoples too, [30]since there is but one God, who will consider the Jews in right standing with Himself, only on condition of their faith, and the heathen peoples on the same condition. [31]Do we then through faith make null and void the law? Not at all; instead, we confirm it.

[m] Lit., *through what sort of law* (in sense of principle of operation).

The RSV's choice of the word "ground" in vs. 30 is unfortunate due to the theological implication involved. It should not read ". . . he will justify the circumcised *on the ground of* their faith and the uncircumcised *because of* their faith"—but rather as the ASV gives it, ". . . he shall justify the circumcision *by* faith and the uncircumcision *through* faith." Compare the ANT. See Note 2, B, C, p. 30f. (notice especially the quotation from Packer in paragraph C) and the chart on page 32 for the distinction between the *Means* of Justification which is "Faith in Christ," and the *Ground* of Justification, which is the "Righteousness of Christ."

a.   The gospel method of justification excludes boasting, for sinners are justified through faith (relying or trusting) in Jesus Christ, *not* by their own works or goodness. 3:27,28

b.   It presents God as the God of all who believe (Jew and Gentile alike). 3:29,30

c.   It upholds the just demands of the law. 3:31

---

[7] Gordon H. Clark, "Romans," *The Biblical Expositor*, p. 243.

B. The case of Abraham is cited as an illustration and proof of the gospel method of Justification by Faith apart from works. 4:1-25

1. Abraham, the father of the Jewish nation, was justified by faith apart from works. 4:1-5

4:1-5 RSV

What then shall we say about[e] Abraham, our forefather according to the flesh? [2]For if Abraham was justified by works, he has something to boast about, but not before God. [3]For what does the scripture say? "Abraham believed God, and it was reckoned to him as righteousness." [4]Now to one who works, his wages are not reckoned as a gift but as his due. [5]And to one who does not work but trusts him who justifies the ungodly, his faith is reckoned as righteousness.

[e] Other ancient authorities read *was gained by*

4:1-5 WT

Then what are we to say about our forefather Abraham?[a] [2]For if he was considered in right standing with God on the condition of what he did, he has something to boast of; but not before God. [3]For what does the Scripture say? "Abraham put his faith in God, and it was credited to him as right standing with God."[b] [4]Now when a workman gets his pay, it is not considered from the point of view of a favor[c] but of an obligation; [5]but the man who does no work, but simply puts his faith in Him who brings the ungodly into right standing with Himself, has his faith credited to him as right standing.

[a] Fol. WH and best Mss.
[b] Gen. 15:6.
[c] Lit., *in accordance with favor.*

a. If Abraham, the father of the Jews according to the flesh, had been justified by works (personal righteousness) he would have had grounds for boasting—even in the sight of God. 4:1,2

But Abraham had no such ground for boasting, for he, like all other men, was sinful and without personal righteousness. Cf. the passages in Part II of Appendix D on "Total Depravity," pp. 152-158.

b. The Scriptures state clearly that he was justified by faith, "Abraham believed God and it was reckoned (imputed) to him as righteousness." 4:3

In explaining the statement concerning faith being reckoned (imputed) to Abraham as righteousness, Clark correctly observes that "The wording here, if detached from the main material of Romans 3:25,26, might give the impression that faith itself is the basis of justification. But Paul allows himself some abbreviation of language in view of the fact that he had spoken so explicitly in the verses above. He had already spoken of faith in Christ and of being justified by faith in His blood. When God acquits a sinner, He does so on the ground of a righteousness that He gives to the sinner. The righteousness comes to the sinner by faith; but from the beginning (1:17) Paul has indicated that it is the righteousness and not the faith which God regards when

He says, Not guilty. One should never forget that it is the object of the faith, and not the faith itself, that produces the result."[8] See Note 2, B,C, p. 30f. and the Chart on p. 32.

  c. The two methods of justification—by works and by faith —are shown to rest on two contrary principles—merit and grace. 4:4,5

  (1) *Justification by works* rests on the principle that men earn their salvation by doing good. Good men are saved by their good works. Salvation then is not a gift but a wage. 4:4

  (2) *Justification by faith* rests on the principle that God imputes righteousness as a free gift to the ungodly who believe in Him. Salvation is not earned by the sinner but is freely given to him when he believes. 4:5

  2. Paul argues from the words of David: (1) that righteousness is reckoned (imputed) to the believing sinner apart from his own works, and quotes from the Psalmist showing (2) that the believer's sins are not reckoned to him (see Psalm 32:1,2). The reason the believer's sins are not imputed to him is that they were imputed to Christ (see Isaiah 53, cf., I Peter 2:24,25). 4:6-8

<table>
<tr><td>4:6-8 RSV</td><td>4:6-8 WT</td></tr>
<tr><td>[6]"So also David pronounces a blessing upon the man to whom God reckons righteousness apart from works:
[7]"Blessed are those whose iniquities are forgiven, and whose sins are covered;
[8]blessed is the man against whom the Lord will not reckon his sin."</td><td>[6]"So David, too, describes[d] the happiness of the man to whom God credits right standing with Himself, without the things he does having anything to do with it:[e]
[7]"Happy are they whose transgressions have been forgiven, Whose sins were covered up;
[8]Happy the man whose sin the Lord does not charge against him!"[f]</td></tr>
</table>

[d] Lit., *mentions.*
[e] Grk., *apart from works.*
[f] Ps. 32:1, 2.

The Outline of Romans is continued on p. 33.

NOTE NO. 2 THE IMPUTATION OF SIN AND RIGHTEOUSNESS IN RELATION TO CHRIST AND THE BELIEVER

A. *Meaning of "Imputation"*

  To impute something to a person means to set it to his account or to number it among the things belonging to him—to reckon it to him. If something is imputed to a person, it is made his legally; it is

---

[8] Clark, "Romans," (above, fn. 7), pp. 243, 244.

counted or imputed as his possession. To impute means to account, charge, credit, reckon, attribute, etc. "It makes no difference, so far as the meaning of imputation is concerned, who it is that imputes, whether man (I Sam. 22:15) or God (Ps 32:2); it makes no difference what is imputed, whether a good deed for reward (Ps 106:30f) or a bad deed for punishment (Lev. 17:4); and it makes no difference whether that which is imputed is something which is personally one's own prior to the imputation, as in the case above cited, where his own good deed was imputed to Phinehas (Ps 106:30f), or something which is not personally one's own prior to the imputation, as where Paul asks that a debt not personally his own be charged to him (Philem. ver 18). In all these cases the act of imputation is simply the charging of one with something . . . . Hence when God is said 'to impute sin' to anyone, the meaning is that God accounts such a one to be a sinner, and consequently guilty and liable to punishment. Similarly, the non-imputation of sin means simply not to lay it to one's charge as a ground of punishment (Ps 32:2). In the same manner, when God is said 'to impute righteousness' to a person, the meaning is that He judicially accounts such a one to be righteous and entitled to all the rewards of a righteous person (Rom 4:6,11)."[9]

B. *The GROUND of Justification*

The twofold imputation of sin and righteousness (in relation to Christ and the believer) forms the *ground* of justification. (1) The believer's sins were imputed to Christ—this is why He suffered and died on the cross (see I Peter 2:24, II Cor. 5:21). Christ became legally responsible for the believer's sins and underwent the believer's just punishment. By dying as the believer's substitute, He satisfied the demands of justice and forever freed the believer from any possibility of condemnation or punishment. When the believer's sins were imputed to Christ, the act of imputation in no way made Him sinful or polluted His nature —it in no way affected His character; it only made Him *legally* responsible for those sins. Imputation does not change one's nature; it only affects one's legal standing. (2) Jesus Christ lived a perfect life—He completely kept God's law. The personal righteousness worked out by Christ during His life on earth is imputed to the sinner the moment he believes. The believer is credited with Christ's righteousness and God views him as if he had done all the good that Christ did. Christ's obedience, His merit, His personal righteousness is imputed to (credited to, set to the account of) the believer. This in no way changes the believer's nature (any more than the imputation of sin to Christ changed His nature); it only affects the believer's legal standing before God.

---

[9] Caspar Wistar Hodge, "Imputation," *The International Standard Bible Encyclopaedia*, p. 1462.

C. *The MEANS of Justification*

The *means* by which the sinner receives the benefits of Christ's saving work (His sinless life and sacrificial death) is *faith in Him.* No one can be justified apart from faith, yet, no one is justified on the basis of his faith. Faith itself does not save the sinner but brings him to Christ who saves him; therefore, faith, though a necessary *means* to justification, is not itself the *cause* or *ground* of justification. "Paul says that believers are justified *dia pisteos* (Rom. 3:25), *pistei* (Rom. 3:28) and *ek pisteos* (Rom. 3:30). The dative and the preposition *dia* represent faith as the instrumental means whereby Christ and his righteousness are appropriated; the preposition *ek* shows that faith occasions, and logically precedes, our personal justification. That believers are justified *dia pistin,* on account of faith, Paul never says, and would deny. Were faith the ground of justification, faith would be in effect a meritorious work, and the gospel message would, after all, be merely another version of justification by works—a doctrine which Paul opposes in all forms as irreconcilable with grace, and spiritually ruinous (cf. Rom. 4:4; 11:6; Gal. 4:21-5:12). Paul regards faith, not as itself our justifying righteousness, but rather as the outstretched empty hand which receives righteousness by receiving Christ."[10] See Note 9, p. 84 on "Saving Faith."

D. *The Distinction between "Imputed" and "Personal" Righteousness*

We must be careful not to confuse *imputed* righteousness (which is received by faith alone and is the only ground of justification) with the *personal acts* of righteousness which are performed by believers as a result of the Holy Spirit's work in their hearts. These personal acts of righteousness in no way secure or add to our justification. To quote the words of Hodge, ". . . the righteousness for which we are justified is neither anything done by us nor wrought in us, but something done for us and imputed to us. It is the work of Christ, what he did and suffered to satisfy the demands of the law . . . . It is nothing that we have either wrought ourselves, or that inheres in us. Hence Christ is said to be our righteousness; and we are said to be justified by his blood, his death, his obedience; we are righteous in him, and are justified by him or in his name, or for his sake. The righteousness of God, therefore, which the gospel reveals, and by which we are constituted righteous, is the perfect righteousness of Christ which completely meets and answers all the demands of that law to which all men are subject, and which all have broken."[11]

For a visual illustration of the relationship between the *ground* of Justification which is the *Work of Christ* and the *means* of Justification which is *Faith in Christ,* see the chart on the following page.

---

[10] Packer, "Justification," (above, fn. 6), pp. 306, 307.
[11] Hodge, *Romans,* p. 31.

The *GROUND* of Justification is THE WORK OF CHRIST

The *MEANS* of Justification is FAITH IN CHRIST

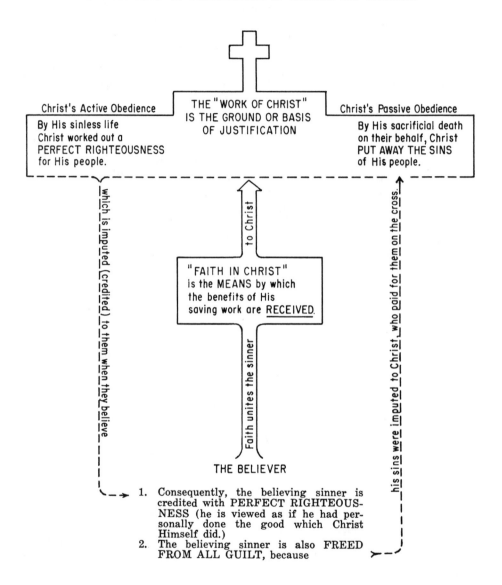

Christ's Active Obedience

THE "WORK OF CHRIST"
IS THE GROUND OR BASIS
OF JUSTIFICATION

Christ's Passive Obedience

By His sinless life
Christ worked out a
PERFECT RIGHTEOUSNESS
for His people.

By His sacrificial death
on their behalf, Christ
PUT AWAY THE SINS
of His people.

which is imputed (credited) to them when they believe

to Christ

his sins were imputed to Christ, who paid for them on the cross.

"FAITH IN CHRIST"
is the MEANS by which
the benefits of His
saving work are RECEIVED.

Faith unites the sinner

THE BELIEVER

1. Consequently, the believing sinner is credited with PERFECT RIGHTEOUS-NESS (he is viewed as if he had personally done the good which Christ Himself did.)

2. The believing sinner is also FREED FROM ALL GUILT, because

For the meaning of "Justification" see Note 1, p. 24.

For the meaning of "Imputed Righteousness" see Note 2, p. 29.

For the meaning of "Saving Faith" see Note 9, p. 84.

As to the necessity of faith for salvation see Note 10, p. 87.

E. *"The Righteousness of God"*

Eight times in the Roman letter reference is made to the righteousness of God. (1) Three times it has reference to God's attribute of justice, see Romans 3:5,25,26. (2) Five times (in 1:17; 3:21,22, and twice in 10:3) it has reference to that righteousness which God gives (imputes) to all who believe in His Son. The righteousness which He gives is apart from works of law (see Romans 3:28, and 4:1-8,23-25); it is not our own (Phil. 3:9); it is the gift of God (Rom. 5:17) and is received by faith (Rom. 1:17, RSV, and 9:30—10:4; Gal. 2:15-21). In I Corinthians 1:30 Paul speaks of Christ as being our "righteousness."

The Outline of Romans is continued from p. 29.

3. Abraham is the father of all who believe, whether Jew (the circumcised) or Gentile (the uncircumcised). 4:9-12

4:9-12 RSV

⁹Is this blessing pronounced only upon the circumcised, or also upon the uncircumcised? We say that faith was reckoned to Abraham as righteousness. ¹⁰How then was it reckoned to him? Was it before or after he had been circumcised? It was not after, but before he was circumcised. ¹¹He received circumcision as a sign or seal of the righteousness which he had by faith while he was still uncircumcised. The purpose was to make him the father of all who believe without being circumcised and who thus have righteousness reckoned to them, ¹²and likewise the father of the circumcised who are not merely circumcised but also follow the example of the faith which our father Abraham had before he was circumcised.

4:9-12 WT

⁹Now does this happiness come to the Jews alone, or to the heathen peoples too? For we say, "Abraham's faith was credited to him as right standing." ¹⁰Under what circumstances[g] was it credited to him as right standing? Was it after he was circumcised, or before? Not after but before he was circumcised. ¹¹Afterward he received the mark of circumcision as God's seal of his right standing with Him on condition of faith[h] which he had before he was circumcised, that he might be the forefather of all who have faith while still uncircumcised,[i] that they might have their faith credited to them as right standing with God; ¹²and the forefather of those Jews who not only belong to the circumcision but also follow in the footsteps of our forefather Abraham in the faith he had before he was circumcised.

[g] Grk., *how* or *when*.
[h] Descriptive gen.
[i] Lit., *during uncircumcision.*

a. The blessing of imputed righteousness does not rest upon circumcision. This is proved by the fact that Abraham had righteousness reckoned to him before he was circumcised. 4:9,10

b. Abraham received circumcision as a "sign" or "seal" of the righteousness which he had received by faith. 4:11a

c. The reason Abraham received righteousness through faith before he was circumcised was to make him *the father of all who believe;* both of the uncircumcised (the Gentiles) and of the circumcised (the Jews). 4:11b,12

4. The promise to Abraham and to his (spiritual) descendants (all true believers) that they would inherit the world never rested on the law but always rested on imputed righteousness which is received by faith. 4:13-17

4:13-17 RSV

[13]The promise to Abraham and his descendants, that they should inherit the world, did not come through the law but through the righteousness of faith. [14]If it is the adherents of the law who are to be the heirs, faith is null and the promise is void. [15]For the law brings wrath, but where there is no law there is no transgression.

[16]That is why it depends on faith, in order that the promise may rest on grace and be guaranteed to all his descendants—not only to the adherents of the law but also to those who share the faith of Abraham, for he is the father of us all, [17]as it is written, "I have made you the father of many nations"—in the presence of the God in whom he believed, who gives life to the dead and calls into existence the things that do not exist.

4:13-17 WT

[13]For the promise made to Abraham and his descendants, that he should own the world, was not conditioned on the law,[j] but on the right standing he had with God through faith. [14]For if the law party is to possess the world, then faith has been nullified and the promise has been made null and void. [15]For the law results[k] in wrath alone; but where there is no law, there can be no violation of it. [16]So it is conditioned on faith,[l] that it might be in accordance with God's unmerited favor, so that the promise might be in force[m] for all the descendants of Abraham, not only for those who belong to the law party but also for those who belong to the faith group of Abraham. He is the father of us all, [17]as the Scripture says, "I have made you the father of many nations."[n] That is, the promise is in force in the sight of God in whom he put his faith, the God who can bring the dead to life and can call to Himself the things that do not exist as though they did.

[j] Grk., *through the law.*
[k] Lit., *produces, effects.*
[l] Grk., *out of faith.*
[m] Used in this sense to describe documents that are valid.
[n] Gen. 17:5.

The law cannot save sinners, it only brings wrath to them; consequently, *the promise* (of salvation given in the Abrahamic Covenant) rests on grace and is assured to all who believe.

5. Abraham's faith illustrates the gospel method of Justification by Faith. (The promise made to him contained the gospel, Gal. 3: 8.) 4:18-25

4:18-25 RSV

[18]In hope he believed against hope, that he should become the father of many nations; as he had been told, "So shall your descendants be." [19]He did not weaken in faith when he considered his own body, which was as good as dead because

4:18-25 WT

[18]Abraham, building on hope in spite of hopeless circumstances, had faith, and so he actually became the father of many nations, just as it had been told him, "So numberless shall your descendants be."[o] [19]Because he never weakened in

[o] In same verse.

34

he was about a hundred years old, or when he considered the barrenness of Sarah's womb. [20]No distrust made him waver concerning the promise of God, but he grew strong in his faith as he gave glory to God, [21]fully convinced that God was able to do what he had promised. [22]That is why his faith was "reckoned to him as righteousness." [23]But the words, "it was reckoned to him," were written not for his sake alone, [24]but for ours also. It will be reckoned to us who believe in him that raised from the dead Jesus our Lord, [25]who was put to death for our trespasses and raised for our justification.

faith, he calmly contemplated his own vital powers as worn out (for he was about one hundred years old) and the inability of Sarah to bear a child, [20]and yet he never staggered in doubt at the promise of God but grew powerful in faith, because he gave the glory to God [21]in full assurance that He was able to do what He had promised. [22]Therefore, his faith was credited to him as right standing with God.

[23]It was not for his sake alone that it was written, "It was credited to him"; [24]it was for our sakes too, for it is going to be credited to us who put our faith in God who raised from the dead our Lord Jesus, [25]who was given up to death because of our shortcomings and was raised again to give us right standing with God.

a. The object of Abraham's faith was God's promise that He would make him the father of many nations. 4:18

b. The strength of his faith is seen in that he believed God's promise, though it seemed impossible that it could come to pass. 4:19, 20

c. The ground of his faith was the ability and faithfulness of God to do what He had promised. 4:21

d. The result of his faith was that he was made righteous (justified). 4:22

e. The record of his faith was given to teach us that all who believe in the death and resurrection of Christ are, like Abraham, counted righteous and therefore justified. 4:23-25

The resurrection of Jesus Christ demonstrates the fact that God has accepted His sacrificial death as the full payment for the believer's sins and thus shows that those who trust in Him are justified.

C. Some of the blessings resulting from justification by faith. 5:1-11

1. Believers have peace with God. 5:1

5:1 RSV

Therefore, since we are justified by faith, we[f] have peace with God through our Lord Jesus Christ.

_____
[f] Other ancient authorities read let us

5:1 WT

Since we have been given right standing with God through faith, then let us continue enjoying[a] peace with God through our Lord Jesus Christ,

_____
[a] Lit., holding or having, so enjoying.

35

2. Believers, because they stand in God's favor through Christ, rejoice in their hope of sharing in God's glory. 5:2

5:2 RSV	5:2 WT
[2]Through him we have obtained access[g] to this grace in which we stand, and we[h] rejoice in our hope of sharing the glory of God.<hr>[g] Other ancient authorities add *by faith* [h] Or *let us*	[2]by whom we have an introduction through faith into this state of God's favor, in which we safely stand;[b] and let us continue exulting in the hope of enjoying the glorious presence of God.<hr>[b] Pf. implies this.

3. Believers rejoice in their suffering, knowing that these sufferings produce endurance (fortitude) which in turn produces character (tried integrity) which in turn produces hope that does not disappoint them, for the Holy Spirit (who has been given to them) assures believers that they are the objects of God's love. 5:3-5

5:3-5 RSV	5:3-5 WT
[3]More than that, we[h] rejoice in our sufferings, knowing that suffering produces endurance, [4]and endurance produces character, and character produces hope, [5]and hope does not disappoint us, because God's love has been poured into our hearts through the Holy Spirit which has been given to us.<hr>[h] Or *let us*	[3]And not only that, but this too: let us continue exulting in our sufferings,[c] for we know that suffering produces endurance, [4]and endurance, tested character, and tested character, hope, [5]and hope never disappoints[d] us; for through the Holy Spirit that has been given us, God's love has flooded[e] our hearts.<hr>[c] Lit., *pressing burdens.* [d] Grk., *puts to shame.* [e] Lit., *poured out into.*

4. Believers are assured of final salvation. 5:6-11

5:6-11 RSV	5:6-11 WT
[6]While we were yet helpless, at the right time Christ died for the ungodly. [7]Why, one will hardly die for a righteous man—though perhaps for a good man one will dare even to die. [8]But God shows his love for us in that while we were yet sinners Christ died for us. [9]Since, therefore, we are now justified by his blood, much more shall we be saved by him from the wrath of God. [10]For if while we were enemies we were reconciled to God by the death of his Son, much more, now that we are reconciled, shall we be saved by his life. [11]Not only so, but we also rejoice in God through our Lord Jesus Christ, through whom we have now received our reconciliation.	[6]For when we were still helpless, Christ at the proper time died for us ungodly men. [7]Now a man will scarcely ever give his life for an upright person, though once in a while a man is brave enough to die for a generous friend.[f] [8]But God proves His love for us by the fact that Christ died for us while we were still sinners. [9]So if we have already been brought into right standing with God by Christ's death, it is much more certain that by Him we shall be saved from God's wrath. [10]For if while we were God's enemies, we were reconciled to Him through the death of His Son, it is much more certain that since we have been reconciled we shall finally[g] be saved<hr>[f] Grk., *a good man,* but qualities of unselfish generosity included. [g] Context shows it is our final salvation at the resurrection.

through His new[h] life. [11]And not only that, but this too: we shall continue exulting in God through our Lord Jesus Christ, through whom we have obtained our reconciliation.

[h] I.e., His resurrection life.

a. God has proved His love for believers (even while they were ungodly sinners) by giving His Son to die in their behalf. 5:6-8

b. Since they have already been justified (declared righteous) and reconciled to God by Christ's death, how much more then shall they be saved from God's wrath through Christ who now lives in their behalf (see John 14:19; Romans 8:11; I Corinthians 15:23; Hebrews 7:25; Matthew 28:18, cf., Ephesians 1:20-22). Believers, because they are reconciled to God, have present and abounding joy. 5:9-11

D. The gospel method of justification illustrated through a comparison of the saving work of Christ with the condemning work of Adam. 5:12-21

Introduction: Paul's design is to show that *just as* the race was condemned on the ground of the imputation of Adam's one sin, *even so* believers are justified on the ground of the imputation of Christ's righteousness. The central idea of the passage is that men are saved in precisely the same manner in which they were lost—through the act of another. As Adam, by his one transgression, brought condemnation to all connected with him, so Christ, by His act of righteousness (His sinless life and substitutionary death) brought justification to all connected with Him.

1. Adam, by his one sin, brought sin and death upon all the race. 5:12-14

5:12-14 RSV	5:12-14 WT
[12]Therefore as sin came into the world through one man and death through sin, and so death spread to all men because all men sinned—[13]sin indeed was in the world before the law was given, but sin is not counted where there is no law. [14]Yet death reigned from Adam to Moses, even over those whose sins were not like the transgression of Adam, who was a type of the one who was to come.	[12]So here is the comparison:[i] As through one man sin came into the world, and death as the consequence of sin, and death spread to all men, because all men sinned. [13]Certainly sin was in the world before the law was given, but it is not charged to men's account where there is no law. [14]And yet death reigned from Adam to Moses, even over those who had not sinned in the way Adam had, against a positive command.[j] For Adam was a figure of Him who was to come.

[i] Lit., *so just as.*
[j] Grk., *in the likeness of Adam's transgression.*

Neither the RSV nor the WT gives a satisfactory rendering of verse 14a. The rendering of the phrase "whose sins [plural] were not like the transgression of Adam" by the RSV, obscures Paul's meaning. Williams' addition "against a positive command" is lacking in the Greek (as is indicated in his footnote J). The ASV gives a much better translation of 14a: "Nevertheless death reigned from Adam until Moses, *even over them that had not sinned after the likeness of Adam's transgression.*" As will be shown below, the apostle is *not* here speaking of the *many personal sins* committed by these individuals, *but of Adam's first sin* which had been *imputed to the race* and which had consequently brought them under the curse of spiritual and physical death.

a. Sin came into the world through the first man Adam, and death, which is the result of sin, spread to all men because all men sinned in Adam (i.e., were constituted sinners on the ground of his one sin). 5:12

It should be noted that the death spoken of in this passage involves more than just the separation of the soul from the body (physical death) ; it also has reference to spiritual or eternal death which also resulted from sin. Hodge states that, "the death here spoken of includes all penal evil, death spiritual and eternal, as well as the dissolution of the body . . . . " After giving several arguments in support of this view he concludes, "As however, natural death is a part, and the most obvious part of the penal evils of sin, it no doubt was prominent in the apostle's mind, as appears from vers. 13, 14."[12]

b. The proof of the assertion of verse 12 (that all men are under the sentence of spiritual and physical death as the result of Adam's one sin) is demonstrated in verses 13 and 14.

The argument is that:

(1)   Since sin is the violation of law, there can be no sin or guilt apart from the breaking of a law. 5:13

(2)   Since death—which is the result of sin (vs. 12)— reigned over all who lived from Adam to Moses (infants included), it follows that all were counted guilty as the result of the violation of some law. 5:14

(a)   The fact that death was universal (from Adam to Moses) cannot be accounted for on the basis of the violation of the law of Moses (the Ten Commandments, etc.), for it had not been given. (5:13a)

(b)   The fact that death was universal cannot be accounted for on the basis of the violation of the law written on the heart (see 2:12-16), for infants cannot break that law, yet they too were subject to death. (5:14a)

(3)   Since all were treated as guilty creatures and were under the sentence of death and condemnation (even those who could not have *personally* broken any law, either the law written on the heart or the law of Moses), it follows that all were constituted sinners and

---

[12] Hodge, *Romans*, p. 148.

treated as guilty because of ADAM'S ONE SIN (i.e., Adam's sin was imputed to them). This idea is repeatedly emphasized in verses 15-19: "many died through *one man's trespass*" (vs. 15) ; "The judgment following *one trespass* brought condemnation" (vs. 16) ; "because of *one man's trespass*, death reigned through that *one man*" (vs. 17) ; "*one man's trespass* led to condemnation for all men" (vs. 18) ; "by *one man's disobedience* many were made sinners," (vs. 19). The point here is that all men are guilty as the result of ONE MAN'S SIN, not as the result of many personal sins!

c. In verse 14b Adam is spoken of as a "type" or "figure" of the One who was to come, namely, Jesus Christ. How was Adam a "type" of Christ? As Hodge shows, "A type, . . . in the religious sense of the term, is not a mere historical parallel or incidental resemblance between persons or events, but a designed resemblance—the one being intended to prefigure or to commemorate the other. It is in this sense that Adam was the type of Christ. The resemblance between them was not casual. It was predetermined, and entered into the whole plan of God. As Adam was the head and representative of his race, whose destiny was suspended on his conduct, so Christ is the head and representative of his people. As the sin of the one was the ground of our condemnation, so the righteousness of the other is the ground of our justification. This relation between Adam and the Messiah was recognized by the Jews, who called their expected deliverer, . . . *the last Adam*, as Paul also calls him in I Cor. 15:45."[13]

2. Before carrying out the comparison between the work of Christ and the work of Adam, Paul shows one outstanding respect in which the two are not parallel. 5:15-17

5:15-17 RSV

[15]But the free gift is not like the trespass. For if many died through one man's trespass, much more have the grace of God and the free gift in the grace of that one man Jesus Christ abounded for many. [16]And the free gift is not like the effect of that one man's sin. For the judgment following one trespass brought condemnation, but the free gift following many trespasses brings justification. [17]If, because of one man's trespass, death reigned through that one man, much more will those who receive the abundance of grace and the free gift of righteousness reign in life through the one man Jesus Christ.

5:15-17 WT

[15]But God's free gift is not at all to be compared with the offense. For if by one man's offense the whole race of men have[k] died, to a much greater degree God's favor and His gift imparted by His favor through the one man Jesus Christ, has overflowed for the whole race of men. [16]And the gift is not at all to be compared with the results of that one man's sin. For that sentence resulted from the offense of one man, and it meant condemnation; but the free gift resulted from the offenses of many, and it meant right standing. [17]For if by one man's offense death reigned through that one, to a much greater degree will those who continue to receive the overflow of His unmerited

[k] Grk., *the many have died.*

[13] Hodge, *Romans*, p. 162.

> favor and His gift of right standing with Himself, reign in real life through One, Jesus Christ.

The works of the two differ in that Christ did *much more* for His people than just to remove the imputed guilt of Adam's one sin; He also made complete satisfaction for all of their personal sins and in addition imputes to them perfect righteousness as a free gift, thus causing them to reign in life! (Verses 13-17 form a parenthesis between verses 12 and 18.)

    3.   The comparison introduced in verse 12 is resumed, and the parallel between the condemning work of Adam and the saving work of Christ is completed. 5:18,19

5:18,19 RSV

[18]Then as one man's trespass led to condemnation for all men, so one man's act of righteousness leads to acquittal and life for all men. [19]For as by one man's disobedience many were made sinners, so by one man's obedience many will be made righteous.

5:18,19 WT

[18]So, as through one offense there resulted condemnation for all men, just so through one act of uprightness there resulted right standing involving life for all men. [19]For just as by that man's disobedience the whole race of men were constituted sinners, so by this One's obedience the whole race of men may be brought into right standing with God.

The phrase *"the whole race of men"* in Williams' translation of vs. 19 is inaccurate and misleading. The ASV gives a much more literal and accurate rendering. "For as through the one man's disobedience *the many* were made sinners, even so through the obedience of the one shall *the many* be made righteous." Compare BV, ANT, and the NEB. (Notice also footnote K in vs. 15, WT.) Verse 19b, when properly translated, does not read "by this One's obedience the whole race of men *may* be brought into right standing with God" as Williams gives it. On the contrary the sense of the verse, when properly translated, is that "the many" *shall* (without fail) be constituted righteous (i.e., justified), as the result of Christ's obedience. See Note 3, C, p. 42.

In commenting on *"made sinners . . . made righteous"* in verse 19, Bishop Moule writes, "Better, constituted, 'put into a position' of guilt and righteousness respectively. Here the whole context points to not a moral change but a legal standing. In Adam 'the many' became, in the eye of the Law, guilty; in Christ 'the many' shall become, in the eye of the Law, righteous. In other words, they shall be justified.—*'Shall be made:'*—the future refers to the succession of believers. The justification of all was, ideally, complete already; but, actually, it would await the times of individual *believing.—'Many:'*—lit., in both cases, 'the many.' "[14]

The heart of the argument of Romans 5:12-21 is contained in verses 12, 18, and 19. These three verses should be given special study.

_____

[14] Bishop H. C. G. Moule, *The Epistle of Paul the Apostle to the Romans*, p. 110. Italics are his.

The point of the argument is to show that men are justified on the ground of the imputed righteousness of Christ just as they were condemned on the ground of the imputed sin of Adam. By means of the comparison between the fall of the race in Adam and the recovery of believers in Christ, Paul illustrates the gospel method of justification. For a scholarly and penetrating discussion of the solidarity that existed between Adam and the race, consult John Murray's book, *The Imputation of Adam's Sin*, published by Wm. B. Eerdmans Publishing Co., (1959).

4. The *law of Moses* was added and thus increased man's transgression, but where sin increased, God's grace overflowed (abounded) all the more by bringing righteousness (justification) and life through Jesus Christ. 5:20,21

5:20,21 RSV	5:20,21 WT
[20]Law came in, to increase the trespass; but where sin increased, grace abounded all the more, [21]so that, as sin reigned in death, grace also might reign through righteousness to eternal life through Jesus Christ our Lord.	[20]Then law crept in to multiply the offense. Though sin has multiplied, yet God's favor has surpassed it and overflowed, [21]so that just as sin had reigned by death, so His favor too might reign in right standing with God which issues in eternal life through Jesus Christ our Lord.

a. The law of Moses came in (was added by God) for the express purpose of increasing man's guilt. 5:20a

Many people think that God gave the law at Mt. Sinai for the purpose of showing men how, through keeping the commandments, they could save themselves. But as 5:20a so clearly reveals, this is a completely wrong idea. Instead of the law aiding man in saving himself, it brought greater guilt and condemnation just as it was designed to do. The law of Moses increased man's transgression by making sin known and thereby increasing his guilt (see 3:20; 7:7-12) and also by arousing in man desires for that which the law forbids (see 7:5,8). For the nature and function of the law, see Note 5, p. 53. Cf. Note 1, B, p. 25.

b. But where sin increased (as the result of law breaking), *grace* abounded all the more and through Jesus Christ brought righteousness and life. 5:20b,21

The Outline of Romans is continued on p. 45.

NOTE NO. 3   THE REPRESENTATIVE WORK OF ADAM AND CHRIST

In Romans 5:12-21 Paul compares the saving work of Christ to the condemning work of Adam. By means of this comparison he illustrates that the methods of justification and condemnation are the same in principle. Sinners are justified through the imputation of Christ's righteousness just as they were condemned through the imputation of Adam's sin. The point of the passage is that just as the race was lost through the representative act of the "first" Adam even so believers are saved through the representative act of the "last" Adam. It was to emphasize the similarity between the representative work of these two that Paul refers to Adam as a "type" of the One who was to come—Jesus Christ. See the Outline on 5:14b.

A. *Adam, the Head and Representative of the Race:*

Adam served not only as the natural head but also as the legal head or guardian of the human race. As the result of the arrangement under which God placed Adam there existed such a solidarity between him and all those who were destined to come from him through natural generation, that Adam's act (while on probation in the garden of Eden) was counted as the act of each of his descendants. Consequently, when Adam transgressed God's commandment (not to eat of the forbidden tree), his sin was imputed or charged to all men as much so as if they had individually and personally committed that sin. Because of Adam's sin we each stand before God from the first moment of our existence as depraved and guilty sinners for we each sinned "in him." For the meaning of Imputation, see Note 2, A, p. 29.

B. *Jesus Christ, the Head and Representative of God's Elect:*

Jesus Christ, "the second man," the "last Adam" (I Cor. 15:45-47) like the first man Adam, served as the head and representative of the people whom the Father had given to Him before the foundation of the world (see John 17). The Son of God became a man and was tested throughout His earthly life. But, unlike the first Adam, Jesus rendered perfect obedience to the Father and worked out a perfect righteousness which is imputed to all who believe in Him. Christ's representative work (His obedience) forms the ground for the justification of His people *just as* Adam's representative work (his transgression) formed the ground for the condemnation of the race. God views all humanity as under one of two heads, either Adam or Christ—the first brought condemnation and death, the second brings justification and life. See the Outline on 5:12-21.

C. It must be noted that there are two distinct groups referred to by the adjective "all" in Romans 5:12-19:

1. Group one refers to "all men" *in Adam,* which, of course, includes every member of the human race.

2. Group two refers to "all men" *in Christ,* which includes all the saved or elect. Only "those who receive the abundance of grace and the free gift of righteousness" can be classed in this group. See verse 17 and Romans 1:16,17.

Bishop Moule's observations on Romans 5:18, "Then as one man's trespass led to condemnation for all men, so one man's act of righteousness leads to acquittal and life for all men," deserve consideration. "What is the reference of these words in the two cases respectively [*all men . . . all men*]? In the first, certainly, *all mankind* is meant. Every man, not in theory only but fact, incurred sentence of death in Adam. In the second case also, many commentators, (e.g. Meyer,) hold that all mankind is intended: not that all actually receive justification, but that all are within the scope of Christ's work. Without entering on the profound question of the Divine Intentions, and merely seeking for St. Paul's *special thought here*, we prefer to take the second 'all men' *with a limit*, as meaning 'all who are connected with the Second Adam;' all 'His brethren.' For through this whole context St. Paul is dealing with results and facts, not with abstract theory. From the dreadful fact of the result of death from the Fall he reasons to the results of Christ's work; and the parallel would be most imperfect (and such as precisely to *contradict* the '*much more*' of vs. 15,17,) if while in the one case condemnation was a fact and act, Justification should be only a possibility in the other. If Adam brings death *in fact* on all concerned, Christ must bring life *in fact* on all concerned also. Again, a limitation is suggested by the whole reasoning of the Epistle, and specifically by 8:30, where the justified are identical with the 'foreknown' and 'glorified,' in the plain sense of the passage.—The use of 'all men' with this change of reference is fairly illustrated by I Cor. 15:22,23. For through that whole ch. the Resurrection *of the Church* is the sole subject; and vs. 23 explicitly refers to 'them that are Christ's:' and yet, when the parallel of Adam and Christ is in view, the word 'all' is equally used there in both cases (*Romans*, p. 109. Italics his). The verses referred to by Moule where Paul changes his reference in the use of "all" read as follows: "For as in Adam all die, so also in Christ shall all be made alive. But each in his own order: Christ the first fruits, then at his coming those who belong to Christ" (I Cor. 15:22,23). Notice that in the first instance the "all" includes *all the race—all in Adam*, whereas in the second instance "all" has reference to *all who belong to Christ—all who are in Him!*

Consult the excellent treatment of Romans 5:12-21 in Hodge's commentary, pp. 142-191. For additional Scriptural testimony concerning the *definite design* of Christ's representative or redemptive work, see Part II of Appendix D, pp. 166-175.

See the illustration of the comparison between the representative work of Adam and Christ on the following page.

THE PARALLEL BETWEEN THE CONDEMNING WORK OF THE
FIRST ADAM AND THE SAVING WORK OF THE LAST ADAM
ILLUSTRATED

Rom. 5:12-21

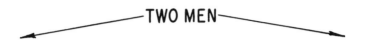

The first Adam (a type of) _____ The last Adam—Christ
Vs. 12.   Vs. 14.

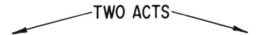

One trespass, one man's sin, one   One man's act of righteousness, one
man's disobedience. Vss. 15,16,17,   man's obedience. Vss. 18,19.
18, & 19.

Sin, death, judgment, condemna-   Free gift, grace, righteousness, life,
tion. Vss. 12,14,15,16,17,18,19, & 21.   justification, acquittal. Vss. 15, 16,
                                                          17,18,19, & 21.

Each REPRESENTED His People

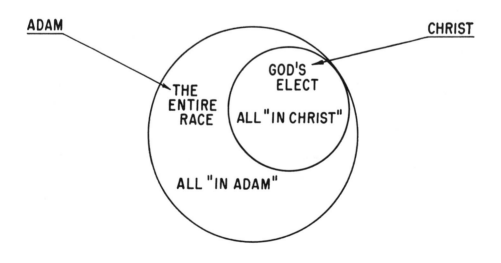

The Outline of Romans is continued from p. 41.

V. PAUL SHOWS HOW UNFOUNDED IS THE OBJECTION THAT BEING JUSTIFIED BY FAITH APART FROM PERSONAL MERIT LEADS ONE TO LIVE A LIFE OF SIN. ON THE CONTRARY, GRACE IS THE SUPREME MOTIVE FOR OBEDIENCE AND INEVITABLY RESULTS IN HOLY LIVING! 6:1—7:6

Introduction: In every age there have been those who have denounced the doctrine of justification by faith on the ground that it logically leads to sin. "If all the believer's sins have already been paid for, if he has already been credited with perfect righteousness, if his good works will not help save him—if all this is true," ask the opponents, "then why worry about sin? why try to do good? why strive to live a righteous life?" Romans 6 answers all such objections showing that the truly justified sinner will take no such attitude. He will not sin that grace may abound (vs. 1), nor will he sin because he is under grace and not under law (vs. 14). On the contrary, the gospel method of salvation by grace leads to true obedience—it inevitably results in good works! But the justified sinner's obedience results from love, not fear; his good works are performed out of gratitude for God's free gift of salvation, not in the hope that these works will help save him. As we shall see in this chapter, justification by faith leads the believer, not to a life of sin, but to a life of grateful obedience.

A.   Those who are justified by faith *cannot continue to live in sin* because through their identification with Christ, they are DEAD TO SIN. 6:1-11

1.   In Romans 5:20, Paul had shown that "where sin increased (as the result of the adding of the Mosaic Law) grace abounded all the more." If then, the increase of sin resulted in an overflow of grace, would it not be a good thing to sin purposely? Would this not magnify God's grace even more? Since some might reason in this manner, Paul himself raises the question, "Are we (who have been justified) to continue in sin that grace may abound?" (vs. 1). The apostle then answers with an emphatic NO! (vs. 2) and shows why this cannot be, "How can we who died to sin still live in it?" 6:1,2

6:1,2 RSV	6:1,2 WT
What shall we say then? Are we to continue in sin that grace may abound? [2]By no means! How can we who died to sin still live in it?	What is our conclusion then? Are we to continue to sin for His unmerited favor to multiply? [2]Not at all! Since[a] we have ended our relation[b] to sin, how can we live in it any longer?

[a] Causal pt.
[b] Lit., *died to sin.*

The Outline of Romans is continued on p. 47.

NOTE NO. 4   THE BELIEVER'S DEATH TO SIN

In Romans 6:2,7, and 11, it is stated that believers have *died to sin:* "we who died to sin" (vs. 2); "he who has died is freed from sin" (vs. 7); "you must consider yourselves dead to sin" (vs. 11). These expressions mean that believers, through their identification with Christ, are dead to the GUILT of sin. They are viewed by God *as if* they themselves *died* in the *death of Christ* and suffered the full penalty of sin's guilt. Sin can no longer make any legal claim on them; thus, they are *dead* to it—free from its condemnation. That believers are *not dead* to the *influence* or *power* of sin in their lives is proved both by the Bible (see for example Romans 7:14-25) and Christian experience. As Haldane points out, the meaning of the phrase "dead to sin" is often extended to include "death to the *power* of sin, to which it has not the smallest reference. It exclusively indicates the justification of believers, and their freedom from the *guilt* of sin, having no allusion to their sanctification, which, however, as the Apostle immediately proceeds to prove, necessarily follows."[15]   Bishop Moule paraphrases verse 7 as follows: "for he who once died to sin now stands free from its claim" and explains that "The *legal claim* of sin is meant here, not its *moral dominion,* for the Greek word rendered 'freed' is literally 'justified.'"[16]   The same idea is expressed in II Corinthians 5:14, "For the love of Christ controls us, because we are convinced that one has died for all; therefore all have died." Smeaton, in commenting on the phrase in Romans 6:2 "we died to sin," observes that "It frequently occurs in the Pauline epistles in different forms, and uniformly alludes not to an inward deliverance from sin, but to the Christian's objective relation, or to his personal standing before God in the vicarious work of Christ; it means that we are legally dead to sin in Christ. This is rendered quite certain by two other expressions occurring in the section. The first of these passages applies the same language to the Lord Himself; for He is said to HAVE DIED TO SIN ONCE (vs. 10). Now the only sense in which the Sinless One can be regarded as dying to sin, is that of dying to its guilt, or to the condemning power which goes along with sin, and which must run its course, wherever sin has been committed. He died to the guilt or criminality of sin, when it was laid on Him; certainly He did not die to its indwelling power. The second of these passages shows that this dying was the ground or meritorious cause of our justification: 'He that is dead has been justified (not FREED, as it is unhappily rendered in the English version) from sin' (vs. 7). The justification of the Christian is thus based on his co-dying with Christ; that is, we are said to have died when Christ died, and to have done what Christ did.

---

[15] Robert Haldane, *Exposition of the Epistle to the Romans,* p. 239. Italics are his.

[16] Moule, *Romans,* p. 115.

The words undoubtedly mean a co-dying with Christ in that one corporate representative deed; that is, they mean that we were one with Christ in His obedience unto death, as we were one with Adam in his disobedience." In a footnote, Smeaton points out that this mode of interpreting the passage is comparatively recent (he cites J. Alting, Klinkenberg, Heringa, Vinke, and Haldane as examples of those who maintain it) and then adds: "The old view advocated by the Reformers and Puritans, failed by making the whole [dying to sin] too much a subjective experience, or an inward renovation. The origin of the misinterpretation must be traced to the separation of the sixth chapter from the fifth, as if a wholly new subject began at Rom. 6:1."[17] Compare the words of Horatius Bonar, who after having defended Haldane's interpretation, states "To be 'dead to sin' is a judicial or legal, not a moral figure. It refers to our release from condemnation, our righteous disjunction from the claim and curse of law. This, instead of giving license to sin, is the beginning and root of holiness."[18]

The believer is not only *dead to sin*, he is also said to be *dead to the law*. See the Outline on Romans 7:1-6, note especially the illustration. See also Note 5, C, p. 54.

The Outline of Romans is continued from p. 45.

2. The *fact* of the believer's *death to sin* is established first by a reference to the significance of baptism and secondly, by showing why Christ was crucified. 6:3-7

6:3-7 RSV	6:3-7 WT
[3]Do you not know that all of us who have been baptized into Christ Jesus were baptized into his death? [4]We were buried therefore with him by baptism into death, so that as Christ was raised from the dead by the glory of the Father, we too might walk in newness of life. [5]For if we have been united with him in a death like his, we shall certainly be united with him in a resurrection like his. [6]We know that our old self was crucified	[3]Or, do you not know that all of us who have been baptized into union with Christ Jesus have been baptized into His death? [4]So through baptism we have been buried with Him in death, so that just as Christ was raised from the dead by the Father's glorious power,[c] an entirely new life.[d] [5]For if we have grown into fellowship with Him by sharing[e] a death like His, surely[f] we shall share a resurrection life like His,[g] [6]for we

[c] Grk., *by the Father's glory* (including power).
[d] Lit., *in newness of life.*
[e] Grk., *by the likeness of His death.*
[f] Lit., *on the other hand.*
[g] Lit., *in likeness of His res.*

---

[17] George Smeaton, *The Apostles' Doctrine of the Atonement*, pp. 163, 164. Capitalizations are his. For further confirmation of this view, consult the excellent comments of Herman N. Ridderbos, *When the Time Had Fully Come*, pp. 53-57.

[18] Horatius Bonar, *God's Way of Holiness*, p. 56.

with him so that the sinful body might be destroyed, and we might no longer be enslaved to sin. ⁷For he who has died is freed from sin.

know that our former self was crucified with Him, to make our body that is liable to sin inactive,ʰ so that we might not a moment longer continue to be slaves to sin. ⁷For when a man is dead, he is freed from the claims of sin.

ʰ Lit., *dead*.

a. *Baptism* symbolizes the believer's death with Christ to sin and the believer's resurrection with Christ to a new life. 6:3,4

When the believing sinner is buried in the watery grave of baptism, he identifies himself with Christ's death (thus confessing that he is dead to sin) ; when he is raised up out of the water, he identifies himself with Christ's resurrection (thus confessing that he is alive and will walk in newness of life).

b. *Christ was crucified* for the purpose of destroying sin—to free His people from its claim. 6:5-7

Because of His death on the cross, Christ's people are justified (freed from the condemnation of sin) in this life and shall be glorified (freed from the presence and influence of sin) in the life to come. See Note 6, p. 60 and the illustration on p. 62.

3. Just as Christ died once to sin (i.e., to its guilt) and now lives to God, so the believer must *consider* (reckon) himself dead to sin and alive to God "in Christ." 6:8-11

6:8-11 RSV

⁸But if we have died with Christ, we believe that we shall also live with him. ⁹For we know that Christ being raised from the dead will never die again; death no longer has dominion over him. ¹⁰The death he died he died to sin, once for all, but the life he lives he lives to God. ¹¹So you also must consider yourselves dead to sin and alive to God in Christ Jesus.

6:8-11 WT

⁸So if we died with Christ, we believe that we shall also live with Him, ⁹for we know that Christ, who once was raised from the dead, will never die again; death has no more power over Him. ¹⁰For by the death He died He died for all ended His relationᵇ to sin, and by the life He now is living He lives in unbrokenⁱ relation to God. ¹¹So you too must consider yourselves as having ended your relation to sin but living in unbroken relation to God.

ᵇ Lit., *died to sin*.
ⁱ Pres. pt. of cont. ac.

Only by realizing that he is dead to the condemning power of sin and alive to God "in Christ" can a sinner truly love or trust God. Only as the believer sees what Christ has done for him can he find the motive to do what God requires of him. Once he sees God's love for him "in Christ" he no longer wants to "live in sin." As Clark observes, "If a man does not thus identify himself with Christ's purpose to destroy sin, and if, instead of grief and hatred of sin, he cherishes the notion that he may continue in sin that grace may abound, the conclusion is inevitable that this man knows nothing of Christ and has not been justified. To speak plainly, it is psychologically impossible to trust Christ's redeeming blood and to want to continue in sin. Sanctification is not merely the purpose of justification, as if the purpose might fail; but rather sanctification is the inevitable result."[19]

B. Because those who are justified by faith are *not under law* (i.e., saved by keeping its commandments) but *under grace* (i.e., saved by the free mercy of God) they are *therefore* called upon to yield themselves to God as His obedient slaves. 6:12—7:6

1. Paul calls upon believers to yield themselves, *not* to sin, *but* to God and as a motive for such action, appeals to the fact that they are under grace, not under law, and thus are free from sin's dominion (power to damn or to destroy them). 6:12-14

6:12-14 RSV

[12]Let not sin therefore reign in your mortal bodies, to make you obey their passions. [13]Do not yield your members to sin as instruments of wickedness, but yield yourselves to God as men who have been brought from death to life, and your members to God as instruments of righteousness. [14]For sin will have no dominion over you, since you are not under law but under grace.

6:12-14 WT

[12]Accordingly sin must not continue to reign over your mortal bodies, so as to make you continue to obey their evil desires, [13]and you must stop offering to sin the parts of your bodies as instruments for wrongdoing, but you must once for all[j] offer yourselves to God as persons raised from the dead to live on perpetually, and once for all[j] offer the parts of your bodies to God as instruments for right-doing. [14]For sin must not any longer exert its mastery over you, for now you are not living as slaves to law but as subjects to God's favor.[k]

---
[j] Aor., so punctiliar ac. *(once for all).*
[k] Lit., *not under law but under unmerited favor.*

Believers are not under law as *a way of salvation* (they are saved by grace through faith, see Ephesians 2:8-10). This, however, does not mean that they are free from God's law as *a rule of duty*—they are under the law of Christ! See Note 5, C, p. 54.

2. The kind of life led by those who are truly justified (those who are not under law but under grace) is *illustrated* by comparing their service to God with *the service of an obedient (self-yielding) slave to a master.* 6:15-23

6:15-23 RSV

[15]What then? Are we to sin because we are not under law but under grace? By no means! [16]Do you not know that if you yield yourselves to any one as obedi-

6:15-23 WT

[15]What are we to conclude? Are we to keep on sinning, because we are not living as slaves to law but as subjects to God's favor? Never! [16]Do you not know

---
[19] Clark, "Romans," (above, fn. 7), p. 248.

ent slaves, you are slaves of the one whom you obey, either of sin, which leads to death, or of obedience, which leads to righteousness? [17]But thanks be to God, that you who were once slaves of sin have become obedient from the heart to the standard of teaching to which you were committed, [18]and, having been set free from sin, have become slaves of righteousness. [19]I am speaking in human terms, because of your natural limitations. For just as you once yielded your members to impurity and to greater and greater iniquity, so now yield your members to righteousness for sanctification.

[20]When you were slaves of sin, you were free in regard to righteousness. [21]But then what return did you get from the things of which you are now ashamed? The end of those things is death. [22]But now that you have been set free from sin and have become slaves of God, the return you get is sanctification and its end, eternal life. [23]For the wages of sin is death, but the free gift of God is eternal life in Christ Jesus our Lord.

that when you habitually offer yourselves to anyone for obedience to him, you are slaves to that one whom you are in the habit of obeying, whether it is the slavery to sin whose end is death or to obedience whose end is right-doing? [17]But, thank God! that though you once were slaves of sin, you became obedient from your hearts to that form of teaching in which you have been instructed, [18]and since you have been freed from sin, you have become the slaves of right-doing. [19]I am speaking in familiar human terms[1] because of the frailty of your nature.[m] For just as you formerly offered the parts of your bodies in slavery to impurity and to ever increasing lawlessness, so now you must once for all offer them in slavery to right-doing, which leads to consecration. [20]For when you were slaves of sin, you were free so far as doing right was concerned. [21]What benefit did you then derive from doing the things of which you are now ashamed? None,[n] for they end in death. [22]But now, since you have been freed from sin and have become the slaves of God, the immediate result is consecration, and the final destiny is eternal life. [23]For the wages paid by sin is death, but the gracious gift of God is eternal life through union with Christ Jesus our Lord.

[1] Grk., *saying a human thing.*
[m] *Flesh* means *human frailty.*
[n] Supplied from context.

"Believers, before conversion, were the servants of sin; after it, they are the servants of righteousness. Formerly they were under an influence which secured their obedience to evil; now they are under an influence which secures their obedience to good. The consequence of the former service was death; of the present, life. The knowledge of these consequences tends to secure the continued fidelity of the Christian to his new Master, . . ."[20] Every man belongs to the master whom he *willingly* serves, whether sin or righteousness. If we are "*obedient* slaves" to sin, we are not saved but if we yield ourselves as "*obedient* slaves" to righteousness we prove ourselves to be true believers, and therefore truly saved. If a man can live at peace with sin, he has no peace with God. He is not justified! "If a man voluntarily sins, on the pretext that he is not under law but under grace, it is a proof that the grace of God is not in him."[21]

Notice the contrast of the end rewards between these two types of servitude; the servants of sin *earn* eternal DEATH for themselves, the servants of God are *given* eternal LIFE through Christ Jesus.

[20] Hodge, *Romans*, p. 203.
[21] Haldane, *Romans*, p. 258.

3. The believer's freedom from the law is illustrated by comparing it to *a married woman's freedom from a dead husband.* 7:1-6

Paul shows that *just as* a married woman is discharged from her husband when he dies and is free to marry another, *even so* the believer, through the death of Christ, has died to the law (and is therefore discharged from its demands as the condition of his salvation) and is now joined to Christ that he might bring forth fruit for God. "Paul here means by the law, the will of God as a rule of duty, no matter how revealed."[22]

7:1-6 RSV

Do you not know, brethren—for I am speaking to those who know the law—that the law is binding on a person only during his life? [2]Thus a married woman is bound by law to her husband as long as he lives; but if her husband dies she is discharged from the law concerning the husband. [3]Accordingly, she will be called an adulteress if she lives with another man while her husband is alive. But if her husband dies she is free from that law, and if she marries another man she is not an adulteress.

[4]Likewise, my brethren, you have died to the law through the body of Christ, so that you may belong to another, to him who has been raised from the dead, in order that we may bear fruit for God. [5]While we were living in the flesh, our sinful passions, aroused by the law, were at work in our members to bear fruit for death. [6]But now we are discharged from the law, dead to that which held us captive, so that we serve not under the old written code but in the new life of the Spirit.

7:1-6 WT

Do you not know, brothers—for I speak to those who are acquainted with the law—that the law can press its claim over a man only so long as he lives? [2]For a married woman is bound by law to her husband while he lives, but if her husband dies, she is freed from the marriage bond.[a] [3]So if she marries another man while her husband is living, she is called an adulteress; but if he dies, she is free from that marriage bond,[b] so that she will not be an adulteress though later married to another man. [4]So, my brothers, you too in the body of Christ have ended your relation to the law, so that you may be married to another husband, to Him who was raised from the dead, in order that we might bear fruit for God. [5]For when we were living in accordance with our lower nature,[c] the sinful passions that were aroused[d] by the law were operating in the parts of our bodies to make us bear fruit that leads to death. [6]But now we have been freed from our relation to law; we have ended our relation to that by which we once were held in bonds, so that we may serve in a new spiritual way and not in the old literalistic way.[e]

[a] Lit., *from the law of the husband.*
[b] Grk., *from the* (that) *law.*
[c] Lit., *in the flesh.*
[d] Vb., implied.
[e] Grk., *in newness of spirit* and *not in oldness of letter.*

See the illustration on the following page.

---

[22] Hodge, *Romans*, p. 217.

a. *THE ILLUSTRATION:*   7:1-3

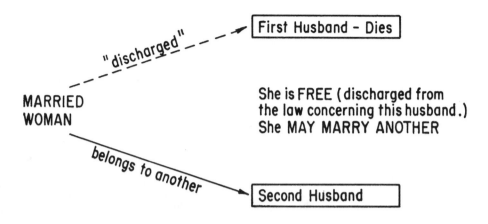

b. *THE APPLICATION:*   7:4-6

LIKEWISE WE (Believers) HAVE DIED TO THE LAW

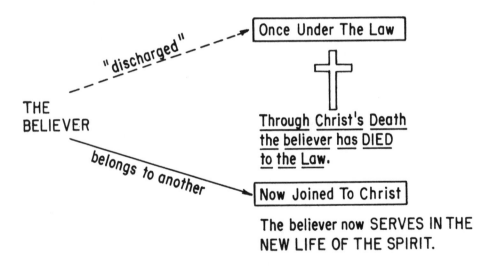

As long as the sinner is under the law (subject to its demands and curse) he brings forth fruit for death but when he is discharged from the law and joined (married) to Christ, he brings forth fruit for God.

The Outline of Romans is continued on p. 56.

NOTE NO. 5   THE LAW OF GOD

A. Definition of the law of God

The law of God is that rule of action which He has prescribed for mankind. In the broad sense of the term, it includes all the commands, regulations, prohibitions, etc., which God has imposed upon the human race. It is important to note, however, that there are many of God's laws that do not apply to all men everywhere and for all time. God has, at various times, given particular commandments to certain people that were binding only upon those people, and were of limited duration. For example, the commandment to circumcise all male children was not given until Abraham's day. It applied only to his descendants, the Jews, and ended with the coming of Jesus Christ.

B. Various revelations of God's law

1. *The law of conscience—the law written on man's heart*

Man was created with the requirements of God's law written on his heart. Before the fall this law was clear and legible, but as the result of Adam's sin the law written on the heart was defaced and marred. Man's spiritual understanding is darkened by sin (see Ephesians 4:17-19). "The heart is deceitful above all things, and desperately corrupt; who can understand it?" (Jer. 17:9). Consequently the law written on the heart is no longer an adequate or reliable guide for fallen man. But this law is still sufficiently clear to make sin known and therefore to render men guilty when they break it, for all men have in their own nature to some degree a knowledge of what is right and wrong (see the Outline on Romans 1:32; 2:12-16).

2. *The law of Moses—the law under the Old Covenant*

This law was given by God to the Jews at Mt. Sinai through Moses, (Ex. 19:1-9; 20:1-20; Deut. 5:1-3). It was *established* as a *covenant* by God with the nation Israel and had no reference whatsoever to the Gentile world.

For convenience the law of Moses is sometimes divided into three parts: (1) The *Ten Commandments* (called the Decalogue) which formed the heart of the Covenant made with Israel (Deut. 4:11-13; 9:9,10,15; I Kings 8:9,21), (2) The Ceremonial Laws which regulated the religious life of the nation, and (3) The Civil Laws which regulated their national life. It must be remembered that all of these laws stood as a single unit and together formed the covenant made with Israel.

This covenant, including all of its parts (laws), was *abolished* by Christ at His death and replaced with a "new" and better covenant under which God's people now live (Jer. 31:31-34; Heb., chs. 8-10; II Cor. 3; Eph. 2:14-16; Col. 2:14-16; Acts 15:1-11, 22-29; I Cor. 9:19-23; Gal. 3:18-25).

In most cases when the word "law" occurs in the Scriptures (especially when the definite article is used—"*the* law") it has reference to the law of Moses. The reason for this is that until Christ came, the law of Moses was the most complete revelation of God's law that had been given to any people since the fall of Adam (see Romans 5:13,20; John 1:17). Therefore, when those acquainted with the Jewish Scriptures thought of God's law, they usually thought of it as expressed in the writings of the great law giver, Moses.

3. *The law of Christ—the law under the New Covenant*

The New Covenant brought still another expression of God's law: the law of Christ, which consists of the teachings, commandments, etc., given by Christ through His own ministry and through the ministry of His chosen apostles and their associates. These laws or principles of conduct are contained in the New Testament (Covenant) Scriptures.

The law of Christ contains a clearer revelation of God's law and a higher standard of conduct for His people than the law of Moses did. And the New Covenant provides certain blessings which the Old Covenant was unable to do: the assurance of sins forgiven, the gift of the Holy Spirit, etc. These blessings supply the motive and strength needed for greater obedience to God's law.

Paul, in Galatians 3:23—4:11, shows that the law of Moses was Israel's custodian (child-trainer, guardian) but now that "the faith" (the New Covenant) has come, God's people are no longer under this custodian. They have received adoption as mature sons and are under the leadership of the Holy Spirit. The saints under the law of Moses were treated as immature children in that they were regulated by detailed laws, whereas the saints under the law of Christ are treated as mature sons and are guided by much broader principles of conduct. Believers living in the present age, therefore, have far more liberty and as a result greater responsibility than the believers who lived under the old system. See John 1:17; Matthew 11:7-15, note verse 11. See Note 11, C, p. 96.

C. Man's relation to God's law

1. As to *salvation:*

a. The unsaved sinner is under God's law regardless of how it is revealed to him—whether written on his heart or revealed in the Scriptures. Lost men are faced with the prospect of being saved through Christ or else suffering the penalty of the broken law. Every unbeliever is obligated to do all that the law commands or to suffer the consequences (Gal. 3:10-12; Rom. 10:5; James 2:10). The more light a lost man lives under, the greater will be his condemnation on the day of judgment. Those who lived with a knowledge of the law of Moses will be judged more strictly than those who had only the law of conscience, and those who have known of the law of Christ will have more to account for than either of the former (Rom. 2:12,13; 5:20; Luke 12:47,48).

b. The saved sinner has been freed from the law as to salvation—discharged from its demands and curse. The believer is not under law but under grace (Rom. 6:14,15; 7:1-6; 10:4).

2. As to *duty* for God's people:

Although all of God's people—believers of all ages—have been freed from the law in relation to salvation, they have never been free from God's law as a rule of duty. *The saints of all ages have been under law to God, but they have not all served under the same revelation of His law.*

a. From Adam to Moses

The rule of duty for the saints living during this time seems to have been primarily the law of conscience (written on man's heart). Some additional laws are recorded in the Biblical record, but little is revealed concerning them.

b. From Moses to Christ

The rule of duty for God's people living during this period was the law of Moses with its many detailed regulations, which was abolished by Christ at His death.[23]

c. From Christ to the end of the age

The rule of duty for believers today is contained in the New Covenant. Though the laws of the Old Covenant are profitable for study, they are no longer binding on God's people. However, many of the moral principles contained in the law of Moses (the Old Covenant) have also been included in the New Covenant Law, (e.g., the laws forbidding murder, adultery, etc.) and thus the two codes of law, though different, have much in common.

See Note 11, on Physical and Spiritual Israel and their relation to the Divine Covenants, p. 94ff.

---

[23] For a good defense of the position that the Mosaic Law, including the Ten Commandments, was *abolished* as a *rule of duty* for God's people living under the New Covenant, see Chs. 2, 4, and 7 of Albertus Pieters' book, *The Seed of Abraham*, published in 1950, by Wm. B. Eerdmans Publishing Company, Grand Rapids, Michigan.

The Outline of Romans is continued from p. 52.

VI. THE FUNCTION OF THE LAW, BOTH BEFORE AND AFTER JUSTIFICATION, IS TO REVEAL AND CONDEMN SIN, BUT IT DOES NOT AND CANNOT PRODUCE HOLINESS. 7:7-25

Thus far in the letter, Paul has shown several things concerning the law: it brings the knowledge of sin, but in no way can it justify the guilty (3:20); it brings wrath (4:15); it increased the trespass (5:20); believers are not under law but under grace (6:14,15); believers are dead to the law—discharged or freed from it (7:4,6); the sinful passions of unbelievers are aroused (incited to evil) by the law, to bear fruit for death (7:5). "What then shall we say (in light of all these facts)? *That the law is sin?*" (7:7). Paul answers with an emphatic *no* and proceeds to show the true function of the law by showing its operation in his own life. First, he explains how the law (before his conversion) had made sin known to him and thereby had made him realize that he was spiritually dead (7:7-13). Then he explains his relationship to the law after his conversion; after he had been made alive spiritually. He delighted in the law and desired to keep its precepts but found that sin still dwelt within him, causing him to do the evil which he had come to hate (7:14-25). Both before and after his conversion, the law had served to identify sin and to condemn it by pointing out God's perfect will, but in neither case had the law given Paul the strength to overcome sin. Thus the law is shown to be ineffective, either for justification (it cannot put the sinner in right standing with God), or for sanctification (it cannot enable the justified sinner to overcome evil while he remains in this body). The law can only command—it cannot give strength to perform; it can only point out sin—it cannot enable one to conquer sin.

A. Before Paul was converted (saved) the law made sin known to him and thus caused him to realize that he was spiritually dead. 7:7-13

1. The law made sin known to Paul. 7:7,8

7:7,8 RSV	7:7,8 WT
[7]What then shall we say? That the law is sin? By no means! Yet, if it had not been for the law, I should not have known sin. I should not have known what it is to covet if the law had not said, "You shall not covet." [8]But sin, finding opportunity in the commandment, wrought in me all kinds of covetousness. Apart from the law sin lies dead.	[7]What are we then to conclude? Is the law sin? Of course not! Yet, if it had not been for[f] the law, I should not have learned what sin was, for I should not have known what an evil desire was, if the law had not said, "You must not have an evil desire."[g] [8]Sin found its rallying point in that command and stirred within me every sort of evil desire, for without law sin is lifeless.

[f] Lit., *through.*
[g] Ex. 20:14, 17; Dt. 5:18, 21.

As Hodge states, the law "produces the conviction of sin by teaching us what sin is, vs. 7, and by making us conscious of the existence and power of this evil in our hearts, vs. 8." He points out in commenting on verse 8 that "Where there is no law, there is no sin; and where there is no knowledge of law there is no knowledge of sin."[24]

2. The law, through making sin known to Paul, made him realize that he was spiritually dead. 7:9-11

7:9-11 RSV

[9]I was once alive apart from the law, but when the commandment came, sin revived and I died; [10]the very commandment which promised life proved to be death to me. [11]For sin, finding opportunity in the commandment, deceived me and by it killed me.

7:9-11 WT

[9]I was once alive when I had no connection with the law, but when the command came, sin revived, and then I died; [10]and so, in my case, the command which should have meant life turned out to mean death. [11]For sin found its rallying point[h] in that command and through it deceived me and killed me.

[h] Favorable point of attack.

3. The law itself is holy and just and good and therefore did not cause Paul's spiritual death. It was *sin* that had caused his death; the law only revealed it. 7:12,13

7:12,13 RSV

[12]So the law is holy, and the commandment is holy and just and good. [13]Did that which is good, then, bring death to me? By no means! It was sin, working death in me through what is good, in order that sin might be shown to be sin, and through the commandment might become sinful beyond measure.

7:12,13 WT

[12]So the law itself is holy, and its specific commands are holy, right, and good. [13]Did that which is good, then, result in death to me? Of course not! It was sin that did it, so that it might show itself as sin, for by means of that good thing it brought about my death, so that through the command sin might appear surpassingly sinful.

B. After Paul was converted (saved) he delighted in the law in his inmost self and served it with his mind but found that sin still dwelt within him and caused him to do the very evil which, as a believer, he had come to hate. 7:14-25

The apostle's testimony was, "the law is spiritual; but I am carnal, sold under sin" (7:14). Hodge in explaining what Paul meant says, "He does not intend to say that he was given up to the willing service of sin; but that he was in the condition of a slave, whose acts are not always the evidence of his inclination. His will may be one way, but his master may direct him another. So it is with the believer. He does what he hates, and omits to do what he approves, ver. 15. This is a description of slavery, and a clear explanation of what is intended by the expression, 'sold under sin.' . . . acts thus performed are not the true criterion of character: 'now then, it is no more I that do it, but

[24] Hodge, *Romans*, pp. 223, 224.

sin that dwelleth in me.' ver. 17. The acts of a slave are indeed his own acts; but not being performed with the full assent and consent of his soul, they are not fair tests of the real state of his feelings."[25] Note well the contrast between the *willing* servant of sin in 6:16,17 (he is lost!) and the *unwilling* servant of sin in 7:14-25 (he is saved!).

1. Paul describes his struggle with indwelling sin. 7:14-23

7:14-23 RSV

[14]We know that the law is spiritual; but I am carnal, sold under sin. [15]I do not understand my own actions. For I do not do what I want, but I do the very thing I hate. [16]Now if I do what I do not want, I agree that the law is good. [17]So then it is no longer I that do it, but sin which dwells within me. [18]For I know that nothing good dwells within me, that is, in my flesh. I can will what is right, but I cannot do it. [19]For I do not do the good I want, but the evil I do not want is what I do. [20]Now if I do what I do not want, it is no longer I that do it, but sin which dwells within me.

[21]So I find it to be a law that when I want to do right, evil lies close at hand. [22]For I delight in the law of God, in my inmost self, [23]but I see in my members another law at war with the law of my mind and making me captive to the law of sin which dwells in my members.

7:14-23 WT

[14]For we know that the law is spiritual, but I am made of flesh that is frail,[i] sold into slavery to sin. [15]Indeed, I do not understand what I do, for I do not practice what I want to do, but I am always doing what I hate. [16]But if I am always doing what I do not want to do, I agree that the law is right. [17]Now really it is not I that am doing these things, but it is sin which has its home[j] within me. [18]For I know that nothing good has its home in me; that is, in my lower self; I have the will but not the power to do what is right. [19]Indeed, I do not do the good things that I want to do, but I do practice the evil things that I do not want to do. [20]But if I do the things that I do not want to do, it is really not I that am doing these things, but it is sin which has its home within me. [21]So I find this law: When I want to do right, the wrong is always in my way. [22]For in accordance with my better inner nature[k] I approve God's law, [23]but I see another power[l] operating in my lower nature in conflict with the power operated by my reason,[m] which makes me a prisoner to the power of sin which is operating in my lower nature.

---

[i] Word emphasizes the frail material of which our lower nature is made.
[j] Pres. of vb. *to live in*, so *to have its home.*
[k] Lit., *according to the inner man.*
[l] Lit., *another law.*
[m] Grk., *mind, reason, higher nature.*

a. The two conflicting principles within Paul.

(1) The *carnal* principle: "I am carnal, sold under sin" vs. 14; "nothing good dwells within me, that is, in my flesh" vs. 18; "with my flesh I serve the law of sin" vs. 25. *"I am carnal,* means I am under the power of the flesh. And by *flesh* is meant not the body, not our sensuous nature merely, but our whole nature as fallen and corrupt."[26]

---

[25] Hodge, *Romans*, p. 227.
[26] Hodge, *Romans*, p. 229. Italics are his.

(2) The *spiritual* principle: "I delight in the law of God, in my inmost self" vs. 22; "I of myself serve the law of God with my mind" vs. 25. "As the apostle recognized in the new man two conflicting principles, he speaks as though there were within him two persons, both represented by I. The one is I, i.e. my flesh; the other is I, i.e. my inner man. By the *inner man* is to be understood the 'new man;' either the renewed principle in itself considered, or the soul considered or viewed as renewed."[27]

   b. The results of these two conflicting principles.

   (1) The *carnal* principle: "I do not do the good I want, but I do the very thing I hate" vs. 15; "with my flesh I serve the law of sin" vs. 25. Note verses 14, 15, 16, 17, 18, 19, 20, 21, 23, 24, and 25.

   (2) The *spiritual* principle: "I want to do right" vs. 21; "I delight in the law of God" vs. 22; "I of myself serve the law of God" vs. 25. Note verses 15, 16, 18, 19, 20, 21, 22, 23, and 25.

   2. Paul, while confessing that he was wretched, nevertheless thanked God that Christ would completely free him from the power and the presence of sin. 7:24, 25a

7:24,25a RSV	7:24,25a WT
[24]Wretched man that I am! Who will deliver me from this body of death? [25]Thanks be to God through Jesus Christ our Lord!	[24]Wretched man that I am! Who can save me from this deadly lower nature? [25]Thank God! it has been done through Jesus Christ our Lord!

   The best commentary on these verses is Romans 8:23, where God's children are said to groan inwardly as they wait for the redemption of their bodies. Complete victory over sin is promised but not while living in this body of sin! See Note 6, D, p. 61. See also Romans 8:10,11 and I Corinthians 15:35-57—note especially verses 56 and 57.

   3. Paul concludes by showing that as long as he remained in this life the warfare between his spiritual nature and his carnal nature would continue. 7:25b

7:25b RSV	7:25b WT
So then, I of myself serve the law of God with my mind, but with my flesh I serve the law of sin.	So in my higher nature[m] I am a slave to the law of God, but in my lower nature, to the law of sin.
	[m] Grk., *mind, reason, higher nature.*

   For proof that Paul in 7:14-25 was writing of his experience as a Christian, see Appendix B, pp. 126-130.

---

[27] Hodge, *Romans*, p. 235. Italics are his.

The Outline of Romans is continued on p. 63.

NOTE NO. 6   INDWELLING SIN

Many, in the present day, leave the impression that the mature or enlightened Christian need not struggle with indwelling sin. All one need do is to yield himself to God by an act of faith and *victory is his!* As a result of this false notion many sincere believers are misled and confused when they fail to experience the "promised victory," and some are even made to doubt their salvation. The truth is that the most mature saint is in constant conflict with indwelling sin even as the apostle Paul was. The one who should doubt the genuineness of his salvation is the one who does not have this struggle, who does not cry out "wretched man that I am," and does not constantly long for deliverance.

A. *Like Paul, every true believer struggles with indwelling sin.* Romans 7:14-25 is the description of their lives. As the apostle John so emphatically states: "If we say we have no sin, we deceive ourselves, and the truth is not in us," (I John 1:8). See Appendix B, footnote 3, p. 129.

B. *No believer is able to understand why he sins; it is a mystery beyond his reach.* The testimony of every saint is the same as that of Paul, "I do not understand my own actions," vs. 15; "I can will what is right, but I cannot do it," vs. 18; "I do not do the good I want, but the evil I do not want is what I do," vs. 19; "I see in my members another law at war with the law of my mind and making me captive to the law of sin which dwells in my members," vs. 23.

C. *The believer in no way excuses sin.* Even though he, like Paul, is "captive to the law of sin," (vs. 23) he feels his responsibility to refrain from sin. He can will what is right but he "cannot do it," (vs. 18) yet, he assumes the obligation to do good and longs for holiness; his continual cry is, "Wretched man that I am!" (vs. 24), and he longs for deliverance. "Inability is consistent with responsibility . . . . As the Scriptures constantly recognize the truth of these two things, so are they constantly united in Christian experience. Every one feels that he cannot do the things that he would, yet is sensible that he is to blame for not doing them. Let any man test his power by the requisition to love God perfectly at all times. Alas! how entire our inability; yet how deep our self-loathing and self-condemnation . . . . The renewed man condemns himself, and justifies God, even while he confesses and mourns his inability to conform to the divine requisitions."[28]

---

[28] Hodge, *Romans*, p. 246.

D. *Every believer is assured of deliverance from indwelling sin through Christ Jesus, but not while living in this body of sin.* Paul asked, "Who will deliver me from this body of death?" (vs. 24) and answered, "Thanks be to God through Jesus Christ our Lord!" (vs. 25). How and when Christ will deliver us is not stated in chapter seven, but in chapter eight we read, " . . . if the Spirit of Christ is in you, although your bodies are dead because of sin, your spirits are alive because of righteousness. If the Spirit of him who raised Jesus from the dead dwells in you, he who raised Christ Jesus from the dead will give life to your mortal bodies . . ." (vs. 10,11). "We . . . groan inwardly (cf. 7:24) as we wait for adoption as sons, the redemption of our bodies," (8:23).

Paul looked for deliverance from indwelling sin but not while in the flesh, and neither can we! Notice his conclusion, "So then I of myself serve the law of God with my mind, but with my flesh I serve the law of sin," (7:25).

E. *Although the believer is plagued with indwelling sin, his sin can never condemn him.* Chapter seven ends with the solemn fact that we are still sinners even after we have been saved (born again) ; but chapter eight opens with the wonderful assurance that "there is therefore now *no* condemnation for those who are in Christ Jesus." Those in Christ are justified on the ground of His righteousness which has been imputed to them. In this blessed truth believers should find hope and comfort to help them in their fight against sin. They have more than sufficient reason to rejoice; their Lord has already delivered them from the condemning power of sin and will, in the resurrection, deliver them from the presence of indwelling sin. "Those Christians are under a great mistake, who suppose that despondency is favourable to piety. Happiness is one of the elements of life. Hope and joy are twin daughters of piety and cannot, without violence and injury, be separated from their parent. To rejoice is as much a duty as it is a privilege."[29]

See the illustration on the following page.

---

[29] Hodge, *Romans*, p. 212.

THE PRESENT COMFORT AND FUTURE DELIVERANCE OF A CHRISTIAN STRUGGLING WITH INDWELLING SIN

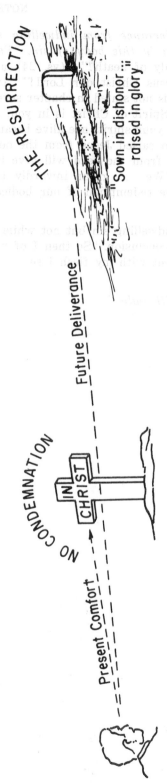

NO CONDEMNATION

IN CHRIST

Present Comfort

Future Deliverance

THE RESURRECTION

"Sown in dishonor... raised in glory"

"Justified"
FREE FROM
SIN'S *GUILT*—NOW
Rom. 6:1-11
8:1-4, 31-39.

"Glorified"
FREE FROM
SIN'S *POWER*—THEN
Rom. 7:24-25
8:10,11,22,23,
29,30. See I Cor.
15:42-57.

The two opposing principles within the Christian's nature:

(1) The *carnal* which serves the law of sin

(2) The *spiritual* which serves the law of God

Result—*Inward conflict.*

Every true saint, like Paul, as long as he remains in this life has an unending struggle with indwelling sin. His Adamic nature (which is subject to sin) is in constant conflict with his renewed nature (which is subject to God's law). He finds within himself a deep yearning to do God's will—this is his innermost desire. He also finds within himself a compelling force that makes him captive to the law of sin and causes him to do the very things he hates. What assurance of salvation can such a one find—what hope is there of final victory? The believer's *present comfort* is found in the saving work of Christ, through whom he has already

been justified (declared righteous) and is thus assured of salvation. His hope for *final deliverance* from the struggle rests in God's promise that He will raise him from the dead in the last day with an incorruptible body completely free from sin. Until that time, however, he must walk by faith and live in hope—ever struggling to put to death the deeds of the body while constantly longing for and striving after the things of the Spirit. Although the believer will be free from sin when he dies, yet his salvation will not be *complete* until his body is resurrected (cf. Rom. 8:22,23).

The Outline of Romans is continued from p. 59.

VII. THE JUSTIFIED, THOUGH PLAGUED WITH SIN AND AFFLICTIONS WHILE IN THIS WORLD, ARE NEVERTHELESS SECURE "IN CHRIST." TO ALL WHO ARE INDWELT BY THE HOLY SPIRIT, SALVATION IS CERTAIN, FOR THE SPIRIT'S WORK IN THEM IS PROOF OF THEIR HAVING BEEN PREDESTINED TO ETERNAL GLORY—NOTHING CAN SEPARATE THEM FROM GOD'S LOVE. 8:1-39

Romans 8 is one of the greatest chapters in all of God's Word. Spener said that if the Holy Scriptures were a ring and the Epistle to the Romans its precious stone, chapter eight would be the sparkling point of the jewel. It is filled with assurance and hope, both for this life and the life to come, for all who trust in Jesus Christ for salvation. As Haldane says, "This chapter presents a glorious display of the power of Divine grace, and of the provision which God has made for the consolation of His people."[30]

Hodge gives as the theme of the chapter "the security of believers" and says, "The salvation of those who have renounced the Law, and accepted the gracious offers of the Gospel, is shown to be absolutely certain. The whole chapter is a series of arguments, most beautifully arranged, in support of this one point. They are all traced back to the great source of hope and security, the unmerited and unchanging love of God in Christ Jesus. The proposition is contained in the first verse. There is no condemnation to those who are in Christ Jesus: they shall never be condemned or perish." [31]

A. Through their identification with Christ, believers (though sinful in themselves) have been freed from the law and therefore cannot be condemned. Hence their salvation is certain. 8:1-4

8:1-4 RSV

There is therefore now no condemnation for those who are in Christ Jesus. [2]For the law of the Spirit of life in Christ Jesus has set me free from the law of sin and death. [3]For God has done what the law, weakened by the flesh, could

8:1-4 WT

So then there is no condemnation at all for those who are in union with Christ Jesus. [2]For the life-giving power[a] of the Spirit through union with Christ Jesus has set us free from the power of sin and death. [3]For though the law

[a] Lit., *law* in sense of *force* or *power*.

---

[30] Haldane, *Romans*, p. 310.

[31] Hodge, *Romans*, p. 247. The outline of this chapter is based on that found in his commentary, pp. 247-248. As he observed in a footnote on page 263, " . . . the division of this chapter into sections is merely arbitrary. For, although there are several very distinct topics introduced, yet the whole is intimately interwoven and made to bear on one point. In passing, too, from one argument to another, the apostle does it so naturally, that there is no abruptness of transition."

not do: sending his own Son in the likeness of sinful flesh and for sin,[1] he condemned sin in the flesh, 'in order that the just requirement of the law might be fulfilled in us, who walk not according to the flesh but according to the Spirit.

[1] Or *and as a sin offering*

could not do it, because it was made helpless[b] through our lower nature, yet God, by sending His own Son in a body similar to that of our lower nature, and as a sacrifice for sin,[c] passed sentence upon sin through His body, 'so that the requirement of the law might be fully met in us who do not live by the standard[d] set by our lower nature, but by the standard set by the Spirit.

[b] Grk., *weak.*
[c] Use of phrase in Sept.
[d] In prep. *kata.*

1.   There is "NO CONDEMNATION" for those who are "in Christ Jesus" (joined to him by faith). 8:1

2.   The reason there is no condemnation for those "in Christ" is that they have been freed (Greek, "justified") from the law of God through the gospel of Jesus Christ. 8:2

a. Hodge observes that "the *law of the Spirit of Life* is the gospel, i.e., the law of which the life giving Spirit is the author."[32] Haldane and Moule concur with this interpretation of the phrase. Moule writes, "It is the Divine Rule of *Justification*, (which alone, as the whole previous reasoning shows, removes 'all condemnation,') and is thus 'a law' in the sense of 'fixed process.' "[33] 8:2a

b. The "law of sin and death" here has reference to God's law, which, as we noted in Romans 7:7-13, brought the knowledge of sin and death to Paul. "If it had not been for the law, I should not have known *sin* . . . . when the commandment came, sin revived and I died; the very commandment which promised life proved to be *death* to me" (7:7,9,10). 8:2b

Hodge interprets verses 1 and 2 as follows: "There is no condemnation to those who are in Christ, because they have been freed in Him by the gospel of the life-giving Spirit from the Law which, although good in itself, is, through our corruption, the source of sin and death."[34]

3.   In order to free believers from the guilt or condemnation of sin, God sent His own Son into the world (in a nature like man's sinful nature, but not itself sinful, see Hebrews 2:14-18; 4:15). Christ gave Himself as a sacrifice for sin, and thereby legally put sin away and thus freed His people from its guilt. 8:3

---

[32] Hodge, *Romans*, p. 250. Italics are his.

[33] Moule, *Romans*, p. 137. Italics are his.

[34] Hodge, *Romans*, p. 251.

4.   As a result of Christ's sacrificial work, the just requirement (demand) of the law has been fulfilled (fully met) in those who are joined to Him. This of course is because of the fact that what Christ did, He did as their substitute or representative, and it is therefore counted (imputed) to them as if they themselves did it. 8:4

B.   Believers are indwelt by the Holy Spirit who *has* regenerated them, who *is* sanctifying them, and who in the last day *will* resurrect them. 8:5-11

8:5-11 RSV

⁵For those who live according to the flesh set their minds on the things of the flesh, but those who live according to the Spirit set their minds on the things of the Spirit. ⁶To set the mind on the flesh is death, but to set the mind on the Spirit is life and peace. ⁷For the mind that is set on the flesh is hostile to God; it does not submit to God's law, indeed it cannot; ⁸and those who are in the flesh cannot please God.

⁹But you are not in the flesh, you are in the Spirit, if the Spirit of God really dwells in you. Any one who does not have the Spirit of Christ does not belong to him. ¹⁰But if Christ is in you, although your bodies are dead because of sin, your spirits are alive because of righteousness. ¹¹If the Spirit of him who raised Jesus from the dead dwells in you, he who raised Christ Jesus from the dead will give life to your mortal bodies also through his Spirit which dwells in you.

8:5-11 WT

⁵For people who live by the standard set by their lower nature are usually thinking the things suggested by that nature,ᵉ and people who live by the standard set by the Spirit are usually thinking the things suggested by the Spirit.ᵉ ⁶For to be thinking the things suggested by the lower nature means death, but to be thinking the things suggested by the Spirit means life and peace. ⁷Because one's thinking the things suggested by the lower nature means enmity to God, for it does not subject itself to God's law, nor indeed can it. ⁸The people who live on the planeᶠ of the lower nature cannot please God. ⁹But you are not living on the plane of the lower nature, but on the spiritual plane, if the Spirit of God has His home within you. Unless a man has the Spirit of Christ, he does not belong to Him. ¹⁰But if Christ livesᵍ in you, although your bodies must die because of sin, your spirits are now enjoying life because of right standing with God. ¹¹If the Spirit of Him who raised Jesus from the dead has His home within you, He who raised Christ Jesus from the dead will also give your mortal bodies life through His Spirit that has His home within you.

ᵉ Subj. gen. gives this meaning.
ᶠ Lit., *are in the flesh, on the plane of the lower nature.*
ᵍ Grk., *if Christ is in you.*

The Holy Spirit's work in the Christian has a threefold aspect— past, present, and future. Through regeneration, the Holy Spirit made the unbeliever spiritually alive and caused him to believe in Jesus Christ. The Spirit continues His work through the process of sanctification by which He imparts spiritual strength and guidance to the believer. Sanctification begins at regeneration and does not end until death. In the resurrection the Spirit will give life to the saint's mortal body when He raises him from the dead.

1. Those who "walk according to" vs. 4; "live according to" vs. 5; and "set their minds on" vs. 6, the *flesh* are *dead spiritually* and therefore hostile to God and His law, vss. 7 and 8. The term "flesh" is used here to denote man's fallen sinful nature. Although the Christian is still influenced by the flesh (his fallen nature), the "flesh" no longer dominates him. It does not characterize his life as it did before he was made alive and energized by the Holy Spirit.

2. The believer "walks" and "lives" according to the *Spirit*, vss. 4,5,6,9-11. The saved man does not live by the standards and dictates of the flesh, but his life is regulated or influenced by the Holy Spirit who dwells within him and who is the dominant ruler of the "inner man." He is still troubled by indwelling sin, but he is not ruled by it as he was before regeneration. Though his body is dead by reason of sin and guilt, his spirit is alive because of the righteousness which has been imputed to him.

C. Believers (through adoption) are, in their present state, the children of God and therefore fellow heirs with Christ. 8:12-17

<table>
<tr><td>8:12-17 RSV</td><td>8:12-17 WT</td></tr>
</table>

8:12-17 RSV

[12]So then, brethren we are debtors, not to the flesh, to live according to the flesh—[13]for if you live according to the flesh you will die, but if by the Spirit you put to death the deeds of the body you will live. [14]For all who are led by the Spirit of God are sons of God. [15]For you did not receive the spirit of slavery to fall back into fear, but you have received the spirit of sonship. When we cry, "Abba! Father!" [16]it is the Spirit himself bearing witness with our spirit that we are children of God, [17]and if children, then heirs, heirs of God and fellow heirs with Christ, provided we suffer with him in order that we may also be glorified with him.

8:12-17 WT

[12]So, brothers, we are under obligation, but not to our lower nature to live by the standard set by it; [13]for if you live by such a standard,[h] you are going to die, but if by the Spirit you put a stop[i] to the doings of your lower nature, you will live. [14]For all who are guided by God's Spirit are God's sons. [15]For you do not have a sense[j] of servitude to fill you with dread again, but the consciousness of adopted sons by which we cry, "Abba,"[k] that is, "Father." [16]The Spirit Himself bears witness with our spirits that we are God's children; [17]and if children, then also heirs, heirs of God and fellow-heirs with Christ—if in reality we share His sufferings, so that we may share His glory too.

[h] Noun repeated in Grk.
[i] Lit., *put to death.*
[j] Grk., *a spirit of servitude.*
[k] *Father* in Paul's native tongue, Ara.

By the Spirit, believers are to put to death the deeds of the body (i.e., works of the flesh, see Gal. 5:16-24). Only those who resist sin, who are led by the Spirit, and who suffer with Christ are true believers! vss. 13,14,17.

D. Believers, though they must suffer various afflictions while in this life, are sustained through them all by the encouragement and help that comes from God. 8:18-28

1. Their present sufferings are not worth comparing with the glory that is to be theirs—and though they now "groan inwardly" because of sin and suffering, they live in hope and patiently wait for the redemption of their bodies when they shall be glorified (made like Christ). 8:18-25

8:18-25 RSV

[18]I consider that the sufferings of this present time are not worth comparing with the glory that is to be revealed to us. [19]For the creation waits with eager longing for the revealing of the sons of God; [20]for the creation was subjected to futility, not of its own will but by the will of him who subjected it in hope; [21]because the creation itself will be set free from its bondage to decay and obtain the glorious liberty of the children of God. [22]We know that the whole creation has been groaning in travail together until now; [23]and not only the creation, but we ourselves, who have the first fruits of the Spirit, groan inwardly as we wait for adoption as sons, the redemption of our bodies. [24]For in this hope we were saved. Now hope that is seen is not hope. For who hopes for what he sees? [25]But if we hope for what we do not see, we wait for it with patience.

8:18-25 WT

[18]For I consider all that we suffer in this present life is nothing to be compared with the glory which by-and-by is to be uncovered for us. [19]For all nature[1] is expectantly waiting for the unveiling of the sons of God. [20]For nature did not of its own accord give up to failure; it was for the sake of Him who let it thus be given up, in the hope [21]that even nature itself might finally be set free from its bondage to decay, so as to share the glorious freedom of God's children. [22]Yes, we know that all nature has gone on groaning in agony together till the present moment. [23]Not only that but this too, we ourselves who enjoy the Spirit as a foretaste of the future,[m] even we ourselves, keep up our inner groanings while we wait to enter upon our adoption as God's sons at[n] the redemption of our bodies. [24]For we were saved in such[o] a hope. [25]But a hope that is seen is not real hope, for who hopes for what he actually sees? But if we hope for something we do not see, we keep on patiently waiting for it.

[1] Lit., *creation*.
[m] Suggested by *foretaste*.
[n] *Redemption* in apposition with *adoption*, but time prominent; hence our trans.
[o] Implied from context.

2. The Holy Spirit helps believers in their weaknesses and sufferings by teaching them how to pray and what to pray for. Hodge in showing the intercessory work of the Holy Spirit states *"to intercede for,* is to act the part of advocate in behalf of any one . . . . As the Spirit is thus said, in the general, to do for us what an advocate did for his client, so he does also what it was the special duty of the advocate to perform, i.e., to dictate to his clients what they ought to say, how they should present their cause. In this sense the present passage is to be understood. We do not know how to pray, but the Spirit teaches us. All true prayer is due to the influence of the Spirit, who not only guides us in the selection of the objects for which to pray, but also gives us the appropriate desires, and works within us that faith without which our prayers are of no avail.

We are not to suppose that the Spirit itself prays, or utters the inarticulate groans of which the apostle here speaks. He is said to do what he causes us to do."[35]   8:26,27

8:26,27 RSV

[26]Likewise the Spirit helps us in our weakness; for we do not know how to pray as we ought, but the Spirit himself intercedes for us with sighs too deep for words. [27]And he who searches the hearts of men knows what is the mind of the Spirit, because[j] the Spirit intercedes for the saints according to the will of God.

[j] Or *that*

8:26,27 WT

[26]In the same way the Spirit, too, is helping us in our weakness, for we do not know how to pray as we should, but the Spirit Himself pleads for us with unspeakable yearnings, [27]and He who searches our hearts knows what the Spirit thinks, for He pleads for His people in accordance with God's will.

3. Believers are assured that God works all things together for their good. 8:28

8:28 RSV

[28]We know that in everything God works for good[k] with those who love him,[l] who are called according to his purpose.

[k]Other ancient authorities read *in everything he works for good,* or *everything works for good*
[l]Greek *God*

8:28 WT

[28]Yes, we know that all things go on working together for the good of those who keep on loving God, who are called in accordance with God's purpose.

Haldane, in commenting on this familiar verse, says "If all things work together for good, there is nothing within the compass of being that is not, in one way or other, advantageous to the children of God . . . . The creation of the world, the fall and the redemption of man, all the dispensations of Providence, whether prosperous or adverse, all occurrences and events—all things, whatsoever they be—work for their good . . . . They do not work thus of themselves: It is God that turns all things to the good of His children. The afflictions of believers, in a peculiar manner, contribute to this end.

"Even the sins of believers work for their good, not from the nature of sin, but by the goodness and power of Him who brings light out of darkness. Everywhere in Scripture we read of the great evil of sin. Everywhere we receive the most solemn warning against its commission; and everywhere we hear also of the chastisements it brings, even upon those who are rescued from its finally condemning power. It is not sin, then, in itself that works the good, but God who overrules its effects to

---

[35] Hodge, *Romans*, pp. 278,279. Italics are his.

His children,—shows them, by means of it, what is in their hearts, as well as their entire dependence on Himself, and the necessity of walking with Him more closely. . . .

"But if our sins work together for our good, shall we sin that grace may abound? Far be the thought. This would be entirely to misunderstand the grace of God, and to turn it into an occasion of offending Him."[36]

The promise contained in Romans 8:28 can only be claimed by those who "love" God, who are "called according to his purpose."

E. Believers are assured of final salvation, for they have been predestined to eternal glory. 8:29,30

8:29,30 RSV	8:29,30 WT
[29]For those whom he foreknew he also predestined to be conformed to the image of his Son, in order that he might be the first-born among many brethren. [30]And those whom he predestined he also called; and those whom he called he also justified; and those whom he justified he also glorified.	[29]For those on whom He set His heart beforehand[p] He marked off[q] as His own to be made like His Son, that He might be the eldest of many brothers; [30]and those whom He marked off as His own He also calls; and those whom He calls He brings into right standing with Himself; those whom He brings into right standing with Himself He also glorifies.

p Lit., *foreknew*, but in Sept. used as translated.
q Root meaning of vb.

Each individual who has been called by God's Spirit and justified by faith can be assured that he was loved by God before the foundation of the world and marked out (ordained) for everlasting life. For as Romans 8:29,30 show, being "called" and "justified" are the result and therefore the evidence of one's having been predestined to eternal glory.

Believers have been predestined to be conformed to the image of God's Son. This conformity (being made like Christ) will take place when the saints are glorified in the resurrection, at Christ's second coming. (Compare Romans 8:17-23; I Cor. 15:49, 51-57; Phil. 3:20, 21; I John 3:2.) They have been predestined to this end so that Christ "might be the first-born among *many* brethren." See Heb. 2:10-17. Compare also Col. 1:15,18; Heb. 1:6; Rev. 1:5. See Note 7, p. 70. For the meaning of "foreknew" in verse 29, see Appendix C, pp. 131-137.

The Outline of Romans is continued on p. 71.

---

36 Haldane, *Romans*, pp. 392, 393.

FOREKNEW	PREDESTINED	CALLED	JUSTIFIED	GLORIFIED
(1)	(2)	(3)	(4)	(5)
Those whom God set His heart on or foreloved;	He marked out or ordained;	He calls (1) Outwardly by the gospel & (2) Inwardly by His Spirit thus giving them life and faith;	He declares them righteous on the ground of Christ's work;	He will glorify them in the resurrection at the last day.
(See Appendix C for meaning of "foreknew," pp. 131-137.)	(See "Unconditional Election" in Appendix D, pp. 158-166.)	(See "Efficacious Grace" in Appendix D, pp. 176-184.)	(See Note 1, p. 24, Note 2, p. 29, and Note 3, p. 41.)	I C o r. 15:35-55; Phil. 3:20,21; II Cor. 5:1-5 (Cf. "Perseverance of the Saints" in Appendix D, pp. 184-188.)

Notice the chain of events: Those whom God (1) knew or fixed His heart upon in ages past, (2) He marked out or ordained, and (3) in time He called (effectually), and (4) He justified, and (5) He glorified. "So indissoluble is the chain that the last link is here viewed as an accomplished fact because the first links are so."[37] The exact number known by God before the world began shall be glorified, no more, no less, and all of them *must* and *will* pass through *each* of these five steps. To illustrate: Suppose God foreknew 100 individuals, then He predestined 100, He called 100, He justified 100, and He glorified 100 individuals. None are gained, none are lost. He will bring to salvation each individual whom He set His heart on (loved) before the world began.

[37] Moule, *Romans*, p. 157.

The Outline of Romans is continued from p. 69.

F. God is for believers—no one can effectually be against them. 8:31-34

8:31-34 RSV	8:31-34 WT
[31]What then shall we say to this? If God is for us, who is against us? [32]He who did not spare his own Son but gave him up for us all, will he not also give us all things with him? [33]Who shall bring any charge against God's elect? It is God who justifies; [34]who is to condemn? Is it Christ Jesus, who died, yes, who was raised from the dead, who is at the right hand of God, who indeed intercedes for us?[m]	[31]What are we then to say to facts like these? If God is for us, who can be against us? [32]Since He did not spare His own Son but gave Him up for us all, will He not with Him graciously give us everything else? [33]Who can bring any charge against those whom God has chosen? It is God who declared them in right standing; [34]who can condemn them? Christ Jesus, who died, or rather, who was raised from the dead, is now at God's right hand, and is actually pleading for us.

[m] Or *It is Christ Jesus . . . for us*

1.   That God is for believers is undeniably true since He has already given His own Son to die for their sins. Certainly, God would not give His most precious possession for His elect and then withhold from them blessings of a lesser nature. 8:31,32

2.   God's people have been cleared in His court of justice from all of their sins. Since God's justice has been completely satisfied, who is there to charge or condemn believers? Would Christ Jesus condemn the very people He loved and gave Himself for, was raised for, and even now intercedes for? 8:33,34

G. God's love for His people is infinite and unchangeable, and nothing in all creation can separate believers from it. 8:35-39

8:35-39 RSV	8:35-39 WT
[35]Who shall separate us from the love of Christ? Shall tribulation, or distress, or persecution, or famine, or nakedness, or peril, or sword? [36]As it is written, "For thy sake we are being killed all the day long; we are regarded as sheep to be slaughtered." [37]No, in all these things we are more than conquerors through him who loved us. [38]For I am sure that neither death, nor life, nor angels, nor principalities, nor things present, nor things to come, nor powers, [39]nor height, nor depth, nor anything else in all creation, will be able to separate us from the love of God in Christ Jesus our Lord.	[35]Who can separate us from Christ's love? Can suffering or misfortune or persecution or hunger or destitution or danger or the sword? [36]As the Scripture says: "For your sake we are being put to death the livelong day, We are treated like sheep to be slaughtered."[r] [37]And yet in all these things we keep on gloriously conquering through Him who loved us. [38]For I have full assurance that neither death nor life nor angels nor principalities nor the present nor the future [39]nor evil forces above or beneath, nor anything else in all creation, will be able to separate us from the love of God as shown in Christ Jesus our Lord.

[r] Ps. 44:22.

"This is the last step in the climax of the apostle's argument; the very summit of the mount of confidence, whence he looks down on his enemies as powerless, and forward and upward with full assurance of a final and abundant triumph. No one can accuse, no one can condemn, no one can separate us from the love of Christ."[38] Compare Paul's language in Romans 8:35-39 with the words of Christ in John 10:27-30.

Haldane concludes his comments on Ch. 8 with these words, "The feelings of the believer, viewed in Christ, as described in the close of this chapter, form a striking contrast with what is said in the end of the former chapter, where he is viewed in himself. In the contemplation of himself as a sinner, he mournfully exclaims, 'O wretched man that I am!' In the contemplation of himself as justified in Christ, he boldly demands, Who shall lay anything to my charge? Who is he that condemneth? Well may the man who loves God defy the universe to separate him from the love of God which is in Christ Jesus his Lord. Although at present the whole creation groaneth and travaileth in pain together, although even he himself groaneth within himself, yet all things are working together for his good. The Holy Spirit is interceding for him in his heart; Jesus Christ is interceding for him before the throne; God the Father hath chosen him from eternity, hath called him, hath justified him, and will finally crown him with glory. The Apostle had begun this chapter by declaring that there is no *condemnation* to them who are in Christ Jesus; he concludes it with the triumphant assurance that there is no *separation* from His love. The salvation of believers is complete in Christ, and their union with Him indissoluble."[39]

For further Scripture references on the "Security of Believers" see the section on the "Perseverance of the Saints" in Part II of Appendix D, pp. 184-188.

For a visual summary of this great chapter, see Note 8, on the following page.

The Outline of Romans is continued on p. 74.

---

[38] Hodge, *Romans*, p. 290.
[39] Haldane, *Romans*, p. 438. Italics are his.

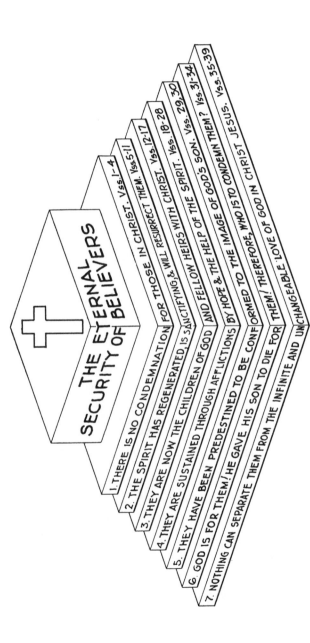

THE ETERNAL
SECURITY OF BELIEVERS

1. THERE IS NO CONDEMNATION FOR THOSE IN CHRIST. Vss. 1-4

2. THE SPIRIT HAS REGENERATED, IS SANCTIFYING, & WILL RESURRECT THEM. Vss. 5-11

3. THEY ARE NOW THE CHILDREN OF GOD AND FELLOW HEIRS WITH CHRIST. Vss. 12-17

4. THEY ARE SUSTAINED THROUGH AFFLICTIONS BY HOPE & THE HELP OF THE SPIRIT. Vss. 18-28

5. THEY HAVE BEEN PREDESTINED TO BE CONFORMED TO THE IMAGE OF GOD'S SON. Vss. 29, 30

6. GOD IS FOR THEM! HE GAVE HIS SON TO DIE FOR THEM! THEREFORE, WHO IS TO CONDEMN THEM? Vss. 31-34

7. NOTHING CAN SEPARATE THEM FROM THE INFINITE AND UNCHANGEABLE LOVE OF GOD IN CHRIST JESUS. Vss. 35-39

THE SEVENFOLD FOUNDATION OF ROMANS EIGHT SUPPORTING
THE BELIEVER'S SECURITY

In Romans Eight Paul rests the doctrine of the eternal security of believers on seven irrefutable arguments. The above visual aid is given in the hope that it will help fix in the mind the theme of this great chapter. Each argument, starting from the top down, rests on the following arguments so that when they are viewed together they form an indestructible foundation. The chapter starts with NO CONDEMNATION "in Christ" and ends with NO SEPARATION from the love of God "in Christ."

PART TWO

THE REJECTION OF THE JEWS AND THE INCLUSION OF THE GENTILES AS GOD'S PEOPLE   Chs. 9-11

Introduction: Chapters 9, 10, and 11 deal with a problem which was quite perplexing in Paul's day, the rejection of Israel and the salvation of the Gentiles. How could the rejection of the great majority of the Jewish people be explained? Had not God made definite promises to Abraham, the father of the Jews, to bless his seed, his descendants? Had not God blessed Israel above all other nations? Of all the peoples of the world, had He not entrusted His written Word, the Old Testament Scriptures, to Jews alone? (See Rom. 3:2 and cf. Heb. 1:1.) Was it not to Israel that God had given the Mosaic Law, the tabernacle and temple worship, the promises, etc.? According to the promises made to Abraham, and under the terms of the covenant made at Mt. Sinai, were not the Jews *His people* and was He not *their God?* In view of such a past, what explanation could be given for Israel's rejection and the inclusion of Gentiles in their place as the people of God? It is this problem which Paul solves in the following three chapters. (1) In 9:1-29, he shows that Jewish rejection was not a failure of God's promise to Abraham to save his seed, for the promise was meant *only* for Abraham's "spiritual" descendants whom God had "chosen" unto salvation. These elect Jews, (who, in Paul's day were but a small portion of Israel) along with elect Gentiles, were being called by God and saved just as He had promised they would be and just as the prophets had foretold it would come to pass. (2) In 9:30—10:21, he shows that the immediate cause of the rejection of Israel and of the salvation of the Gentiles was the different manner in which the two groups were responding to the Gospel; the Jews were stumbling at Christ whereas the Gentiles were believing in Him. The Jews had misunderstood and were misusing the Law. Instead of seeing their own sinfulness by contrasting their conduct with the Law's holy requirements and turning to God for mercy and pardon, they were trying to establish a righteousness of their own by keeping its commands. They were looking to the Law, and not to the Gospel, for salvation and thus were perishing! (3) In chapter 11, Paul explains that Israel's rejection is neither total (some Jews were being saved) nor final (the time will come when God will show mercy to the nation at large and so all Israel will be saved).

VIII.   THE ULTIMATE OR ETERNAL REASON FOR THE REJECTION OF THE GREATER PART OF ISRAEL AND THE CALLING OF THE GENTILES TO SALVATION IS GOD'S SOVEREIGN ELECTION. 9:1-29

A. Before entering on the discussion of the rejection of the Jews, Paul expresses his deep concern and love for them and his respect for their national privileges. 9:1-5

9:1-5 RSV

I am speaking the truth in Christ, I am not lying; my conscience bears me witness in the Holy Spirit, ²that I have great sorrow and unceasing anguish in my heart. ³For I could wish that I myself were accursed and cut off from Christ for the sake of my brethren, my kinsmen by race. ⁴They are Israelites, and to them belong the sonship, the glory, the covenants, the giving of the law, the worship, and the promises; ⁵to them belong the patriarchs, and of their race, according to the flesh, is the Christ. God who is over all be blessed for ever.ⁿ Amen.

___
ⁿ Or *Christ, who is God over all, blessed for ever*

9:1-5 WT

I am telling the truth as a Christian man,ᵃ I am telling no lie, because my conscience enlightenedᵇ by the Holy Spirit is bearing me witness to this fact, ²that I have deep grief and constant anguish in my heart; ³for I could wish myself accursed, even cut offᶜ from Christ, for the sake of my brothers, my natural kinsmen. ⁴For they are Israelites; to them belong the privileges of sonship, God's glorious presence,ᵈ the special covenants, the giving of the law, the temple service, the promises, ⁵the patriarchs, and from them by natural descent the Christ has come, who is exalted over all, God blessed forever. Amen!

___
ᵃ Lit., *speaking the truth in Christ.*
ᵇ Grk., *by the Holy Spirit.*
ᶜ In the prep.
ᵈ Lit., *glory* (Shekinah).

Notice the marginal rendering, in footnote "n" of verse 5 in the RSV, which reads "Christ, who is God over all, blessed for ever." For a defense of this rendering of the verse rather than the one given in the main text of the RSV, see Hodge's Commentary, pp. 300-302. He argues that according to the rules of construction the verse must be translated to teach that Christ is God over all. Cf. the ANT and the BV.

1.   Paul loved his kinsmen after the flesh, so much that he could wish himself cut off (accursed) from Christ for their sake, if this could mean salvation for them.   9:1-3

2.   He reviews briefly their glorious privileges of the past. Israel was God's adopted nation. He had manifested His presence to them. He had made special covenants with them and had given them the law of Moses and the temple worship. His promises had been directed to them and finally, of their nation according to the flesh, had come the Christ, who is God over all!   9:4,5

B.   In introducing the subject of God's rejection of the nation Israel, and of God's calling the Gentiles to salvation, Paul establishes the absolute right of God to do with His fallen, sinful creatures as He pleases. The apostle explains that God's promise to save Abraham's descendants had reference only to his "spiritual" or "elect" seed (9:6-8) and that it was God who determined which of Abraham's descendants according to the flesh were to be included in this elect group (9:9-13). Salvation results from God's showing mercy, not from man's will or actions (9:14-18). God, like a potter, makes out of the clay (the fallen mass of humanity) vessels for beauty or vessels for menial use (9:19-21). Paul concludes the section by showing that no one has the right to question God's sovereignty in rejecting some men and saving others. In order to display His wrath (His displeasure against sin) God will punish the vessels of wrath made for destruction (9:22); in this way He will make known the riches of His glory for the vessels of mercy, His elect people (9:23) whom He has called *not only* from the JEWS *but also* from the GENTILES (9:24). Who can object to God's acting in this fashion with His sinful creatures? 9:6-24

1. The rejection of national Israel, the Jews according to the flesh, was not a failure of God's promise to save Abraham's seed. 9:6-13

How could Israel's lost condition be explained in view of the promise God had made to Abraham to bless (save) his seed? Had God gone back on His word? This is the question which Paul now answers.

a. God's promise to save Abraham's descendants was limited in scope—it did not mean that God would show mercy to all of Abraham's *natural* descendants (i.e., "the children of the flesh") but had reference only to Abraham's *spiritual* seed (i.e., "the children of promise"). 9:6-8

9:6-8 RSV	9:6-8 WT
⁶But it is not as though the word of God had failed. For not all who are descended from Israel belong to Israel, ⁷and not all are children of Abraham because they are his descendants; but "Through Isaac shall your descendants be named." ⁸This means that it is not the children of the flesh who are the children of God, but the children of the promise are reckoned as descendants.	⁶But it is not that God's word has failed. For not everybody that is descended from Israel really belongs to Israel, ⁷nor are they all children of Abraham, because they are his descendants, but the promise was, "In the line of Isaac your descendants will be counted."ᵉ ⁸That is, it is not Abraham's natural descendants who are God's children, but those who are made children by the promiseᶠ are counted his true descendants.
	ᵉ Gen. 21:12.
	ᶠ Subj. gen.

"For not all who are descended from Israel (after the flesh) belong to (spiritual) Israel . . . . This means that it is *not the children of the flesh* who are THE CHILDREN OF GOD, *but the children of the promise are reckoned* (counted) *as descendants,*" (9:6b,8). From among the physical nation Israel, God has elected certain Jews unto salvation. These elect Jews (which only make up a part of national Israel) are the *true* descendants of Abraham, and they make up the true "Israel of God" (Gal. 6:16), that *spiritual* nation which is composed of all true believers. It was to *these* elect or believing Jews, and to them only, that the promise applied. Although the majority of the Jews were perishing in unbelief in Paul's day, those Jews whom God had sovereignly selected out of the physical nation to be His children were being saved through faith; therefore, God's promise to Abraham (to save his seed) was being fulfilled. See Note 11, pp. 94-99, and the diagram on p. 100 for the distinction between national Israel which is made up of Abraham's physical descendants and spiritual Israel which is made up of Abraham's spiritual descendants (spiritual Israel now includes saved Gentiles as well as saved Jews).

76

b. Paul illustrates God's sovereign election of some Jews and rejection of others as heirs of the promise by citing examples from the immediate descendants of Abraham. 9:9-13

9:9-13 RSV

[9]For this is what the promise said, "About this time I will return and Sarah shall have a son." [10]And not only so, but also when Rebecca had conceived children by one man, our forefather Isaac, [11]though they were not yet born and had done nothing either good or bad, in order that God's purpose of election might continue, not because of works but because of his call, [12]she was told, "The elder will serve the younger." [13]As it is written, "Jacob I loved, but Esau I hated."

9:9-13 WT

[9]For this is the language of the promise, "About this time next year I will come back, and Sarah will have a son."[g] [10]Not only that but this too: there was Rebecca who was impregnated by our forefather Isaac. [11]For even before the twin sons[h] were born, and though they had done nothing either good or bad, that God's purpose in accordance with His choice might continue to stand, conditioned not on men's actions but on God's calling them, [12]she was told, "The elder will be a slave to the younger."[i] [13]As the Scripture says, "Jacob I have loved, but Esau I have hated."[j]

[g] Gen. 18:10.
[h] Implied with pt. from the account in Gen.
[i] Gen. 25:23.
[j] Mal. 1:2,3.

(1) Abraham had two sons, Ishmael who was born of Hagar, and Isaac "the son of promise" who, fourteen years later, was born of Sarah. Though both were his sons according to the flesh, the former was *rejected* and the latter was *chosen by God* to share in the promise made to Abraham, thus clearly showing that God determines who among Abraham's descendants will inherit the blessing. 9:9

(2) The example of God's choice between Isaac's twin sons, Esau and Jacob, is cited by Paul to show that God alone determines who is to receive His blessings. God's choice of Jacob and rejection of Esau was announced to Rebecca before the twins were born, before they had done anything either good or bad, so that all might know that God's choice was not based on man's actions. Many think that before the foundation of the world, God looked down through time and picked out for salvation those whom He saw would respond to Him (i.e., do what was required of them) and that election therefore is based on God's foreknowledge of what each individual would do. But Paul's language will not admit of such an interpretation (cf. Rom. 11:5,6). See Appendix C, pp. 131-137. 9:10-13

Although God's choice of Jacob and rejection of Esau was not based on the personal acts (good or bad) of either, both were *guilty in Adam.* As the result of the imputation of Adam's first sin to all the race, and thus to Jacob and Esau, they were both justly exposed to God's wrath. (See the Outline on 5:12-21 and Note 3, pp. 41-44.)

THE PRINCIPLE OF ELECTION ILLUSTRATED
FROM THE OLD TESTAMENT

The principle of God's selection is clearly seen within the immediate descendants of Abraham, the father of the Jewish nation.

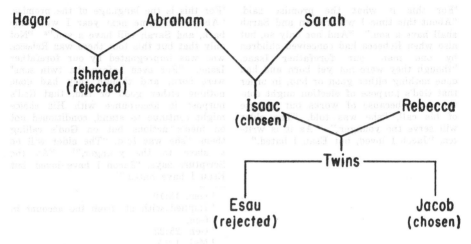

Both Ishmael and Isaac were the sons of Abraham, but one was rejected while the other was blessed by God. Isaac's twin sons were equally the descendants of Abraham, but God cut off Esau and blessed Jacob, not because of anything good or bad done by either of them, but in order to demonstrate His purpose of election. God's choice does not depend on man's will or actions but rests solely in Himself.

    2.   After having established the fact of unconditional election, Paul *defends* it! 9:14-24

        He states and answers the two main objections which are made against the doctrine of *unconditional election* (the doctrine that God's choice of who will be saved is *not determined* by man's actions but rests solely in God's sovereign will). It should be noted that if Paul were establishing election unto external privileges only and not election unto salvation, or if he meant by election that God chose those to eternal life whom He saw would meet the conditions which He had stipulated, then the two objections which he raises and answers would be meaningless. Paul would have needed only to explain that he was not talking about election unto salvation or that election was conditional and therefore determined by man's own actions; in either case the objections which follow would cease to exist. The fact that he raises the objections and answers them as he does shows clearly that Paul is teaching that each individual's destiny was determined by Almighty God, that some were by grace chosen unto eternal life and others in justice were left to suffer the consequences of their sin, eternal death.

a. The *first* objection: *It would be unjust for God to show mercy to one and not to another* (9:14). 9:14-18

9:14-18 RSV

[14]"What shall we say then? Is there injustice on God's part? By no means! [15]For he says to Moses, "I will have mercy on whom I have mercy, and I will have compassion on whom I have compassion." [16]So it depends not upon man's will or exertion, but upon God's mercy. [17]For the scripture says to Pharaoh, "I have raised you up for the very purpose of showing my power in you, so that my name may be proclaimed in all the earth." [18]So then he has mercy upon whomever he wills, and he hardens the heart of whomever he wills.

9:14-18 WT

[14]"What are we then to conclude? It is not that there is injustice in God, is it? Of course not! [15]For He says to Moses, "I will have mercy on any man that I choose to have mercy on, and take pity on any man that I choose to take pity on."[k] [16]So one's destiny[1] does not depend on his own willing or strenuous actions but on God's having mercy on him. [17]For the Scripture says to Pharaoh, "I have raised you to your position for this very purpose of displaying my power in dealing with you, of announcing my name all over the earth."[m] [18]So He has mercy on any man that He chooses to, and He hardens any man that He chooses to harden.

[k] Ex. 33:19.
[1] Lit., *it is not of him who wills or runs.*
[m] Ex. 9:16.

Paul's answer is twofold:

(1) God Himself declares that He shows mercy to whom He will. Paul quotes the words which God spoke to Moses: "I will have mercy on whom I will have mercy and I will have compassion (pity) on whom I will have compassion" (9:15). See Exodus 33:19. Paul then concludes from these words that election depends on God's mercy, not man's merit. "So it depends not upon man's will or exertion (efforts) but upon God's mercy" (9:16).

(2) God exercised this right in His dealings with Pharaoh, the ruler of Egypt during the time of Israel's deliverance from bondage. For as God said to him, "I have raised you up for the very purpose of showing my power in you, so that my name may be proclaimed in all the earth" (9:17). From these words Paul concludes that God not only shows mercy to whomever He wills but also "hardens the heart of whomever he wills" (9:18).

b. The *second* objection: Since the destiny of all men is in the hands of God and He extends mercy to one while withholding it from another, *why does God still hold men responsible for their actions* (9:19)? 9:19-23

9:19-23 RSV

[19]You will say to me then, "Why does he still find fault? For who can resist his will?" [20]But, who are you, a man, to answer back to God? Will what is

9:19-23 WT

[19]So you will ask me, "Why does He still find fault? For who can resist His will?" [20]On the contrary, friend, who are you anyway that you would answer back

molded say to its molder, "Why have you made me thus?" [21]Has the potter no right over the clay, to make out of the same lump one vessel for beauty and another for menial use? [22]What if God, desiring to show his wrath and to make known his power, has endured with much patience the vessels of wrath made for destruction, [23]in order to make known the riches of his glory for the vessels of mercy, which he has prepared beforehand for glory,

to God? Can the clay that is molded ask the man who molds it, "Why did you make me like this?" [21]Has not the potter the right with his clay to make of the same lump one vessel for ornamental purposes, another for degrading service? [22]And what if God, though wishing to display His anger and make known His power, yet has most patiently borne with the objects of His anger, already ripe for destruction,[n] [23]so as to make known the riches of His glory for the objects of His mercy, whom He prepared in ages past to share His glory—

[n] Lit., *vessels made ready* (pf. pt.) *for destruction.*

Paul's answer is twofold:

(1)   It is irreverent for creatures to criticize or contradict the actions of their Creator, especially when one considers that God has both claimed (vs. 16) and exercised (vss. 17,18) the right which is being objected to (9:20,21). "The objection is founded on ignorance or mis-apprehension of the true relation between God and his sinful creatures. It supposes that he is under obligation to extend his grace to all. Whereas he is under obligation to none. All are sinners, and have forfeited every claim to his mercy; it is, therefore, the prerogative of God to spare one and not another; to make one vessel to honour, and another to dishonour. He, as their sovereign Creator, has the same right over them that a potter has over the clay. It is to be borne in mind, that Paul does not here speak of the right of God over his creatures as creatures, but as sinful creatures, as he himself clearly intimates in the next verses (vss. 22,23)."[40] 9:20,21

(2)   God, in dealing with His sinful creatures by punishing some and pardoning others, is doing nothing unreasonable or unjust, for both classes of vessels serve the highest end; the punishing of the vessels of wrath manifests God's displeasure against sin whereas the pardoning of the vessels of mercy manifests the riches of His glory.   9:22,23

"God only punishes the wicked for their sins, while he extends undeserved mercy to the objects of his grace. There is no in-justice done to one wicked man in the pardon of another, especially as there are the highest objects to be accomplished both in the punishment of the vessels of wrath, and the pardon of the vessels of mercy. God does nothing more than exercise a right inherent in sovereignty, viz., that of dispensing pardon at his pleasure, . . ."[41]

[40] Hodge, *Romans*, p. 318.

[41] Hodge, *Romans*, p. 304.

c. *Conclusion:* God, who has mercy on whom He chooses to have mercy, is now calling men from among the Gentiles as well as from among the Jews. 9:24

9:24 RSV	9:24 WT
[24]even us whom he has called, not from the Jews only but also from the Gentiles?	[24]even us whom He has called, not only from among the Jews but from among the heathen too?

Hodge, in his comments on verse 24, gives a splendid summary of Paul's argument, "How naturally does the apostle here return to the main subject of discussion! How skilfully is the conclusion brought out at which he has continually aimed! God chose Isaac in preference to Ishmael, Jacob in preference to Esau; it is a prerogative which he claims and exercises, of selecting from among the guilty family of men, whom he pleases as the objects of his mercy, and leaving whom he pleases to perish in their sins, unrestricted in his choice by the descent or previous conduct of the individuals. He has mercy upon whom he will have mercy. He calls men, therefore, from among the Gentiles and from among the Jews indiscriminately. This is the conclusion at which the apostle aimed. The Gentiles are admitted into the Messiah's kingdom, vers. 25,26; and the great body of the Jews are excluded, vers. 27. This conclusion he confirms by explicit declarations of Scripture."[42]

C. Paul shows that the salvation of the Gentiles and the rejection of the greater part of Israel was foretold by the prophets. 9:25-29

1. Hosea wrote concerning the time when those who were not God's people (i.e., Gentiles) would be called "sons of the living God" (see Hosea 2:23 and 1:10). 9:25,26

9:25,26 RSV	9:25,26 WT
[25]As indeed he says in Hose'a, "Those who were not my people I will call 'my people,' and her who was not beloved I will call 'my beloved.' " [26]"And in the very place where it was said to them, 'You are not my people,' they will be called 'sons of the living God.' "	[25]Just as He says in Hosea: "I will call a people that was not mine, my people, And her who was not beloved, my beloved, [26]And in the place where it was said, 'You are no people of mine,' They shall be called sons of the living God."[o]
	[o] Hos. 2:23.

2. Isaiah foretold that the time would come when only a remnant (i.e., a small fragment or portion) of Israel would be saved (see Isa. 10:22,23; 1:9 and 11:11). 9:27-29

---

[42] Hodge, *Romans*, p. 322.

81

9:27-29 RSV	9:27-29 WT
[27]And Isaiah cries out concerning Israel: "Though the number of the sons of Israel be as the sand of the sea, only a remnant of them will be saved; [28]for the Lord will execute his sentence upon the earth with rigor and dispatch." [29]And as Isaiah predicted, "If the Lord of hosts had not left us children, we would have fared like Sodom and been made like Gomor'rah."	[27]And Isaiah cries out about Israel, "Although the sons of Israel are as numberless as the sands of the sea, only a remnant of them will be saved, [28]for the Lord will completely and quickly execute His sentence on the earth."[p] [29]As Isaiah again has foretold, "Unless the Lord of hosts had left us some descendants, we would have fared as Sodom did and would have been like Gomorrah."[q]

[p] Isa. 10:22; 28:22.
[q] Isa. 1:9.

Both of these prophecies had already begun to be fulfilled in Paul's day!

Notice that throughout this whole discourse the Apostle is discussing the election and calling of individuals to *salvation* and not to external privilege or service. These individuals were selected by God to be made His "children" (9:8) and to be shown "mercy" (9:15,16,18). They were made "vessels of mercy" and prepared "for glory" (9:21-23). They were made "God's people" and called "sons of the living God" (9:25,26). Notice that "only a remnant of Israel will be *saved*" (9:27). For further Biblical proof that individuals were elected by God unto salvation before the foundation of the world, see Point II in the second part of Appendix D, pp. 158-166.

IX. THE IMMEDIATE CAUSE OF ISRAEL'S REJECTION AND OF THE GENTILES' SALVATION WAS THE DIFFERENT MANNER IN WHICH THEY WERE RESPONDING TO THE GOSPEL (the good news that righteousness is obtained through faith in Jesus Christ). 9:30—10:21

A. The Gentiles were receiving God's free gift of righteousness by faith and were being justified whereas the Jews, ignorant of God's gift of righteousness, were trying to work out a righteousness of their own and were perishing. 9:30—10:4

1. The Gentiles who had not sought after righteousness were now obtaining it through faith. 9:30

9:30 RSV	9:30 WT
[30]What shall we say, then? That Gentiles who did not pursue righteousness have attained it, that is, righteousness through faith;	[30]What are we then to conclude? That heathen peoples who were not in search for right standing with God have obtained it, and that a right standing conditioned on faith;

In 1:18-32, Paul describes the terrible condition of the Gentile world and explains why they had been abandoned by God and left without

any supernatural revelation of His person or of the way of life. They had suppressed the truth about God and turned to idols and served the creature rather than the Creator; therefore, God had given them up to all kinds of evil. Only what could be known about God through nature (creation) was available to them and this knowledge, though it left them without excuse for their idolatry, was not sufficient to bring them to salvation. Left to themselves they had not pursued righteousness! But now the situation had changed; God was turning to them in mercy and calling (effectually drawing) them unto Himself (9:24-26) and revealing unto them the gift of righteousness which is received through faith in His Son (9:30).

2. The Jews who had tried to work out a righteousness of their own based on obedience to the law had failed to obtain righteousness—for they ignorantly sought it by works, instead of by faith. 9:31—10:4

9:31—10:4 RSV   9:31—10:4 WT

³¹but that Israel who pursued the righteousness which is based on law did not succeed in fulfilling that law. ³²Why? Because they did not pursue it through faith, but as if it were based on works. They have stumbled over the stumbling-stone, ³³as it is written,

"Behold I am laying in Zion a stone
    that will make men stumble,
a rock that will make them fall;
and he who believes in him will not
    be put to shame."

Brethren, my heart's desire and prayer to God for them is that they may be saved. ²I bear them witness that they have a zeal for God, but it is not enlightened. ³For, being ignorant of the righteousness that comes from God, and seeking to establish their own, they did not submit to God's righteousness. ⁴For Christ is the end of the law, that every one who has faith may be justified.

³¹while Israel, though ever in pursuit of a law that would bring right standing, did not attain to it. ³²Why? Because they did not try through faith but through what they could do. They have stumbled over the stone that causes people to stumble, ³³as the Scripture says:

"See, I put on Zion a stone for causing
    people to stumble, a rock to trip
    them on,
But no one who puts his faith in it will
    ever be put to shame."ʳ

Brothers, my heart's good will goes out for them, and my prayer to God is that they may be saved. ²For I can testify that they are zealous for God, but they are not intelligentlyᵃ so. ³For they were ignorant of God's way of right standing and were trying to set up one of their own, and so would not surrender to God's way of right standing. ⁴For Christ has put an end to lawᵇ as a way to right standing for everyone who puts his trust in Him.

ʳ Isa. 8:14; 28:16.
ᵃ Lit., *in accordance with knowledge.*
ᵇ Grk., *is the end of the law.*

a. The Jews were trying to save themselves through their own works but were failing. 9:31,32a

b. The Jews were stumbling over Christ, the stumbling-stone, as Isaiah had predicted they would (see Isa. 28:16; 8:14). 9:32b,33

c. Paul expresses his desire for Israel's salvation and bears witness to their zeal for God, but shows that this zeal was not enlightened, for they were ignorant (without knowledge) of the righteousness that God gives (imputes) and were trying to establish a righteousness of their own. They failed to understand that Christ is the end of the law as the means of justification for all who believe. 10:1-4

The Outline of Romans is continued on p. 85.

NOTE NO. 9   SAVING FAITH

The basic idea conveyed by the word faith is *trust*. As the introduction to *The Amplified New Testament* states, the original Greek rendered "to believe" means " 'To adhere to, cleave to, to trust, to have faith in, to rely on.' " Whether or not one's faith will save him depends upon its object. One can have faith without having "saving faith." Trust or reliance can be wrongly placed—if it is it will not result in justification. The only faith that will put a sinner into a position of acceptance with God is faith in Jesus Christ, His eternal Son. But faith in Him presupposes a knowledge of His Person as the Son of God, the Lord of Heaven, and of His work (His sacrificial death for sinners and resurrection from the dead). Without knowing who He is and what He did, one could not trust Him or rely on Him for salvation (see Note 10, p. 87). Berkhof defines saving faith as "a certain conviction, wrought in the heart by the Holy Spirit, as to the truth of the gospel, and a hearty reliance (trust) on the promises of God in Christ."[43]

Saving faith is not something residing in the soul of each individual needing only to be directed toward Christ in order to become effective, but is created in the soul by the Holy Spirit when the sinner is made alive. Saving faith, like repentance, is a fruit of regeneration; it is not man's gift to God but rather is itself a *gift from God*. Packer, speaking of faith as a supernatural divine gift, correctly observes that "Sin and Satan have so blinded fallen men (Eph. 4:18; II Cor. 4:4), that they cannot discern dominical and apostolic witness to be God's word, nor 'see' and comprehend the realities of which it speaks (John 3:3; I Cor. 2:14), nor 'come' in self-renouncing trust to Christ (John 6:44, 65), till the Holy Spirit has enlightened them (cf. II Cor. 4:6). Only the recipients of this divine 'teaching,' 'drawing' and 'anointing' come to Christ and abide in him (John 6:44-45; I John 2:20, 27). God is thus the author of all saving faith (Eph. 2:8; Phil. 1:29) . . ."[44]

The Bible makes it clear that faith is not a meritorious work performed by the sinner. Faith, like all the other facets of salvation, flows from the cross; it is a part of the salvation that Christ earned for His people. Faith is created in the hearts of God's elect when they are made alive by the almighty power of the Holy Spirit, who works when and where He wills.

---

[43] L. Berkhof, *Systematic Theology*, p. 503.

[44] James I. Packer, "Faith," *Baker's Dictionary of Theology*, p. 210.

Therefore the sinner, in believing in Christ, has no ground to boast, for he was enabled to believe in Him by the grace of God. See Point IV in Part Two of Appendix D on "Efficacious Grace," pp. 176-184.

The Outline of Romans is continued from p. 84.

B.   The LEGAL and GOSPEL methods of justification are contrasted for the purpose of showing that the legal method is beyond the reach of sinful men, but that the gospel method is simple and easy and adapted to all men without distinction.   10:5-13

1.   The legal system demands of men perfect obedience to God's law for justification (see Galatians 3:10-13).   10:5

10:5 RSV

[5]Moses writes that the man who practices the righteousness which is based on the law shall live by it.

10:5 WT

[5]For Moses says of the law-way to right standing with God that whoever can perform the law will live by it.

2.   The gospel method of justification prescribes no such severe terms; it simply requires heart faith and open confession of Christ as the risen Lord.   10:6-11

10:6-11 RSV

[6]But the righteousness based on faith says, Do not say in your heart, "Who will ascend into heaven?" (that is, to bring Christ down) [7]or "Who will descend into the abyss?" (that is, to bring Christ up from the dead). [8]But what does it say? The word is near you, on your lips and in your heart (that is, the word of faith which we preach); [9]because, if you confess with your lips that Jesus is Lord and believe in your heart that God raised him from the dead, you will be saved. [10]For man believes with his heart and so is justified, and he confesses with his lips and so is saved. [11]The scripture says, "No one who believes in him will be put to shame."

10:6-11 WT

[6]But here is what the faith-way to right standing[c] says, "Do not say to yourself, 'Who will go up to heaven?'" that is, to bring Christ down; [7]or "'Who will go down into the depths?'" that is, to bring Christ up from the dead. [8]But what does it say? "God's message is close to you, on your very lips and in your heart"; that is, the message about faith which we preach. [9]For if with your lips you acknowledge the fact that Jesus is Lord, and in your hearts you believe that God raised Him from the dead, you will be saved. [10]For in their hearts people exercise the faith that leads to right standing, and with their lips they make the acknowledgment which means[d] salvation. [11]For the Scripture says, "No one who puts his faith in Him will ever be put to shame."[e]

[c] Lit., the right standing conditioned on faith.
[d] Grk., unto salvation.
[e] Isa. 28:16.

"But the righteousness based on faith—imputed by God and bringing right relationship with Him—says, Do not say in your heart, Who will ascend into heaven? that is, to bring Christ down, Or who will descend into the abyss? that is, to bring Christ up from the dead· [as if we could be saved by our own efforts], [Deut. 30:12,13.]

But what does it say? The Word (God's message in Christ) is near you, on your lips and in your heart; that is, the Word—the message, the basis and object —of faith, which we preach. [Deut. 30:14.] Because if you acknowledge *and* confess with your lips that Jesus is Lord and in your heart believe (adhere to, trust in and rely on the truth) that God raised Him from the dead, you will be saved. For with the heart a person believes (adheres to, trusts in and relies on Christ) and so is justified (declared righteous, acceptable to God), and with the mouth he confesses— declares openly and speaks out freely his faith—*and* confirms [his] salvation. The Scripture says, No man who believes in Him—who adheres to, relies on and trusts in Him—will ever be put to shame *or* be disappointed. [Is. 28:16; 49:23; Jer. 17:7; Ps. 34:22.]" (10:6-11, *The Amplified New Testament*)

3. Justification is offered to all men (Jew and Gentile alike) on the same terms. The promise is clear and certain—"all who call upon *the Lord* (i.e., Jesus, see vs. 9) shall be saved." 10:12,13

10:12,13 RSV	10:12,13 WT
[12]For there is no distinction between Jew and Greek; the same Lord is Lord of all and bestows his riches upon all who call upon him. [13]For, "every one who calls upon the name of the Lord will be saved."	[12]But there is no distinction between Jew and Greek, for the same Lord is over them all, because He is infinitely kind[f] to all who call upon Him. [13]For everyone who calls upon the name of the Lord will be saved.

f Lit., *rich* (in kindness).

C. The Gospel of Christ is not only adapted to all men but *must be sent* (preached) *to all men if they are to be saved!* 10:14-17

10:14-17 RSV	10:14-17 WT
[14]But how are men to call upon him in whom they have not believed? And how are they to believe in him of whom they have never heard? And how are they to hear without a preacher? [15]And how can men preach unless they are sent? As it is written, "How beautiful are the feet of those who preach good news!" [16]But they have not all heeded the gospel; for Isaiah says, "Lord, who has believed what he has heard from us?" [17]So faith comes from what is heard, and what is heard comes by the preaching of Christ.	[14]But how can people call upon One in whom they have not believed? And how can they believe in One about whom they have not heard? And how can people hear without someone to preach to them? [15]And how can men preach unless they are sent to do so? As the Scripture says, "How beautiful are the feet of men who bring the glad news of His good things!"[g] [16]However, they have not all given heed to the good news, for Isaiah says, "Lord, who has put faith in what we told?"[h] [17]So faith comes from hearing what is told, and hearing through the message about Christ.

g Isa. 52:7.
h Isa. 53:1.

Notice carefully the chain of reasoning set forth by Paul in verses 14-17:

1. Sinners must CALL upon Jesus as Lord if they are to be saved.

2. But they cannot call upon Him unless they BELIEVE in Him.

3. They cannot believe in Him without HEARING about Him.

4. And they cannot hear about Him unless the message of CHRIST IS PREACHED to them.

5. Therefore the message must be SENT *if sinners are to be saved.*[45]

Conclusion: "So faith comes from what is heard, and what is heard comes by the preaching of Christ" (10:17).

The Outline of Romans is continued on p. 89.

NOTE NO. 10   THE CONDITION OF THOSE WHO HAVE NEVER HEARD THE GOSPEL

All men are guilty before God on two counts. First, because of Adam's sin which has been imputed to the race (see the Outline on 5:12-19 and Note 3, p. 41) and second, because of their own personal sins which they commit by breaking God's law (see the Outline on 2:12-16; and 3:9-12, 20 and Note 5, C,1, p. 54). The only way sinners can be freed from their guilt is through faith in Jesus Christ. But what of those who have never heard of Jesus and therefore cannot possibly believe in Him? Are they lost? Will they perish in hell? Paul's answer is YES! For as he explains in Rom. 10:14-17, unless the Gospel is preached to the lost (this includes *all* the lost, heathen as well as the Jews) and believed by them, they cannot possibly escape God's wrath. Speaking of Christ in Acts 4:12, Peter states, "There is salvation in no one else, for there is no other name under heaven, given among men *by which we must be saved.*"

Those who have not lived under the clear light of God's Word will not be as strictly judged as those who have lived under that Word and yet have refused to heed its warnings and embrace its promises. Christ teaches this in Luke 12:47,48, "And that servant who knew his master's will, but did not make ready or act according to his will, shall receive a severe beating. But he who did not know, and did what deserved a beating, shall receive a light beating. Every one to whom much is given, of him will much be required; and of him to whom men commit much, they will demand the more." As Hodge states, "Men are to be judged

---

[45] For an excellent discussion of *evangelism*, its definition, its message, its motives, the methods and means by which it should be practiced, and its relation to the sovereignty of God in saving sinners, see J. I. Packer's splendid book, *Evangelism and the Sovereignty of God* (126 pages) published by the Inter-Varsity Press, 1519 North Astor, Chicago 10, Illinois. This work stresses the proper Biblical balance between those doctrines contained in chapters 9 and 10 of Romans. God determines who will be saved; this is emphatically taught in Romans 9:1-29. Nonetheless, it is the lost sinner's responsibility to accept the Gospel through faith or else remain under the curse of the broken law (9:30—10:13). It is also the Christian's responsibility to actively engage in aggressive evangelism and to spread the Gospel to all men everywhere or else they perish (10:14-17). Packer shows that these two concepts, God's sovereignty and man's responsibility, are taught side by side in the Bible; both are true and both must be believed and stressed if we are to do justice to the Biblical message.

by the light they have severally enjoyed. The ground of judgment is their works; the rule of judgment is their knowledge."[46] Since the heathen sin against God by breaking the law written on their hearts, they will perish unless the message of Christ is carried to them. There is no justification for sinners apart from faith in Christ! Those whom God has chosen to save He saves through the *means* of the Gospel of Jesus Christ; He calls them outwardly by the message of the Gospel and inwardly by the Holy Spirit who enables them to believe the message. "But we are bound to give thanks to God always for you, brethren beloved by the Lord, because God chose you from the beginning to be saved, through sanctification by the Spirit and belief in the truth. To this he called you through our gospel, so that you may obtain the glory of our Lord Jesus Christ," (II Thess. 2:13,14).

There are some who believe that those who never hear the Gospel *cannot* be damned. They argue that "God would not be so unjust as to condemn to hell those who have never been given a chance to accept or to reject Christ." Yet they advocate the sending of missionaries to those who have never heard and who, therefore, according to their view, could not possibly be lost. It seems contradictory to hold that the heathen are safe because they have never heard of Christ, and yet to support the missionary movement. For if the heathen cannot be lost without first hearing the Gospel and if after hearing it some of them reject it, then, would it not follow that missionaries, instead of bringing the possibility of salvation to the heathen are, in fact, bringing only condemnation to those who reject Christ after hearing the message? But, as Paul shows in Romans, men are lost, not by their rejection of Christ, but because of their sins. And if they are to believe the Gospel of Christ which frees them of the guilt of their sins, they must first hear it. Thus, the sending of missionaries is absolutely imperative if the heathen are to be saved.

As to the question of the salvation of those incapable of understanding and believing the Gospel (i.e., infants, the mentally incompetent, etc.) the Scriptures are silent—it is. enough to know that the Judge of the world will do right. That they stand in need of salvation is clear from the fact that Adam's sin has been charged to all the race (5:12-19); but we are given no information as to what provision has been made for them. This much is certain: If they enter heaven it must be through the merits of Christ, and not because they are innocent or free from guilt. When considering such matters we should ever keep before us the words of Deuteronomy 29:29, "The secret things belong to the Lord our God; but the things that are revealed belong to us and to our children for ever, . . ." See Note 9, "Saving Faith," p. 84.

---

[46] Hodge, *Romans*, p. 53.

The Outline of Romans is continued from p. 87.

D. The Old Testament prophets foretold of the universal spread of the Gospel and of the inclusion of Gentiles as God's people as well as of the rejection of the Gospel by Israel. 10:18-21

10:18-21 RSV	10:18-21 WT
[18]But I ask, have they not heard? Indeed they have; for "Their voice has gone out to all the earth, and their words to the ends of the world." [19]Again I ask, did Israel not understand? First Moses says, "I will make you jealous of those who are not a nation; with a foolish nation I will make you angry." [20]Then Isaiah is so bold as to say, "I have been found by those who did not seek me; I have shown myself to those who did not ask for me." [21]But of Israel he says, "All day long I have held out my hands to a disobedient and contrary people."	[18]But may I ask, they had no chance to hear, did they?[1] Yes, indeed: "All over the earth their voices[j] have gone, To the ends of the world their words."[k] [19]But again I ask, Israel did not understand, did they? For in the first place Moses says: "I will make you jealous of a nation that is no nation; I will provoke you to anger at a senseless nation."[l] [20]Then Isaiah was bold enough to say: "I have been found by a people who were not searching for me, I have made known myself to people who were not asking to know me."[m] [21]But of Israel he said: "All day long I have held out my hands to a people that is disobedient and obstinate."[n]

[1] Grk. expects ans. *No.*
[j] Nature's voices.
[k] Ps. 19:4.
[l] Dt. 32:21.
[m] Isa. 65:1.
[n] Isa. 65:2.

X. THE REJECTION OF THE JEWS, AS TO NUMBER, IS NOT TOTAL, AS TO TIME, IS NOT FINAL. 11:1-36

A. The rejection of the Jew as to *number* is *not total.* 11:1-10

Though God has rejected the greater part of the Jewish nation, He has not cast away His people (i.e., His elect), those "whom He foreknew" (i.e., set His heart on beforehand—see 8:29,30 and Appendix C, pp. 131-137).

1. Paul himself (11:1) as well as other Jews of his day had been shown grace. Just as in Elijah's day when God had "kept for Himself" seven thousand men, "so too at the present time there is a remnant (i.e., a small fragment) chosen by grace." The elect were chosen, not because of what they had done or would do but solely on the basis of God's unmerited favor. 11:1-6

11:1-6 RSV

I ask, then, has God rejected his people? By no means! I myself am an Israelite, a descendant of Abraham, a member of the tribe of Benjamin. [2]God has not rejected his people whom he foreknew. Do you not know what the scripture says of Eli'jah, how he pleads with God against Israel? [3]"Lord, they have killed thy prophets, they have demolished thy altars, and I alone am left, and they seek my life." [4]But what is God's reply to him? "I have kept for myself seven thousand men who have not bowed the knee to Ba'al." [5]So too at the present time there is a remnant, chosen by grace. [6]But if it is by grace, it is no longer on the basis of works; otherwise grace would no longer be grace.

11:1-6 WT

I say then, God has not disowned His people, has He? Of course not! Why, I am an Israelite myself, a descendant of Abraham, a member of the tribe of Benjamin.[a] [2]No,[b] God has not disowned His people, on whom He set His heart beforehand. Do you know what the Scripture says in Elijah's case, how he pleaded with God against Israel? [3]"Lord, they have killed your prophets, they have demolished your altars; I alone have been left, and they are trying to kill me."[c] [4]But how did God reply to him?[d] "I have reserved for myself seven thousand men who have never bent their knees to Baal." [5]So it is at the present time; a remnant remains, in accordance with God's unmerited favor. [6]But if it is by His unmerited favor, it is not at all conditioned on what they have done.[e] If that were so, His favor would not be favor at all.

[a] Lit., *of the seed of A., of the tribe of B.*
[b] Strongly implied.
[c] I Kg. 19:10.
[d] Lit., *what did the oracle*, etc.
[e] Grk., *is not out of works.*

2. Those of Israel who were not chosen by grace, who were not numbered among His elect, God hardened and blinded. 11:7-10

11:7-10 RSV

[7]What then? Israel failed to obtain what it sought. The elect obtained it, but the rest were hardened, [8]as it is written,
"God gave them a spirit of stupor, eyes that should not see and ears that should not hear,
down to this very day."
[9]And David says,
"Let their feast become a snare and a trap,
a pitfall and a retribution for them;
[10]let their eyes be darkened so that they cannot see,
and bend their backs for ever."

11:7-10 WT

[7]What are we then to conclude? Israel has failed to obtain what it is still in search for, but His chosen ones have obtained it. The rest have become insensible[f] to it, [8]as the Scripture says,
"God has given them over to an attitude[g] of insensibility, so that their eyes cannot see and their ears cannot hear, down to this very day."[h] [9]And David said:
"Let their food become a snare and a trap to them,
Their pitfall and retribution;
[10]Let their eyes be darkened, so they cannot see,
And forever bend their backs beneath the load."[i]

[f] Lit., *hardened.*
[g] Grk., *spirit.*
[h] Isa. 29:10; Dt. 29:4.
[i] Ps. 69:22, 23.

It must be remembered that God, in "hardening" certain individuals (as in Romans 9:17,18; 11:7,8), is dealing with fallen sinful creatures—not with innocent people. This hardening is a *judicial punishment* (i.e., a punishment resulting from a judgment of God inflicted as the result of sin). God abandons sinners to their own corrupt nature. When God hardens an individual He is not forcing a good person, who wants to do right, to do evil but is punishing a sinner by giving him up to sin. See the Outline on 1:24-31. "God does not punish without an existing cause in the guilty. Condemnation supposes positive criminality. Men are in themselves sinful, and commit sin voluntarily; and for their punishment, they are hardened, and finally perish in their sins, and their destruction is the execution of a just sentence of God against sin . . . . God knows what men left to their own inclinations will do; and as to those who are finally condemned, He determines to abandon them to their depraved inclinations, and hardens them in their rebellion against Him."[47]

B.   The rejection of the Jews as to *time* is *not final.* 11:11-32

1.   The re-inclusion of the Jews, as God's people, is both a desirable and probable event. 11:11-24

a.   The temporary rejection of the Jews was designed to bring salvation to the Gentiles—to the world. 11:11-16

11:11-16 RSV

[11]"So I ask, have they stumbled so as to fall? By no means! But through their trespass salvation has come to the Gentiles, so as to make Israel jealous. [12]Now if their trespass means riches for the world, and if their failure means riches for the Gentiles, how much more will their full inclusion mean! [13]Now I am speaking to you Gentiles. Inasmuch then as I am an apostle to the Gentiles, I magnify my ministry [14]in order to make my fellow Jews jealous, and thus save some of them. [15]For if their rejection means the reconciliation of the world, what will their acceptance mean but life from the dead? [16]If the dough offered as first fruits is holy, so is the whole lump; and if the root is holy, so are the branches.

11:11-16 WT

[11]"I say then, they did not stumble so as to fall in utter ruin,[j] did they? Of course not! On the contrary, because of their stumbling, salvation has come to heathen peoples, to make the Israelites[k] jealous. [12]But if their stumbling has resulted in the enrichment of the world, and their overthrow becomes the enrichment of heathen peoples, how much richer the result will be when the full quota of Jews[l] comes in! [13]Yes, I now am speaking to you who are a part of the heathen peoples. As I am an apostle to the heathen peoples, I am making the most[m] of my ministry to them, to see[n] [14]if I can make my fellow-countrymen jealous, and so save some of them. [15]For if the rejection of them has resulted in the reconciling of the world, what will the result be of the final reception of them but life from the dead?

[j] Lit., *so as once for all to fall.*
[k] Implied in pro.
[l] Lit., *their fullness.*
[m] Grk., *glorifying, magnifying.*
[n] Implied with particle.

---

[47] Haldane, *Romans,* p. 528.

¹⁶If the first handful of dough is con-
secrated,° so is the whole mass; if the
tree's root is consecrated, so are the
branches.

° Lit., *holy.*

b. The Gentiles are in no position to boast of their inclusion
into the olive tree (the people of God) as if their inclusion had come about
as the result of their being superior to the Jews. The Jews were broken
off because of unbelief; the Gentiles stand fast only through faith!
11:17-22

11:17-22 RSV

¹⁷But if some of the branches were
broken off, and you, a wild olive shoot,
were grafted in their place to share the
richness° of the olive tree, ¹⁸do not boast
over the branches. If you do boast, remember it is not you that support the
root, but the root that supports you. ¹⁹You
will say, "Branches were broken off so
that I might be grafted in." ²⁰That is
true. They were broken off because of
their unbelief, but you stand fast only
through faith. So do not become proud,
but stand in awe. ²¹For if God did not
spare the natural branches, neither will
he spare you. ²²Note then the kindness
and the severity of God: severity toward
those who have fallen, but God's kindness
to you, provided you continue in his kindness; otherwise you too will be cut off.

° Other ancient authorities read *rich
root*

11:17-22 WT

¹⁷If some of the branches have been
broken off, and yet you, although you
were wild olive suckers,^p have been grafted in among the native branches, and
been made to share the rich sap of the
native olive's root, ¹⁸you must not be
boasting against the natural branches.
And if you do, just consider,^q you do
not support the root, but the root supports you. ¹⁹Then you will say, "Branches
have been broken off for us to be grafted
in." ²⁰Very well; but it was for lack of
faith that they were broken off, and
it is through your faith that you now
stand where you are. Stop your haughty
thinking; rather continue to be reverent,
²¹for if God did not spare the natural
branches, certainly^r He will not spare
you. ²²So take a look at the goodness
and the severity of God; severity to those
who have fallen, but goodness to you,
on condition that you continue to live by
His goodness; otherwise, you too will be
pruned away.

^p Grk., uses sg. for pl.
^q Implied.
^r Very strong neg. thus trans.

As Haldane observes, "The Jewish nation was God's olive
tree. They were all the people of God in a typical sense, and the greater
part of God's true people had been chosen out of them; but now, by their
unbelief, some of the branches were broken off from the tree . . . . And
among, or rather instead of, those that were broken off, the Gentiles, who
were a wild olive, having had no place in the good olive tree, are now made
the children of Abraham by faith in Christ Jesus, Gal. 3:26-29. They
were grafted into the good olive tree, whose root Abraham was, and were
made partakers of his distinguished privileges . . . . Whenever Gentile
Christians feel a disposition to boast with respect to the Jews, let them
remember not only that the Jews were first the people of God, but that
the first Christians were also Jews. The Jews received no advantage from

the Gentiles; but, on the contrary, the Gentiles have received much from the Jews, from whom the Gospel sounded out—its first preachers being Jews, and of whom even Christ Himself, as concerning the flesh, came. The Gentile believers become the children of Abraham, and all the blessings they enjoy are in virtue of that relation."[48]

c. The Jews can and will be grafted back into the olive tree, if they do not persist in their unbelief. 11:23, 24

11:23,24 RSV	11:23,24 WT
[23]And even the others, if they do not persist in their unbelief, will be grafted in, for God has the power to graft them in again. [24]For if you have been cut from what is by nature a wild olive tree, and grafted, contrary to nature, into a cultivated olive tree, how much more will these natural branches be grafted back into their own olive tree.	[23]And they too, if they do not continue to live by their unbelief, will be grafted in, for God is amply able to graft them in. [24]For if you were cut off from an olive wild by nature, and contrary to nature were grafted on to a fine olive stock, how much easier will it be for the natural branches to be grafted on to their own olive stock?

2. God has, in fact, determined to graft the Jews back into their own olive tree at a future time. But this grafting back in will not take place until the full number of the Gentiles have come in, then God will show mercy to Israel as a nation (i.e., to the Jews living in that day). 11:25-32

a. When the full number of the Gentiles have been grafted into God's people, national Israel will be saved. 11:25,26a

11:25,26a RSV	11:25,26a WT
[25]Lest you be wise in your own conceits, I want you to understand this mystery, brethren: a hardening has come upon part of Israel, until the full number of the Gentiles come in, [26]and so all Israel will be saved;	[25]For to keep you from being self-conceited, brothers, I do not want to have a misunderstanding of this uncovered secret, that only temporary insensibility has come upon Israel until the full quota of the heathen peoples comes in, [26]and so in that way all Israel will be saved,

"Lest you be self-opinionated—wise in your own conceits—I do not want you to miss this hidden truth *and* mystery, brethren: a hardening (insensibility) has [temporarily] befallen a part of Israel [to last] until the full number of the ingathering of the Gentiles has come in, And so all Israel will be saved." (11:25,26a, *The Amplified New Testament)*

b. The future conversion of Israel was predicted in the Old Testament. (See such passages as Isaiah 27:9; 59:20, 21; Jeremiah 31: 33, 34; cf., Hebrews 8:8-12; 10:16, 17.) 11:26b, 27

---

[48] Haldane, *Romans*, pp. 537, 538.

11:26b,27 RSV	11:26b,27 WT
as it is written, "The Deliverer will come from Zion, he will banish ungodliness from Jacob"; [27]"and this will be my covenant with them when I take away their sins."	just as the Scripture says: "From Zion the deliverer will come; He will remove ungodliness from Jacob; [27]And this my covenant I make with them, When I shall take away their sins."[s]
	[s] Isa. 59:20,21.

c. The greater number of the Jews are now enemies of God, but as regards God's election the nation is beloved and will yet be shown mercy. 11:28-32

11:28-32 RSV	11:28-32 WT
[28]As regards the gospel they are enemies of God, for your sake; but as regards election they are beloved for the sake of their forefathers. [29]For the gifts and the call of God are irrevocable. [30]Just as you were once disobedient to God but now have received mercy because of their disobedience, [31]so they have now been disobedient in order that by the mercy shown to you they also may[p] receive mercy. [32]For God has consigned all men to disobedience, that he may have mercy upon all. [p] Other ancient authorities add *now*	[28]As measured by the good news the Jews are God's enemies for your sakes, but as measured by God's choice they are His beloved because of their forefathers, [29]for the gracious gifts and call of God are never taken back.[t] [30]For just as you once disobeyed God, but now have had mercy shown you because of their disobedience, [31]so they too are now disobedient because of the mercy shown you, that they too may now have mercy shown them. [32]For God has locked up all mankind in the prison of disobedience so as to have mercy on them all. [t] Lit., *never regretted because of change of mind.*

The Outline of Romans is continued on p. 102.

NOTE NO. 11 PHYSICAL AND SPIRITUAL ISRAEL AND THEIR RELATION TO THE DIVINE COVENANTS

Introduction: The information contained in this note is designed to show in outline form: (A) The origin of the Jewish people (the nation Israel) ; (B) The twofold nature of the covenant made with Abraham (the father of the Jews) ; (C) The past, present, and future state of the physical nation Israel and its relation to the covenants; and (D) The identity of spiritual Israel and its relation to the covenants.

A. *The Origin of the Jews*

Approximately 2,000 years before the birth of Christ, God called a man named Abram out of Ur of the Chaldees into the land of Canaan. God established a covenant with him and changed his name to Abraham. As the result of this covenant, Abraham eventually became the father of the Hebrew nation—the Jewish people. The story of his life is recorded in Genesis 11-25.

B. *The Twofold Nature of the Covenant Made with Abraham*

When God called Abraham He established a covenant with him in which He promised to do three things: (1) to give Abraham a *seed*, i.e., to make of him a great nation, (2) to give him a *land*, and (3) to *bless* him and through him to bless all the families of the earth. See Genesis 12:1-3.

This covenant had a twofold or dual aspect; the promises were to be fulfilled both *physically* and *spiritually*.

1. The *Physical* fulfillment of the Abrahamic Covenant

a. The *Seed.* Through the miraculous birth of Isaac, God gave Abraham a son—an heir of the covenant blessings (Gen. 15:1-6; 17:15-21; 21:1-7). Through Isaac and his descendants, God made of Abraham a great nation (Gen. 12:2; 13:16; 17:2; 22:15-18; 46:2-4; Deut. 26:5; Heb. 11:12). Abraham's seed have been identified by various names; they are known as the nation Israel, the twelve tribes of Israel, Israelites, Hebrews, Jews, etc.

b. The *Land.* God gave Abraham the land of Canaan for his physical descendants (the Jews) to dwell in. See Genesis 12:1,7; 13:14-17; 15:7,18-21; 17:8; 48:3,4,21; 50:24. Later, when God established a second covenant with the Seed of Abraham at Mt. Sinai, Israel's abiding in the promised land was made conditional. In order to *possess the land* and *remain in it*, the nation had to *obey the laws of the Mosaic Covenant* (Lev. 20:22ff; 26:3-46; Deut. 4:20-40; 5:33; 8:19,20; 11:8-32; 29:22-28; 30:1-20; Joshua 1:1-11; II Kings 17:13-23; Neh. 1:1-9; 9:6-37).

c. The *Blessing.* The physical aspect of the blessing promised to Abraham by God involved material prosperity (see Gen. 12:3; 24:34,35; 26:12,13) as well as divine protection. For examples of how God blessed those who befriended Abraham and his posterity and how He cursed those who opposed them, see Gen. 12:10-20 and I Sam. 15:1-6.

2. The *Spiritual* fulfillment of the Abrahamic Covenant

Each of these three promises was to also receive a spiritual fulfillment.

a. The *Seed.* In Galatians 3:16, Paul tells us that Jesus Christ was THE seed (offspring, RSV) promised to Abraham. In the same chapter he explains that all believers, through their union with Christ, are Abraham's spiritual seed, Gal. 3:6-9,22,26-29, note verses 9, 22, and 29.

b. The *Land.* The land promised to Abraham's spiritual seed is the new heaven and new earth, Romans 4:13; Hebrews 11:8-10; 13-16; II Peter 3:11-13; Revelation 21:1-4.

c. The *Blessing*. The spiritual aspect of the blessing which was promised is the Gospel of Jesus Christ through which, indeed, all the nations of the earth are being blessed, Galatians 3:8.

C. *Physical Israel and its Relation to the Covenants*

Abraham, in fulfillment of God's promise, became the father of the nation Israel. The nation was made up of all his household whether they were his blood descendants or not. For example, slaves bought with money were included in Abraham's "seed." The males who were thus included, as well as those directly descended from Abraham by birth, were required to receive the sign or seal of the Abrahamic Covenant which was circumcision (Gen. 17:9-14).

It was not until several hundred years after the establishment of the Abrahamic Covenant that God formed Abraham's seed into the nation Israel. At that time God established a second covenant with Abraham's descendants—the Mosaic Covenant. This second covenant neither abolished nor replaced the Abrahamic Covenant but was simply "added" to it, Galatians 3:15-18 (see Note 5,B,2, p. 53). Israel failed miserably to keep the Mosaic Covenant and consequently failed to inherit the blessings offered under its terms. By the time Jesus Christ came into the world the Jewish people, for the most part, had become proud and vain and thought that God would save no one but Jews (and their proselytes). They believed too, that God had so bound Himself in His promise to bless Abraham's seed that they (the Jews) were certain of salvation. They thought that mere physical connection with the nation Israel (being Abraham's descendants according to the flesh) meant that God would save and keep them. See Luke 3:7-9 and John 8:31-47.

When Jesus made His appearance as the Christ, the Son of God, the Jewish nation rejected Him and insisted that He be put to death! With the crucifixion of Christ *the Mosaic Covenant* made with Israel at Mt. Sinai *was abolished* and a *New Covenant was established*. (See Note 5, B,2,3, p. 53f., also Jeremiah 31:31-34; Matthew 26:27,28; I Corinthians 11:25; Hebrews 8:6-13; 9:15-24; 10:5-18; II Corinthians 3.) Because of Israel's rejection of the Christ and of the covenant sealed in His blood, God rejected the nation.

It is with Israel's rejection and the Gentiles' acceptance that Paul is concerned in Romans 9, 10, and 11. He shows that this rejection is not a failure of God's word (9:6-8), that it had been predicted (9:25-29), that it was neither total (11:1-10), nor final (11:11-32), for God will yet bring the nation to faith in Christ and the blessings of the New Covenant (11:25-27) and so all Israel will be saved.

D. *Spiritual Israel and its Relation to the Covenants*

Abraham was the father of not only the physical nation Israel but also of a great spiritual nation—a nation made up of all those who are truly saved. The New Testament speaks of him as the father of *all who believe,* regardless of whether they are Jews or Gentiles. See Romans 4:9-17; 9:6-8; Galatians 3:6-9,14,22,27-29; 6:15,16; Philippians 3:2,3; Ephesians 2:11—3:6. During Old Testament times this faith nation was contained within physical Israel (see the diagram on p. 100).

Contained within the threefold *physical* promise made to Abraham (viz., the promise of a seed, a land, and a blessing) there was a threefold *spiritual* promise (see B, 2, above). The threefold physical aspect of this promise was fulfilled to the physical nation Israel during the Old Testament period. But the threefold spiritual aspect of the promise was not, and indeed could not be *fulfilled until* Jesus Christ came into the world and through His death established the New Covenant. This is evident from the following considerations: (1) The spiritual *seed* promised to Abraham was Jesus Christ and "in Him" all true believers. "Now the promises were made to Abraham and to his offspring. It does not say, 'And to offsprings,' referring to many; but, referring to one, 'And to your offspring,' which is Christ" (Gal. 3:16). Cf. the ANT. (2) The spiritual counterpart of the promised *land* is the new heaven and new earth which Christ secured for His people through His redemptive work, but which cannot be inherited by them until He comes again and ushers in the new order. See Heb. 11:8-16,39,40; note especially vss. 39,40. (3) The spiritual *blessing* promised to Abraham in the words "in you all the families of the earth shall be blessed" (Gen. 12:3b BV) is explained by Paul in Galatians 3:8 to mean that the blessing of salvation (i.e., the Gospel) would be extended to all nations, to the Gentiles as well as to the Jews. The point is that the *spiritual counterpart of the threefold physical promise* made to Abraham could not be FULFILLED or REALIZED until Jesus Christ (Abraham's true seed) came into the world and through His redeeming work established the New Covenant under which the Gospel has been extended to all nations, cf., Matt. 26: 26-29 and 28:18-20. Study carefully Eph. 2:11—3:12. Notice how Paul concludes this section in speaking of God's "eternal purpose which he has *realized* in Christ Jesus our Lord" (Eph. 3:11). This is not to be understood to mean that Abraham had no spiritual descendants under the Old Testament economy, before Christ came, for he did. Men were saved by faith then just as they are now. But the situation was drastically changed with Christ's coming and the spiritual fulfillment of the Abrahamic Covenant took on a new dimension with the establishment of the New Covenant by Christ. For example, until Christ came, the physical aspect of the Abrahamic promises had received much greater emphasis than had the spiritual element of that covenant. But with the establishment of the New Covenant the situation was changed—the spiritual content of the Abrahamic promises came to the forefront whereas the physical element faded into insignificance and dropped out of sight. The transition from the physical to the spiritual began, in point of time, with the crucifixion of Christ (when He sealed the New Covenant with His blood), but the awareness of what was happening came gradually. As the purpose of God was progressively revealed to the apostles and prophets by the Holy Spirit, the physical nation and the promised land in which it dwelt ceased to retain their previous importance. It soon became evident that unbelieving Israel had been cut off from the Abrahamic blessing and that both believing Jews and Gentiles were the true heirs of the Abrahamic promise—not of a physical land or outward protection but of the promise of eternal salvation, of a new heaven and a new earth!

This however does not mean that God is through with physical Israel, for Paul makes it clear in Romans eleven (esp. vss. 25-32) that the day will come when God will bring all Israel (the physical nation) into the blessings of the New Covenant by bringing the individual members of the nation living at that time to faith in Christ, and thus "all Israel will be saved" (vss. 26,27). For the present, a hardening has come upon part of Israel, but that hardening will be removed. As regards the Gospel the Jews are the enemies of God for the Gentiles' sake; but as regards His election they are beloved for the sake of their forefathers and will, before the age closes, be shown mercy and by faith will be "grafted" into spiritual Israel and made partakers of the blessings of the New Covenant.

It is of first importance to see that the New Covenant was *not* established with a physical group (either on the basis of external connections or outward visible conditions) as had been the physical aspect of the Abrahamic Covenant. The New Covenant was *not* established with national Israel *nor* with the professing visible church as such—but was established *only* with those who possess true faith, with the true Israel of God, with the faith nation of which Abraham is the spiritual father. This is evident from the contents of the New Covenant itself, for under its terms God declares that He will take away the sins of His covenant people and remember these sins against them no more; He will be their God and they will be His people, and He will write His laws upon their hearts. See Jeremiah 31:31-34 and Hebrews 8:6-12. Only believers share in such blessings!

With the establishment of the New Covenant there came many changes in God's dealings with His people (see Note 5,B and C, pp. 53,54), but these changes did not bring an end to spiritual Israel. The same faith nation that had existed during Old Testament times continued its existence during the New Testament period and still exists today. The people of God are *one body* regardless of which dispensation (age) they have lived in or which covenants they have lived under—they are *all* members of the same spiritual community. Packer, in showing the consequence which Christ's coming had on God's people, observes that "the life of the Church of God was reconstructed in its permanent and final form. As a result, the Church came to look very different from what it had been before. It became a mainly Gentile body, in which most Jews had no place. It lost its national life and became an international society. Its characteristic rites were no longer circumcision and the annual passover, but baptism and the weekly Lord's Supper; and whereas the synagogue had met on the seventh day, Christians came together on the first day of the week. They had no priestly caste nor central shrine: they offered no animal sacrifices. They had abandoned all the elaborate Old Testament machinery for bringing sinners near to a holy God; they claimed that it had been done away by the Messiah's priestly sacrifice of Himself, which won permanent access to God for all believers everywhere. The outward differences between the Old and the New order were thus considerable; yet the apostles insisted that the Christian community was essentially the same church as before. Gentile converts were told that in Christ they had become 'the Israel of God', 'Abraham's seed' and heirs of the Abrahamic promise, for they had now been grafted into the one olive tree (the covenant community, of which the patriarchs were the root and first-fruits) in place of those of Abraham's lineal seed who were broken off through unbelief."[49]

This spiritual nation is, in the present age, contained within the visible or professing church even as it was contained in physical Israel during Old Testament times. It is called by various names in the New Testament; it is referred to as the church which is Christ's body (Eph. 1:22,23; 2:16; 3:6,9,10; 4:4,15,16; 5:23; I Cor. 12:12-28; cf., Rom. 12: 4-8; Col. 1:18,24; 2:19; 3:15), the bride of Christ (Eph. 5:23-32), the Israel of God (Gal. 6:14-16, note verse 16 in the RSV), the true circumcision (Phil. 3:2,3; cf., Col. 2:11; Rom. 2:28,29), the household of God (Eph. 2:19; I Tim. 3:15), a spiritual house (I Pet. 2:4-9), a chosen race, a royal priesthood, a holy nation, God's own people, (I Pet. 2:9,10; cf., Ex. 19:5,6), a holy city, new Jerusalem (Rev. 21:1-4, 9-14; Heb. 12:22-24), etc. But regardless of what name the people of God are called by in either the Old or New Testament, they are ALL *members of the same spiritual nation* and by faith are ALL *the children of Abraham and heirs of the same spiritual promise.* See the chart on the following page.

---

[49] J. I. Packer, *Fundamentalism and the Word of God,* pp. 52, 53.

PHYSICAL AND SPIRITUAL ISRAEL

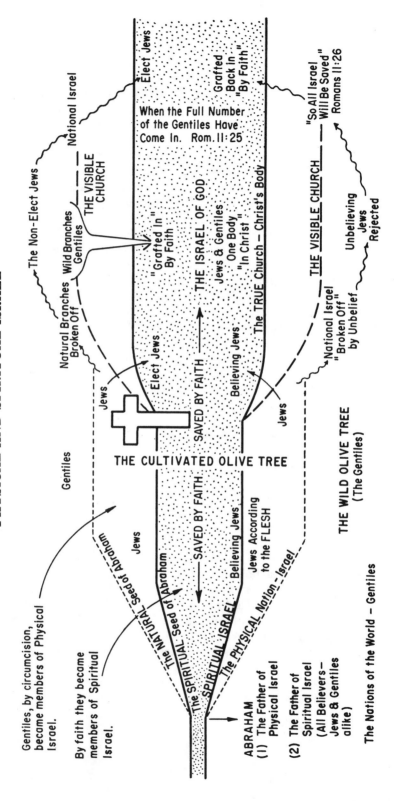

PHYSICAL AND SPIRITUAL ISRAEL

This chart is designed to show two things: (1) The origin, history, and future state of PHYSICAL ISRAEL. The nation had its beginning with the call of Abraham, continued through Old Testament times as God's special people (though many of its members were *not saved*) and with its rejection of Jesus as God's Christ was itself rejected by God. The rejected nation was scattered among the other nations of the world but will in the future be shown mercy by God and brought to a saving knowledge of Jesus Christ. (2) The identity of SPIRITUAL ISRAEL. Abraham was the father of a faith nation as well as of physical Israel. This faith nation is composed of the true people of God—of all who are saved regardless of their racial descent. This spiritual nation was contained within physical Israel during Old Testament times and was made up almost entirely of Jews. Since the coming of Christ and the establishment of the New Covenant, this faith nation has been contained within the visible or professing church and is made up almost entirely of Gentiles. When the full number of the Gentiles have been brought into spiritual Israel, God will "graft" physical Israel into the spiritual nation and thus save the Jews living in that day.

The Outline of Romans is continued from p. 94.

C. Paul ascribes adoring praise to the all-wise and almighty Sovereign (whose resources, wisdom, decisions, and methods are beyond man's comprehension), Who Himself is the Originator, Director, and End of all things! 11:33-36

11:33-36 RSV

[33]O the depth of the riches and wisdom and knowledge of God! How unsearchable are his judgments and how inscrutable his ways!
[34]"For who has known the mind of the Lord,
    or who has been his counselor?"
[35]"Or who has given a gift to him that he might be repaid?"
[36]For from him and through him and to him are all things. To him be glory for ever. Amen.

11:33-36 WT

[33]How fathomless the depths of God's resources, wisdom, and knowledge! How unsearchable His decisions, and how mysterious" His methods! [34]For who has ever understood the thoughts of the Lord, or has ever been His adviser? [35]Or who has ever advanced God anything to have Him pay him back? [36]For from Him everything comes, through Him everything lives, and for Him everything exists. Glory to Him forever! Amen.

" Grk., literally means *untraceable.*

Hodge's comments on these verses deserve quoting. "The reason why man can lay God under no obligation is, that God is himself all and in all; the source, the means, and the end. By him all things are; through his power, wisdom, and goodness, all things are directed and governed; and to him, as their last end, all things tend . . . . God is the source, the constantly working cause, and end of all things . . . . When Paul asks, Who hath first given to God? the answer is, No one, *for* of him, through him, and to him, are all things. It is for the display of his character everything exists, and is directed, as the highest and noblest of all possible objects. Creatures are as nothing, less than vanity and nothing in comparison with God. Human knowledge, power, and virtue, are mere glimmering reflections from the brightness of the divine glory. That system of religion, therefore, is best in accordance with the character of God, the nature of man, and the end of the universe, in which all things are of, through, and to God; and which most effectually leads men to say, NOT UNTO US, BUT UNTO THY NAME BE ALL THE GLORY ! . . .

"The leading principle of all is, that God is the source of all good; that in fallen man there is neither merit nor ability; that salvation, consequently, is all of grace, as well sanctification as pardon, as well election as eternal glory. For of him, and through him, and to him, are all things; to whom be glory for ever. Amen."[50]

---

[50] Hodge, *Romans*, pp. 379, 380. Italics and capitalization are his.

PART THREE
PRACTICAL EXHORTATIONS AND PERSONAL MATTERS
DIRECTED TO THE SAINTS AT ROME
Chs. 12-16

Introduction: Paul in Romans, as in almost all of his letters, deals with the doctrinal foundation of Christianity before turning his attention to the obligations required of those who acknowledge the truth of the Christian faith. His order is first doctrine and then duty. This order is important because right thinking must precede right living. Only as we understand and receive by faith what God has done for us can we find the right motive and adopt the right methods for serving Him. To preach duty without a sound doctrinal foundation or to preach doctrine without duty to God as its ultimate goal is a vain and worthless undertaking. The words of Matthew Henry are certainly true, "The foundation of Christian practice must be laid in Christian knowledge and faith. We must first understand how we receive Christ Jesus the Lord, and then we shall know the better how to walk in him."[51]

Thus far in the letter (chs. 1-11) the apostle has dealt with human guilt and depravity; he has carefully explained the gospel method of justification by faith, the Spirit's work of sanctification, the security of believers and the principle of sovereign election. In the remainder of the letter (chs. 12-16), Paul turns his attention to the various duties which have been imposed by God upon those whom He has saved. The apostle, in this section of Romans, sets forth rules and principles by which Christians are to regulate their lives. He reasons with, exhorts, encourages, warns and instructs them as to how they should conduct themselves in this world. If the reader has been given the grace to understand and to receive the doctrines taught thus far in Romans, if he feels himself to be an object of God's saving mercy, then he is under the most solemn obligation to study these closing chapters with great care so that he might know and do what is required of him—so that he might *honor* sound doctrine by *practicing* Christian duty!

XI. PRACTICAL EXHORTATIONS. 12:1—15:13

A. Duties to God and to the Church. 12:1-8

1. Believers, because of the mercy shown them by God, should devote themselves to Him as living sacrifices and be conformed to His will—not to this world. 12:1,2

12:1,2 RSV	12:1,2 WT
I appeal to you therefore, brethren, by the mercies of God, to present your bodies	I beg you, therefore, brothers, through these mercies God has shown you, to make

---

[51] Matthew Henry, *Commentary on the Whole Bible*, Vol. VI, p. 454.

as a living sacrifice, holy and acceptable to God, which is your spiritual worship. ²Do not be conformed to this world^q but be transformed by the renewal of your mind, that you may prove what is the will of God, what is good and acceptable and perfect.^r

---

^q Greek *age*
^r Or *what is the good and acceptable and perfect will of God*

a decisive^a dedication of your bodies as a living sacrifice, devoted^b and well-pleasing to God, which is your reasonable service. ²Stop living in accordance with the customs of this world, but by the new ideals that mold your minds^c continue to transform yourselves, so as to find and follow^d God's will; that is, what is good, well-pleasing to Him, and perfect.

---

^a Aor. infin., *once for all offer.*
^b Lit., *holy,* so *devoted.*
^c Lit., *stop conforming to this world, but by renewing of your mind continue, etc.*
^d Vb. means *test and approve,* so *find and follow.*

2.   Believers are *warned* not to think too highly of their individual importance, for each, with all the rest, is a part of Christ's One Body, the Church (12:3-5). They are also instructed as to how to use the individual gifts God has assigned them (12:6-8). (Compare I Corinthians, chs. 12-14 and Ephesians 4:1-16.)   12:3-8

12:3-8   RSV

³For by the grace given to me I bid every one among you not to think of himself more highly than he ought to think, but to think with sober judgment, each according to the measure of faith which God has assigned him. ⁴For as in one body we have many members, and all the members do not have the same function, ⁵so we, though many, are one body in Christ, and individually members one of another. ⁶Having gifts that differ according to the grace given to us, let us use them: if prophecy, in proportion to our faith; ⁷if service, in our serving; he who teaches, in his teaching; ⁸he who exhorts, in his exhortation; he who contributes, in liberality; he who gives aid, with zeal; he who does acts of mercy, with cheerfulness.

12:3-8   WT

³ Now through the unmerited favor God has shown me I would say to every one of you not to estimate himself above his real value,^e but to make a sober rating of himself, in accordance with the degree of faith which God has apportioned to him. ⁴For just as we have many parts united in our physical^f bodies, and the parts do not all have the same function, ⁵so we, though many, are united in one body through union with Christ, and we are individually parts of one another. ⁶As we have gifts that differ in accordance with the favor God has shown us, if it is that of preaching, let it be done in proportion to our faith; ⁷or of practical service, in the field of service; or of a teacher, in the field of teaching; ⁸or of one who encourages others, in the field of encouragement; or one who gives his money, with liberality; or one who leads others, with earnestness; or one who does deeds of charity, with cheerfulness.^g

---

^e Lit., *what he ought to think.*
^f Implied in contrasting two kinds of bodies.
^g An involved sentence in both Grk. and Eng.; meaning clear.

B. Duties to fellow believers and to the world. 12:9-21

1. To fellow believers. 12:9-13

12:9-13 RSV

⁹Let love be genuine; hate what is evil, hold fast to what is good; ¹⁰love one another with brotherly affection; outdo one another in showing honor. ¹¹Never flag in zeal, be aglow with the Spirit, serve the Lord. ¹²Rejoice in your hope, be patient in tribulation, be constant in prayer. ¹³Contribute to the needs of the saints, practice hospitality.

12:9-13 WT

⁹Your love must be true. You must always turnʰ in horror from what is wrong, but keep on holding to what is right. ¹⁰In brotherly love be affectionate to one another, in personal honors put one another to the fore,ⁱ ¹¹never slack in earnestness, alwaysʲ on fireᵏ with the Spirit, always serving the Lord, ¹²everʲ happy in hope, always patient in suffering, ever persistent in prayer, ¹³always supplying the needs of God's people, ever practicing hospitality.

ʰ In prep. *apo.*
ⁱ Lit. meaning of phrase.
ʲ These words exactly tr. Grk. pres. (pt. and impv.).
ᵏ Lit., *boiling.*

2. To the world, especially to enemies. 12:14-21

12:14-21 RSV

¹⁴Bless those who persecute you; bless and do not curse them. ¹⁵Rejoice with those who rejoice, weep with those who weep. ¹⁶Live in harmony with one another; do not be haughty, but associate with the lowly;ˢ never be conceited. ¹⁷Repay no one evil for evil, but take thought for what is noble in the sight of all. ¹⁸If possible, so far as it depends upon you, live peaceably with all. ¹⁹Beloved, never avenge yourselves, but leave itᵗ to the wrath of God; for it is written, "Vengeance is mine, I will repay, says the Lord." ²⁰No, "if your enemy is hungry, feed him; if he is thirsty, give him drink; for by so doing you will heap burning coals upon his head." ²¹Do not be overcome by evil, but overcome evil with good.

ˢ Or *give yourselves to humble tasks*
ᵗ Greek *give place*

12:14-21 WT

¹⁴Keep on blessing your persecutors; keep on blessing and stop cursing them. ¹⁵Practiceʲ rejoicing with people who rejoice, and weeping with people who weep. ¹⁶Keep on thinking in harmonyˡ with one another. Stop being high-minded but keep on associating with lowly people. Stop being conceited. ¹⁷Stop returning evil for evil to anyone. Always see to it that your affairs are right in the sight of everybody. ¹⁸If possible, so far as it depends on you, live in peace with everybody. ¹⁹Stop taking revenge on one another, beloved, but leave a place for God'sᵐ anger, for the Scripture says, "Vengeance belongs to me; I will pay them back, says the Lord."ⁿ ²⁰Do the opposite.° If your enemy is hungry, give him something to eat. If he is thirsty, give him something to drink. For ifᵖ you act in this way, you will heap burning coals upon his head! ²¹Stop being conquered by evil, but keep on conquering evil with good.

ʲ These words exactly tr. Grk. pres. (pt. and impv.).
ˡ Grk., *the same thing.*
ᵐ Implied.
ⁿ Dt. 32:35.
° Lit., *on the contrary* (vb. implied).
ᵖ Cond. adv. pt.

C. Duties to civil authorities. 13:1-7

13:1-7 RSV

Let every person be subject to the governing authorities. For there is no authority except from God, and those that exist have been instituted by God. ²Therefore he who resists the authorities resists what God has appointed, and those who resist will incur judgment. ³For rulers are not a terror to good conduct, but to bad. Would you have no fear of him who is in authority? Then do what is good, and you will receive his approval, ⁴for he is God's servant for your good. But if you do wrong, be afraid, for he does not bear the sword in vain; he is the servant of God to execute his wrath on the wrongdoer. ⁵Therefore one must be subject, not only to avoid God's wrath but also for the sake of conscience. ⁶For the same reason you also pay taxes, for the authorities are ministers of God, attending to this very thing. ⁷Pay all of them their dues, taxes to whom taxes are due, revenue to whom revenue is due, respect to whom respect is due, honor to whom honor is due.

13:1-7 WT

Everybody must obey the civil[a] authorities that are over him, for no authority exists except by God's permission; the existing authorities have been established by Him, ²so that anyone who resists the authorities sets himself against what God has established, and those who set themselves against Him will get the penalty due them. ³For civil authorities are not a terror to the man who does right, but they are to the man who does wrong. Do you want to have no dread of the civil authorities? Then practice doing right and you will be commended for it. ⁴For the civil authorities[b] are God's servants to do you good.[c] But if you practice doing wrong, you should dread them, for they do not wield the sword for nothing, they are God's servants to inflict punishment[d] upon people who do wrong. ⁵Therefore, you must obey them, not only for the sake of escaping punishment,[e] but also for conscience' sake; ⁶for this is the reason why you pay your taxes, for the civil authorities are God's official servants faithfully devoting themselves to this very end. ⁷Pay all of them what is due them—tribute to the officer[f] to receive it, taxes to the officer to receive them, respect to the man entitled to it, and honor to the man entitled to it.

[a] Implied in context.
[b] To be supplied.
[c] Lit., *for good.*
[d] Grk., *avengers for wrath.*
[e] Lit., *because of wrath.*
[f] Only implied.

Clark's comments on this passage are to the point. "Government is not merely a human invention; it is ordained of God for the good of the governed; and therefore a Christian is obliged to obey the laws, not only from fear of civil penalties, but chiefly for conscience toward God. The employment of the sword and the collection of taxes are, briefly, the two chief functions of the State. By the term 'sword,' Paul means the penalties of disobedience, obviously including capital punishment, and doubtless war as well.

"From this passage James I of England and other absolute monarchs have argued for the divine right of kings, and some theologians have concurred that subjects must invariably submit. John Calvin and John Knox, on the contrary, pointed out that rulers also have obligations, and when they fail to discharge their obligations, they may be disobeyed and even replaced. Peter (Acts 5:29) said, 'We ought to obey God rather than men.' The midwives of Egypt also (Ex. 1:17) and Moses' parents (Ex. 2:3) disobeyed Pharaoh. If then government is ordained of God, it would seem reasonable that it has no authority contrary to God's commands.

"But in all ordinary cases, and this is most of the time, a Christian should obey the law."[52]

D.   The duty to love one another; "Love is the fulfilling of the law." 13:8-10

13:8-10 RSV

[8]Owe no one anything, except to love one another; for he who loves his neighbor has fulfilled the law. [9]The commandments, "You shall not commit adultery, You shall not kill, You shall not steal, You shall not covet," and any other commandment, are summed up in this sentence, "You shall love your neighbor as yourself." [10]Love does no wrong to a neighbor; therefore love is the fulfilling of the law.

13:8-10 WT

[8]Stop owing anybody anything, except the obligation to love one another, for whoever practices loving others has perfectly satisfied[g] the law. [9]For the commandments, "You must not commit adultery, You must not murder, You must not steal, You must not have an evil desire," and any other commandment if there is any, are summed up in this command, "You must love your neighbor as you do yourself." [10]Love never does a wrong to one's neighbor; so love is the perfect satisfaction of the law.

[g] Grk., *has fulfilled or filled to the full.*

E.   All these as well as the following duties should be viewed in the light of the fact that salvation is nearer than when we first believed; "the night is far gone, the day is at hand."   13:11-14

13:11-14 RSV

[11]Besides this you know what hour it is, how it is full time now for you to wake from sleep. For salvation is nearer to us now than when we first believed; [12]the night is far gone, the day is at hand. Let us then cast off the works of darkness and put on the armor of light; [13]let us conduct ourselves becomingly as in the day, not in reveling and drunkenness, not in debauchery and licentiousness, not in quarreling and jealousy. [14]But put on the Lord Jesus Christ, and make no provision for the flesh, to gratify its desires.

13:11-14 WT

[11]Do[h] this in particular because you know the present crisis,[i] that it is high time for you to wake up out of your sleep, for our salvation is now nearer[j] to us than when we first believed. [12]The night has almost passed; the day is at hand. So let us put aside the deeds of darkness, and put on the weapons of light. [13]Let us live becomingly for people who are in the light of day, not in carousing and drunkenness, nor in sexual immorality and licentiousness, nor in quarreling and jealousy. [14]Instead, put on the Lord Jesus Christ, and put a stop to gratifying the evil desires that lurk in your lower nature.

[h] Implied.
[i] Lit., *time.*
[j] Final deliverance at Christ's sec. coming is nearer.

---

[52] Clark, "Romans," (above, fn. 7), pp. 254, 255.

F.   Instructions concerning Christian liberty. 14:1—15:13

The Problem: A dispute had arisen among believers as to whether the use of certain things was in itself sinful. There were some (probably a scrupulous class of Jewish Christians) who felt that the followers of Christ were under obligation to observe certain days as holy, to refrain from eating meats, drinking wine, etc. These believers insisted that the *use* of such things was sinful and therefore should be avoided by all Christians.

There were equally sincere believers who disagreed with this view. They felt that the *use* of such things was not in itself sinful; that in fact their use was "a matter of indifference." In their opinion things such as "food" and "drink" and "days" had no moral qualities in themselves, and since God had given no instructions prohibiting their use, Christians were free to use them at their own discretion.

Paul, in this section, lays down some basic principles as to how Christians who differ over such "opinions" should look upon each other. He shows that even though the things under dispute were "matters of indifference" (their use was not in itself sinful) that nevertheless the "strong in faith" (those who understood this) should not use these things in such a way as to offend "the weak in faith" (those who mistakenly believed their use to be sinful). The weak in faith abstain from certain things (food, wine, etc.) *on religious grounds.* They abstain from these things thinking that this is necessary if they are to please the Lord. It is important to see that the *weakness* of the weak is not a weakness of a tendency to overindulge (as is mistakenly claimed by many "temperance" writers) but it is *a weakness which arises from religious scruples*—from a lack of knowledge. [53]

See Note 12, pp. 112-118 on "Christian Liberty" for further information relating to the principles covered in 14:1—15:13.

1.   The manner in which the strong and the weak in faith are to treat and regard each other. 14:1-12

14:1-12 RSV

As for the man who is weak in faith, welcome him, but not for disputes over opinions. [2]One believes he may eat anything, while the weak man eats only vegetables. [3]Let not him who eats despise him who abstains, and let not him who abstains pass judgment on him who eats; for God has welcomed him. [4]Who are you

14:1-12 WT

Make it your practice to receive into full Christian fellowship[a] people who are overscrupulous,[b] but not to criticize their views. [2]One man believes that he can eat anything, another who is overscrupulous eats nothing but vegetables. [3]The man who eats anything must not look down on the man who does not do so, nor must

---

[a] In prep.—perfective ac.
[b] Lit., *weak in faith.*

---

[53] Compare John Murray's article "The Weak and the Strong" in the *Westminster Theological Journal*, May, 1950, pp. 136-153.

to pass judgment on the servant of another? It is before his own master that he stands or falls. And he will be upheld, for the Master is able to make him stand. ⁵One man esteems one day as better than another, while another man esteems all days alike. Let every one be fully convinced in his own mind. ⁶He who observes the day, observes it in honor of the Lord. He also who eats, eats in honor of the Lord, since he gives thanks to God; while he who abstains, abstains in honor of the Lord and gives thanks to God. ⁷None of us lives to himself, and none of us dies to himself. ⁸If we live, we live to the Lord, and if we die, we die to the Lord; so then, whether we live or whether we die, we are the Lord's. ⁹For to this end Christ died and lived again, that he might be Lord both of the dead and of the living.

¹⁰Why do you pass judgment on your brother? Or you, why do you despise your brother? For we shall all stand before the judgment seat of God; ¹¹for it is written,

"As I live, says the Lord, every knee shall bow to me,
and every tongue shall give praise^u to God."

¹²So each of us shall give account of himself to God.

———
^u Or *confess*

the man who does not do so condemn the man who does, for God has fully^c accepted him. ⁴Who are you to criticize another man's servant? It is his own master's business^d whether he stands or falls, and he will stand, for the Lord has power to make him stand. ⁵One man rates one day above another, another rates them all alike. Let every man be fully convinced in his own mind. ⁶The man who keeps a certain day keeps it for the Lord. The man who eats anything does it for the Lord too, for he gives God thanks. The man who refuses to eat anything does it for the Lord too, and gives God thanks.

⁷For none of us can^e live alone by himself, and none of us can die alone by himself; ⁸indeed,^f if we live, we always live in relation^g to the Lord, and if we die, we always die in relation to the Lord. So whether we live or die we belong to the Lord. ⁹For Christ died and lived again for the very purpose of being Lord of both the dead and the living. ¹⁰Then why should you criticize your brother? Or, why should you look down on your brother? Surely,^f we shall all stand before God to be judged, ¹¹for the Scripture says:

" 'As surely as I live,' says the Lord, 'every knee shall bend before me, And every tongue shall make acknowledgment to God.' "^h

¹²So each of us must give an account of himself to God.

———
^c Expressed by prep.
^d Dat. of interest.
^e Implied.
^f Intensive *gar*.
^g Dat. of relation.
^h Isa. 45:23.

a. The weak are to be received into the Christian fellowship but not for disputes over opinions. 14:1

b. The strong and the weak are not to despise or pass judgment on each other; both belong to the Lord and will be upheld by Him. 14:2-4

c. Each does what he does in such matters in honor of the Lord and each belongs to the Lord. 14:5-9

d. All such matters will be dealt with in the final judgment when each one gives an account of himself to God. 14:10-12

2. The manner in which Christian liberty is to be used by the strong in faith. 14:13-23

14:13-23 RSV

¹³Then let us no more pass judgment on one another, but rather decide never to put a stumbling-block or hindrance in the way of a brother. ¹⁴I know and am persuaded in the Lord Jesus that nothing is unclean in itself; but it is unclean for any one who thinks it unclean. ¹⁵If your brother is being injured by what you eat, you are no longer walking in love. Do not let what you eat cause the ruin of one for whom Christ died. ¹⁶So do not let what is good to you be spoken of as evil. ¹⁷For the kingdom of God does not mean food and drink but righteousness and peace and joy in the Holy Spirit; ¹⁸he who thus serves Christ is acceptable to God and approved by men. ¹⁹Let us then pursue what makes for peace and for mutual upbuilding. ²⁰Do not, for the sake of food, destroy the work of God. Everything is indeed clean, but it is wrong for any one to make others fall by what he eats; ²¹it is right not to eat meat or drink wine or do anything that makes your brother stumble.ᵛ ²²The faith that you have, keep between yourself and God; happy is he who has no reason to judge himself for what he approves. ²³But he who has doubts is condemned, if he eats, because he does not act from faith; for whatever does not proceed from faith is sin.ʷ

ᵛ Other ancient authorities add *or be upset or be weakened*
ʷ Other authorities, some ancient, insert here Ch. 16.25-27

14:13-23 WT

¹³Then let us stop criticizing one another; instead, do this,ᵉ determine to stop putting stumbling blocks or hindrances in your brother's way. ¹⁴I know, and through my union with the Lord Jesus I have a clear conviction, that nothing is unclean in itself; that a thing is unclean only to the person who thinks it unclean. ¹⁵For if your brother is hurt because of the food you eat, you are not living by the standardⁱ of love. Stop ruining, by what you eat, the man for whom Christ died. ¹⁶Then stop abusing your rights. ¹⁷For the kingdom of God does not consist in what we eat and drink, but in doing right, in peace and joy through the Holy Spirit; ¹⁸whoever in this way continues serving Christ is well-pleasing to God and approved by men. ¹⁹So let us keep on pursuing things that make for peace and our mutual upbuilding. ²⁰Stop undoing the work of God just for the sake of food. Everything is clean, but it is wrong for a man to eat anything when it makes another stumble.ʲ The right thing to do is not to eat meat or drink wine, or do anything else, that makes your brother stumble.ʲ ²²On your part, you must exercise your faith by the standard of yourself in the sight of God. Happy is the man who need not condemn himself for doing the thing that he approves. ²³But the man who has misgivings about eating, if he then eats, has already condemned himself by so doing, because he did not follow his faith, and any actionᵏ that does not follow one's faith is a sin.

ᵉ Implied.
ⁱ Expressed by prep. *kata* with acc.
ʲ In first clause, lit., *through a cause to stumble;* in second, lit., *by which stumbles.*
ᵏ Lit., *anything not from faith,* etc.

(Notice that Christian liberty is not to be given up or denied but rather to be used with great discretion.)

a. The law of love is to be followed; therefore, Christian liberty must not be used to harm a brother for whom Christ died. 14:13-15

b. Christian liberty is not to be used in such a way as to bring reproach on the faith. 14:16

c. The Christian faith does not consist of physical things such as food or drink but of righteousness and peace and joy in the Holy Spirit. 14:17,18

   d. Christians should pursue what makes for peace and for mutual upbuilding. 14:19

   e. It is wrong for anyone to make others fall by the use of things in themselves indifferent, such as meat or wine. 14:20,21

   f. Though the strong are free to use things which God has not pronounced sinful, they should not encourage the weak in faith to use them against their conscience, for whatever does not come from faith is sin. 14:22,23

   3. In order to glorify God, Christians are to follow the example of Christ and, like Him, are not to please themselves but to please others. 15:1-13

15:1-13 RSV

We who are strong ought to bear with the failings of the weak, and not to please ourselves; ²let each of us please his neighbor for his good, to edify him. ³For Christ did not please himself; but, as it is written, "The reproaches of those who reproached thee fell on me." ⁴For whatever was written in former days was written for our instruction, that by steadfastness and by the encouragement of the scriptures we might have hope. ⁵May the God of steadfastness and encouragement grant you to live in such harmony with one another, in accord with Christ Jesus, ⁶that together you may with one voice glorify the God and Father of our Lord Jesus Christ.

⁷Welcome one another, therefore, as Christ has welcomed you, for the glory of God. ⁸For I tell you that Christ became a servant to the circumcised to show God's truthfulness, in order to confirm the promises given to the patriarchs, ⁹and in order that the Gentiles might glorify God for his mercy. As it is written,

"Therefore I will praise thee among the Gentiles,
 and sing to thy name";
¹⁰and again it is said,
"Rejoice, O Gentiles, with his people";
¹¹and again,
"Praise the Lord, all Gentiles,
 and let all the peoples praise him";

15:1-13 WT

It is the duty of us who are strong to bear with the weaknesses of those who are not strong, and not merely to please ourselves. ²Each one of us must practice pleasing his neighbor, to help in his immediate* upbuilding for his eternal* good. ³Christ certainly did not please Himself; instead, as the Scripture says, "The reproaches of those who reproach you have fallen upon me."ᵇ ⁴For everything that was written in the earlier times was written for our instruction, so that by our patient endurance and through the encouragement the Scriptures bring we might continuously cherish our hope. ⁵May God, who gives men patient endurance and encouragement,ᶜ grant you such harmony with one another, in accordance with the standard which Christ Jesus sets, ⁶that with united hearts and lips you may praise the God and Father of our Lord Jesus Christ.

⁷Therefore, practice receiving one another into full Christian fellowship, just as Christ has so received you to Himself. ⁸Yes, I mean that Christ has become a servant to Israel to prove God's truthfulness,ᵈ to make valid His promises to our forefathers, ⁹and for the heathen peoples to praise God for His mercy, as the Scripture says:

"For this I will give thanks to you
      among the heathen,
 And will sing praises to your name."ᵉ

* Former in *pros*, latter in *eis*.
ᵇ Ps. 69:9.
ᶜ Obj. gen.
ᵈ Lit., *for God's truth.*
ᵉ Ps. 18:49.

[12]and further Isaiah says,
"The root of Jesse shall come,
he who rises to rule the Gentiles;
in him shall the Gentiles hope."
[13]May the God of hope fill you with all joy and peace in believing, so that by the power of the Holy Spirit you may abound in hope.

[10]And again:
"Rejoice, you heathen peoples, with His people!"[f]
[11]And again:
"All you heathen peoples, praise the Lord,
Yea, let all peoples sing His praise."[g]
[12]And again Isaiah says:
"The noted Son[h] of Jesse will come,
Even He who rises to rule the heathen;
On Him the heathen will set their hope."[i]
[13]May the hope-inspiring God[j] so fill you with perfect joy and peace through your continuing faith, that you may bubble over with hope by the power of the Holy Spirit.

---

[f] Dt. 32:43.
[g] Ps. 117:1.
[h] Lit., *the* (well-known) *Root of Jesse.*
[i] Isa. 11:1, 10.
[j] Obj. or descriptive gen.

a. The strong must bear with the failings of the weak and help them. 15:1,2

b. Believers must follow the self-denying example of Christ and thereby live in harmony with one another. 15:3-6

c. Believers are to welcome (receive) one another as Christ has received both Jews and Gentiles (causing them to glorify God and to abound in hope). 15:7-13

The Outline of Romans is continued on p. 118.

NOTE NO. 12 CHRISTIAN LIBERTY

Distinguishing between right and wrong in matters of personal conduct is often difficult. This is evident from the fact that there is so much disagreement among Christians as to what acts are sinful. Practices which are approved by some groups are rejected by others as being inconsistent with Christian duty. For example, in some circles, smoking is considered sinful while in other circles it is viewed as a matter of indifference (i.e., as not being sinful in itself). The same is true of card playing, attending movies, watching television, dancing, the use of cosmetics, eating certain foods, drinking certain beverages, as well as many other things. Given below are three Biblical rules by which one can test any given act to see whether it is sinful. But before discussing the rules themselves, we need first to examine some basic principles concerning the nature of sin.

A. BASIC PRINCIPLES CONCERNING THE NATURE OF SIN

1. *Sin defined.*

Sin is the *transgression* (stepping out of the bounds) *of the law of God.* Smith's *Dictionary of the Bible* defines sin as " 'any want of conformity unto, or transgression of any law of God, given as a rule to the reasonable creature.' (Rom. 3:23; I John 3:4; Gal. 3:10-12). A sin of omission is the neglect to do what the law of God commands; a sin of commission is the doing of anything which it forbids."

2. *The Bible alone determines what is sinful.*

God has made known to man what is required of him by (1) the law written on man's heart and (2) the law revealed in His written word. Because of Adam's sin, the law written on man's heart has been defaced and therefore is no longer a clear or reliable guide. (See Note 5,A and B,1, p. 53.) For this reason one must look to the written Word of God as the only infallible rule for determining what is sinful. Neither men nor churches have the right, independently of the Bible, to declare a given act as being either lawful or unlawful in the eyes of God. The Bible is the only and all-sufficient rule for determining such matters. By properly applying the commands and principles set forth within the Scriptures, under the guidance of the Spirit, one can know the proper course of action in any given set of circumstances. Therefore, no Christian ought to regard any rule or law as binding on his conscience if it cannot be substantiated by the written Word of God. This is but to say that the Bible is the only authoritative rule for the faith and practice of God's people.

3. *Material objects are never sinful within themselves.*

Sin, because of its nature, cannot reside in physical matter. Sin, by definition, is an attitude or an act; it is the violation of God's law by a rational creature; it is not a physical substance nor does it have physical existence. No material object, therefore, is sinful within itself. An object may be *used wrongly* but the object itself is not sinful. For example, a knife may be used to murder someone, but this does not make the knife sinful. The sin is in the heart of the one who violates God's law by willfully and maliciously taking the life of his fellow man. The same is true of a deck of cards, a glass of whiskey, a bottle of poison, or any other material object. Regardless of how such things are used (or misused!), they can never be sinful within themselves.

Christ made it clear that it is not what goes into a man that defiles him but what comes *out of his heart!* " 'Do you not see that whatever goes into a man from outside cannot defile him, since it enters, not his heart but his stomach, and so passes on?' (Thus he declared all foods clean.) And he said, 'What comes out of a man is what defiles a man. For from within, out of the heart of man, come evil thoughts, fornication, theft, murder, adultery, coveting, wickedness, deceit, licentiousness, an evil eye, slander, pride, foolishness. All these evil things come from within, and they defile a man' " (Mark 7:18b-23). Paul acknowledges this same principle in Romans 14:14, "I know and am persuaded in the Lord Jesus that nothing is unclean in itself; but it is unclean for anyone who thinks it unclean."

B. THREE RULES FOR TESTING AN ACT TO SEE IF IT IS SINFUL

The following questions are given to serve as a guide to help the individual Christian in determining whether a particular act in a given set of circumstances is permissible for him. When one wishes to know *"Is it wrong for me to do so and so under the present circumstances?"* (regardless of what it might be, whether it is playing checkers, watching television, dancing, drinking wine, stealing, committing murder, etc.) he should ask himself the following three questions: (1) Does the Bible forbid my doing this? (2) Would this cause me to be tempted to sin? and (3) Would my doing this offend a weak brother so as to cause him to stumble? If the first question can be answered no, then the second question is applicable; if the second question can also be answered no, the third question is applicable. If all three questions can be truthfully answered in the negative, then it is not wrong for him—although it may be wrong for someone else. But if any one of the three questions *must* be answered *yes*, then the practice under investigation must be avoided by him.

1. *Does the Bible forbid my doing this?*

If the Bible gives an unqualified command forbidding a Christian to do a certain thing, then that act is sinful. For example, if one should ask, "Is it wrong to murder? to commit adultery? to steal? or to get drunk?" the answer is absolutely *yes!* for these acts are clearly forbidden in the Bible. No Christian can knowingly and willfully do such things without breaking God's law.

In addition to the *specific* commands contained within the Bible there are also broad *general* commands which set limitations upon what a Christian may do. For example, there is no specific commandment in the Bible forbidding a Christian to drive an automobile ninety miles an hour in a twenty mile speed zone, yet if he should do this he would be disobeying the Scriptures—he would be violating the general command which states that he must "be subject to the governing authorities," (that he must obey civil laws). See the Outline on Romans 13:1-7.

However, simply because someone declares that a particular thing is sinful on the ground that it violates some general command of the Bible does not make that act a sin! All such claims must be proved or else must be disregarded. This means that unless such claims can be substantiated by sound principles of Biblical interpretation they are to be viewed as mere opinions and thus as having no authority over the conscience. [54] For example, using lipstick is not to be considered wrong just because some individual or some church declares that it is "worldly" and therefore sinful. The burden of proof rests upon the one who makes such a claim. Vos is certainly correct in insisting that "A matter must be regarded as indifferent until proved to be sinful, not *vice versa*. A man is regarded as innocent until proved guilty. Nothing could be more false and dangerous than the contention of some religious teachers that a matter must be regarded as sinful until proved to be indifferent. When there is any doubt that the matter is sinful in itself, it must be left to the individual conscience. If the teaching of Scripture about a particular matter appears to be doubtful or obscure, or even seems to be contradictory, this is all the more reason for church assemblies *not* to make authoritative pronouncements or laws about such a matter. What God has not clearly revealed, let the church not presume to determine. God grant that we may be preserved from trying to have a clearer standard than the Bible, or a more complete set of moral laws than that contained in the Word of God!"[55]

"Why do you submit to regulations, 'Do not handle, Do not taste, Do not touch' (referring to things which all perish as they are used), according to human precepts and doctrines? These have indeed an appearance of wisdom in promoting rigor of devotion and self-abasement and severity to the body, but they are of no value in checking the indulgence of the flesh" (Col. 2:20b-23).

2. *Although it is not a sin in itself, would my doing this lead me into temptation and cause me to sin?*

The words of Christ, recorded in Matthew 5:29,30, plainly teach that Christians are under obligation to avoid occasions of temptation to sin. " 'If your right eye causes you to sin, pluck it out and throw it away; it is better that you lose one of your members than that your whole body be thrown into hell. And if your right hand causes you to sin, cut it

---

[54] Ramm states this principle when he writes "that *any interpretation of Scripture must have adequate justification*," and that "The grounds for the interpretation *must be made explicit.*" Bernard Ramm, *Protestant Biblical Interpretation*, p. 101. Italics are his. For further help in the field of Biblical Interpretation see L. Berkhof, *Principles of Biblical Interpretation* and Alan M. Stibbs, *Understanding God's Word.*

[55] Johannes G. Vos, *The Separated Life*, p. 18. Italics are his. This booklet, published by the Committee on Christian Education, Orthodox Presbyterian Church, Philadelphia 2, Pa., is the best treatment of the subject of Christian Liberty that we have come upon.

off and throw it away; it is better that you lose one of your members than that your whole body go into hell.' " Vos, in commenting on this passage, observes that "these words are not to be understood literally; the Lord does not intend us to attempt to avoid sin by actually mutilating our bodies. The real meaning is that the Christian is bound to cut off occasions of temptation to sin.

"It will be noted that the command is conditional: 'If thy right eye causeth thee to stumble,' etc. Therefore no universal rule can be made in this matter, for what is an overwhelming temptation to one person may be no temptation at all to another person. For a Chinese just converted from heathenism to keep a small brass image of the Buddha in his house, would be to tolerate a serious occasion of temptation to sin. For him the only safe course, even the only right course, is to get rid of the abomination as soon as possible. For a retired missionary living in America to have an image of the Buddha in his house as a curio cannot possibly be an occasion of temptation to him or to anyone else; to dispose of such an object in order to avoid temptation would be absurd. The image itself is 'nothing in the world' (I Cor. 8:4); it is simply 'a piece of brass' (II Kings 18:4); but to the man just saved from paganism it is a symbol of all the abominations of idolatry and a constant invitation to return to the old ways."[56]

Each individual must judge for himself what constitutes a temptation *to him* and thus what needs to be avoided *by him*. For as Vos stated, "what is an overwhelming temptation to one person may be no temptation at all to another person." For example, suppose two Christian friends, visiting in France, were invited to dinner and were each served a glass of wine before the meal. Would it be wrong for them to drink it? The answer could very well be "yes" for one and "no" for the other. It may be possible for one of them to drink the wine without being tempted in the least to overindulgence or drunkenness. But suppose the other friend had, at one time, been an alcoholic and knew that in all probability he would not want to stop with the one glass. Would it be safe for him to drink the wine in light of his past experience? Of course *not*, for it would constitute a temptation to overindulge and possibly cause him to get drunk. And drunkenness, let it be remembered, is absolutely forbidden in the Bible, (see Romans 13:13; I Corinthians 5:11; Galatians 5:19-21; Ephesians 5:18; Titus 1:7; I Peter 4:3) whereas drinking wine, in moderation, is not (see Psalm 104:14,15; Matthew 11:18,19; Luke 7:33,34; John 2:1-10; I Corinthians 11:20-22; I Timothy 3:8; 5:23; Titus 2:3). Thus one of them could drink the glass of wine without being tempted to overindulgence or drunkenness, but the other could not; therefore, it would not be wrong for one, but it would be wrong for the other.

---

[56] Vos, *The Separated Life*, p. 4. Italics are his.

3. *Would my doing this cause me to offend a weak brother so as
to make him stumble?*

A Christian is not only obliged to avoid acts of sin (things forbidden by the Bible) and the occasions of temptation to sin (things not
sinful within themselves but which lead to sin) but he is also told to avoid
practices which would offend a weak brother so as to cause him to stumble.
Note the admonition of Romans 14:13,21, "Then let us no more pass judgment on one another, but rather decide never to put a stumbling-block or
hindrance in the way of a brother . . . . it is right not to eat meat or drink
wine or do anything that makes your brother stumble." Paul lays down
this principle repeatedly in Romans 14:1—15:13; I Corinthians 8:1-13;
9:19-23; and 10:23—11:1. These passages should be given careful study.

To illustrate this principle, suppose in the example given above,
there had been three Christian friends invited to dinner and each was
served a glass of wine. (We shall refer to them as *A, B,* and *C.*) *A* felt free,
before God, to drink the wine—to him it was no temptation to drunkenness
nor was it wrong in itself. *B,* though he knew there was no sin in drinking a glass of wine, knew that it was unsafe for him in light of his past
experience as an alcoholic. If they were the only ones involved then *A*
could drink the wine if he so desired even though *B* could not. But suppose *C* was weak in faith; he thought that the use of wine in any amount
was sinful and therefore its use by *A* would offend him and cause him
to stumble. For example, it might wound *C's* conscience and lead him
to do what he believed to be wrong, or it might make him prejudiced
toward and critical of *A* and disrupt their fellowship and testimony. The
question now arises as to whether *A,* under these circumstances, would
be free to drink it. The Biblical answer is *no,* he would not; not because
the drinking of wine is sinful (it is not), nor because it would tempt *A*
to drunkenness (it would not), but because it would offend *C* (the weak
brother) and cause him to stumble. As Paul states, "Everything is indeed
clean, but it is wrong for anyone to make others fall by what he eats;
it is right not to eat meat or *drink wine* or do anything that makes your
brother stumble" (Rom. 14:20b-21).

It must be emphasized that by its very nature *Christian liberty is
limited to things not sinful in themselves.* There is danger of confusion at
this point, for Paul, in Romans 14:21, uses wine as an *example* of the type
of thing which should be given up IF its use offends others. The danger
of confusion lies in the fact that many Christians today think that drinking wine is a sin in itself. Some think that the Bible forbids its use
even in moderation; others mistakenly identify drinking wine with drunkenness and thus wrongly conclude that because the latter is a sin so is
the former. But inasmuch as Paul uses wine as an example of the kind
of thing that a Christian is *free to use, unless it offends others,* it is
evident that its use is not itself a violation of God's law and therefore
is not a sin. Note carefully that Romans 14:21 *does not read:* "it is

right not to eat meat or *get drunk* or do anything that makes your brother stumble." The reason is evident; *getting drunk is a sin* whether it offends a brother or not whereas *drinking wine is not wrong unless* it results in drunkenness or causes others to stumble.

"So, whether you eat or drink, or whatever you do, do all to the glory of God. Give no offense to Jews or to Greeks or to the church of God" (I Cor. 10:31,32).

Conclusion: These three questions are given as an outline for testing an act to see if it is sinful. But what if one were faced with a situation of which he was uncertain? Perhaps he does not know if the Bible forbids his doing the thing in question, or perhaps he is uncertain as to whether it would tempt him or offend a brother. In such a case what must he do? The Biblical answer is *when in doubt about a thing, don't do it.* "The faith that you have, keep between yourself and God; happy is he who has no reason to judge himself for what he approves. *But he who has doubts is condemned,* if he eats, because he does not act from faith; for *whatever does not proceed from faith is sin"* (Rom. 14:22,23).

Using these three principles for determining Christian liberty demands that each believer know the Scriptures for himself. It also demands that he make decisions for himself and not allow any man or church to dictate to his conscience. Every Christian must declare with Luther, "I am bound by the text of the Bible, my conscience is captive to the word of God." Each believer must also determine for himself how and when to use the liberty given him. But he must make his judgments in the full realization that he is responsible to God for all his decisions and in the last day will have to give an account of himself to Him who knows the secrets of the heart.

The Outline of Romans is continued from p. 112.

XII. PERSONAL MATTERS 15:14—16:23

A. Paul explains his own feelings and relationship toward the saints at Rome. 15:14-33

1. He expresses confidence in their goodness, knowledge, and ability to instruct others. 15:14

15:14 RSV

¹⁴"I myself am satisfied about you, my brethren, that you yourselves are full of goodness, filled with all knowledge, and able to instruct one another.

15:14 WT

¹⁴"As far as I am concerned about you, my brothers, I am convinced that you especially are abounding in the highest goodness, richly supplied with perfect knowledge and competent to counsel one another.

2. He justifies the boldness with which he had written to them on the ground of his office as a minister (an apostle) of Jesus Christ

and explains that his purpose was to remind them of truths, with which they were already familiar. 15:15-17

15:15-17 RSV

[15]But on some points I have written to you very boldly by way of reminder, because of the grace given me by God [16]to be a minister of Christ Jesus to the Gentiles in the priestly service of the gospel of God, so that the offering of the Gentiles may be acceptable, sanctified by the Holy Spirit. [17]In Christ Jesus, then, I have reason to be proud of my work for God.

15:15-17 WT

[15]And yet, to refresh your memories, I have written you rather freely on some details, because of the unmerited favor shown me by God [16]in making me a minister of Christ Jesus to the heathen peoples, to have me act as a sacrificing minister of the good news, in order that my offering of the heathen peoples to God may be acceptable, consecrated by the Holy Spirit. [17]So, as a Christian, I am proud[k] of the things that I have done for God.

[k] Lit., *I am boasting in Christ.*

3. He briefly reviews his missionary labors and explains that he had made it a practice to preach the gospel in fields where Christ had not yet been named. 15:18-21

15:18-21 RSV

[18]For I will not venture to speak of anything except what Christ has wrought through me to win obedience from the Gentiles, by word and deed, [19]by the power of signs and wonders, by the power of the Holy Spirit, so that from Jerusalem and as far round as Illyr'icum I have fully preached the gospel of Christ, [20]thus making it my ambition to preach the gospel, not where Christ has already been named, lest I build on another man's foundation, [21]but as it is written,
"They shall see who have never been told of him,
and they shall understand who have never heard of him."

15:18-21 WT

[18]For I would venture to mention only what Christ has accomplished through me in bringing the heathen peoples to obedience, by word and by work, [19]by the power of signs and wonders, by the power of the Holy Spirit. So I have completed the telling of the good news of Christ all the way from Jerusalem around to Illyricum. [20]In this matter it has ever been my ambition to tell the good news where Christ's name had never been mentioned, so as not to build upon foundations laid by other men, [21]but, as the Scripture says:
"They will see who were never told of Him,
And they will understand who have not heard."[1]

[1] Isa. 52:15.

4. This was why he had never been to Rome though he had often longed to visit the saints there. 15:22,23

15:22,23 RSV

[22]This is the reason why I have so often been hindered from coming to you. [23]But now, since I no longer have any room for work in these regions, and since I have longed for many years to come to you,

15:22,23 WT

[22]This is the reason why I have so often been prevented from coming to see you. [23]But now, as there are no more places for me to occupy in this part of the world, and as I have for many years been longing to come to see you,

5. His plan was to visit them on his way to Spain; but first he had to deliver the Gentiles' contribution to the needy saints at Jerusalem. 15:24-29

15:24-29 RSV

²⁴I hope to see you in passing as I go to Spain, and to be sped on my journey there by you, once I have enjoyed your company for a little. ²⁵At present, however, I am going to Jerusalem with aid for the saints. ²⁶For Macedo'nia and Acha'ia have been pleased to make some contribution for the poor among the saints at Jerusalem; ²⁷they were pleased to do. it, and indeed they are in debt to them, for if the Gentiles have come to share in their spiritual blessings, they ought also to be of service to them in material blessings. ²⁸When therefore I have completed this, and have delivered to them what has been raised,ˣ I shall go on by way of you to Spain; ²⁹and I know that when I come to you I shall come in the fulness of the blessingʸ of Christ.

ˣ Greek *sealed to them this fruit*
ʸ Other ancient authorities insert *of the gospel*

15:24-29 WT

²⁴when I make my trip to Spain, I certainly hope to see you on my way there and to be helped forward by you, after I have enjoyed being with you awhile. ²⁵But just now I am on my way to Jerusalem to help God's people. ²⁶For Macedonia and Greece were delighted to make a contribution to the poor among God's people in Jerusalem. ²⁷They certainly were delighted to do it, and they really are under obligation to them, for if the heathen peoples have shared in their spiritual blessings, they ought to serve them in material blessings. ²⁸So, after I have finished this matter and made sure of the results of this contributionᵐ for them, I shall come by you on my way to Spain. ²⁹And I feel sure that when I do come to you, I shall come with Christ's abundant blessingⁿ on me.

ᵐ Lit., *made sure this fruit to them.*
ⁿ Lit., *in fullness of Christ's blessing.*

6.   He requested their prayers in his behalf that if it were God's will, this plan might be brought to completion. 15:30-33

15:30-33 RSV

³⁰I appeal to you, brethren, by our Lord Jesus Christ and by the love of the Spirit, to strive together with me in your prayers to God on my behalf, ³¹that I may be delivered from the unbelievers in Judea, and that my service for Jerusalem may be acceptable to the saints, ³²so that by God's will I may come to you with joy and be refreshed in your company. ³³The God of peace be with you all. Amen.

15:30-33 WT

³⁰Now I beg you, brothers, for the sake of our Lord Jesus Christ and by the love that the Spirit inspires, to wrestle with me in prayers to God on my behalf, ³¹that I may be delivered from those in Judea who are disobedient, and that the help which I am taking to Jerusalem may be well received by God's people there, ³²so that, if it is God's will, I may come with a happy heartᵒ to see you and have a refreshing rest while with you. ³³The peacegiving God be with you all! Amen.

ᵒ Lit., *in joy.*

B.   Paul commends Phoebe to the church and sends personal greetings to various individuals. 16:1-16

16:1-16 RSV

I commend to you our sister Phoebe, a deaconess of the church at Cen'chre-ae, ²that you may receive her in the Lord as befits the saints, and help her in whatever she may require from you, for she has been a helper of many and of myself as well.

16:1-16 WT

Now I introduceᵃ to you our sister Phoebe, who is a deaconess in the church at Cenchreae, ²that you may give her a Christianᵇ welcome in a manner becoming God's people, and give her whatever help she needs from you, for she herself has

ᵃ Grk., *commend.*
ᵇ Lit., *welcome in the Lord.*

³Greet Prisca and Aquila, my fellow workers in Christ Jesus, ⁴who risked their necks for my life, to whom not only I but also all the churches of the Gentiles give thanks; ⁵greet also the church in their house. Greet my beloved Epae'netus, who was the first convert in Asia for Christ. ⁶Greet Mary, who has worked hard among you. ⁷Greet Andron'icus and Ju'nias, my kinsmen and my fellow prisoners; they are men of note among the apostles, and they were in Christ before me. ⁸Greet Amplia'tus, my beloved in the Lord. ⁹Greet Urba'nus, our fellow worker in Christ, and my beloved Stachys. ¹⁰Greet Apel'les, who is approved in Christ. Greet those who belong to the family of Aristob'ulus. ¹¹Greet my kinsman Hero'dion. Greet those in the Lord who belong to the family of Narcis'sus. ¹²Greet those workers in the Lord, Tryphae'na and Trypho'sa. Greet the beloved Persis, who has worked hard in the Lord. ¹³Greet Rufus, eminent in the Lord, also his mother and mine. ¹⁴Greet Asyn'critus, Phlegon, Hermes, Pat'robas, Hermas, and the brethren who are with them. ¹⁵Greet Philol'ogus, Julia, Nereus and his sister, and Olym'pas, and all the saints who are with them. ¹⁶Greet one another with a holy kiss. All the churches of Christ greet you.

given protection⁰ to many, including myself. ³Remember me⁰ to Prisca and Aquila, my fellow-workers in the work of Christ Jesus, ⁴who once risked their very necks for my life. I am so thankful to them; not only I but also all the churches among the heathen thank them. ⁵Remember me to the church too, that meets at their house. Remember me to my dear Epaenetus, who was the first convert⁰ to Christ in the province of Asia. ⁶Remember me to Mary, who has toiled so hard for you. ⁷Remember me to Andronicus and Junias, my fellow-countrymen, who also served in prison with me; they are held in high esteem among the apostles, and became Christians⁰ before I did. ⁸Remember me to Ampliatus, my dear Christian friend.⁰ ⁹Remember me to Urbanus, my fellow-worker in the work of Christ, and to my dear friend Stachys. ¹⁰Remember me to Apelles, that most venerated Christian. Remember me to the members of Aristobulus' family. ¹¹Remember me to Herodion, my fellow-countryman. Remember me to the Christian members of Narcissus' family. ¹²Remember me to Tryphaena and Tryphosa, who continued to toil in the work of the Lord. Remember me to my dear friend Persis, who toiled so hard in the work of the Lord. ¹³Remember me to Rufus, that choicest Christian, and to his mother, who has been a mother to me too. ¹⁴Remember me to Asyncritus, Phlegon, Hermes, Patrobas, Hermas, and the brothers who are associated with them. ¹⁵Remember me to Philologus and Julia, to Nereus and his sister, and to Olympas, and all God's people who are associated with them. ¹⁶Greet one another with a consecrated kiss. All the churches of Christ wish to be remembered to you.

ᶜ Lit., *been protectress.*
ᵈ Grk., *greet.*
ᵉ Lit., *first fruits.*
ᶠ *Became in Christ before me.*
ᵍ *My beloved in the Lord.*

Many believe that Phoebe, a deaconess of the church at Cenchreae (a seaport of Corinth), delivered this letter to the Roman church.

C. The apostle WARNS the saints to have nothing to do with those who cause dissensions and difficulties by *opposing sound doctrine*—such persons are false teachers, they are not true servants of Christ! 16:17-20

16:17-20 RSV

¹⁷I appeal to you, brethren, to take note of those who create dissensions and

16:17-20 WT

¹⁷But I beg you, brothers, to keep on the lookout for those who stir up divisions

difficulties, in opposition to the doctrine which you have been taught; avoid them. [18] For such persons do not serve our Lord Christ, but their own appetites,[z] and by fair and flattering words they deceive the hearts of the simple-minded. [19] For while your obedience is known to all, so that I rejoice over you, I would have you wise as to what is good and guileless as to what is evil; [20]then the God of peace will soon crush Satan under your feet. The grace of our Lord Jesus Christ be with you.[a]

---

[z] Greek *their own belly* (Phil. 3. 19)
[a] Other ancient authorities omit this sentence

and put hindrances in your way, in opposition to the instruction that you had, and always avoid them. [15]For such men are really not serving our Lord Christ but their own base appetites,[h] and by their fair and flattering talk[i] they are deceiving the hearts of unsuspecting people. [19]Yes, your obedience has been told to everybody; so I am delighted about you, but I want you to be wise about what is good and innocent about what is bad. [20]Now the peace-giving God will soon crush Satan under your feet. The spiritual blessing of our Lord Jesus be with you.

---

[h] Lit., *their own belly.*
[i] Grk., *smooth talk and blessing.*

D. He conveys the greetings of his companions to the Roman saints. (Tertius, the apostle's amanuensis, or secretary, who had written the letter at Paul's direction, sends his greetings in the Lord.) 16:21-23

16:21-23 RSV

[21] Timothy, my fellow worker, greets you; so do L u c i u s and J a s o n and Sosip'ater, my kinsmen.
[22] I Tertius, the writer of this letter, greet you in the Lord.
[23] Ga'ius, who is host to me and to the whole church, greets you. Eras'tus, the city treasurer, and our brother Quartus, greet you. [b]

---

[b] Other ancient authorities insert verse 24,*The grace of our Lord Jesus Christ be with you all. Amen.*

16:21-23 WT

[21] Timothy, my fellow-worker, wishes to be remembered to you; so do L u c i u s, J a s o n, and Sosipater too, my fellow-countrymen. [22]I, Tertius, who write this letter, wish to be remembered to you as a fellow-Christian. [23]Gaius, my host, and host of the whole church here, wishes to be remembered to you. Erastus, the treasurer of the city, wishes to be remembered to you, and so does our brother Quartus.[j]

---

[j] V.24 not in best Mss.

XIII. THE CONCLUDING DOXOLOGY 16:25-27

16:25-27 RSV

[25] Now to him who is able to strengthen you according to my g o s p e l and the preaching of Jesus Christ, according to the revelation of the mystery which was kept secret for long ages [26] but is now disclosed and through the prophetic writings is made known to all nations, according to the command of the eternal God, to bring about obedience to the faith —[27]to the only wise God be glory for evermore through Jesus Christ! Amen.

16:25-27 WT

[25] To Him who can make you strong in accordance with the good news I bring and in accordance with the m e s s a g e preached about Jesus Christ, in accordance with the uncovering of the secret which for ages past had not been told, [26] but now has been fully brought to light by means of the prophetic Scriptures, and in accordance with the command of the eternal God has been made known to all the heathen, to win them to obedience inspired by faith—[27]to the one wise God be glory forever through Jesus Christ. Amen.

Paul gives praise to the eternal, all-wise God who, through the prophetic Scriptures, has made known the gospel of Jesus Christ—the good news of salvation by faith freely offered to all men, Gentiles as well as Jews. Compare Romans 1:16,17.

APPENDIX A

JAMES AND PAUL ON JUSTIFICATION

Throughout church history there have been two opposing views as to how sinners are justified, that is, how they are made righteous before God and thus declared acceptable by Him.

One view is that justification is by *faith alone* apart from works of the law. Sinners are declared righteous and thus justified solely on the ground of Christ's righteousness which is imputed to them the moment they believe in Him. Salvation is by grace through faith and in no sense results from, nor depends upon, the sinner's good works. Personal acts of obedience neither secure nor add to one's justification; it is based entirely on the righteousness which God freely gives to all who believe.

The other view is that sinners, in order to be justified, must do more than believe in Christ; they must also render personal obedience to God's law. Thus justification is said to be by *faith plus works*. The sinner is made acceptable to God on the ground of what he believes coupled with what he does, not on the sole ground of what Christ did in his behalf. One can share in the benefits of Christ's saving work only by believing the gospel *and* obeying the law of Christ. Either, without the other, is inadequate to render the sinner acceptable to God; He requires both faith and works of those whom He justifies.

The advocates of both schools of thought appeal to the Scriptures for support of their views. The former quote the words of Paul in Romans 3:28 as a clear statement of their position. "For we hold that a man is justified by faith apart from works of law." The latter cite the words of James as proof of their doctrine of justification by faith plus works. "You see that a man is justified by works and not by faith alone" (2:24). On the surface these two statements *appear* to contradict each other. Must one agree with James and thus reject Paul or vice versa? Or can the two statements be reconciled?

The purpose of this appendix is to show that the conflict is not real but only apparent. When both verses (Rom. 3:28 and James 2:24) are read in their proper setting they actually complement rather than contradict each other. Both statements are correct when understood as their authors intended that they be understood. A sinner is justified by faith apart from works of the law as Paul asserts, and yet the saved sinner is justified by works and not by faith alone as James states. To understand how this can be, we must examine the two verses in their context.

Paul's purpose in Romans 3:9—5:21 is to show that a guilty sinner who has no righteousness of his own can obtain perfect righteousness through faith in Jesus Christ.[1] The moment the sinner believes, Christ's righteousness is credited to him and consequently he is declared righteous (he is justified) by God. The ground of the sinner's justification before God is the imputed righteousness of Christ. The means by which this righteousness is received is faith alone. The point which Paul wishes to establish is that sinners are rendered completely acceptable to God through faith in Christ apart from personal merit. One's works have nothing to do with his justification before God! It is in this context that the apostle states "For we hold that a man is justified by faith apart from works of law," (Rom. 3:28).

James' goal is quite different. The purpose of his letter is to show how Christians must live before men. They must be doers of the word, not hearers only, lest they deceive themselves (1:22-25). This theme is stressed throughout his epistle. In 2:14-26 James is showing that faith which does not produce works is dead faith and cannot save. It does no good to *claim* to have faith unless the claim is supported by evidence. In 2:14 he asks "What does it profit my brethren if a man *says* he has faith *but has not works?* Can *his faith* save him?" The answer of course is *no!* Notice the challenge which James makes in 2:18: "Show me your faith apart from your works and I by my works will show you my faith." He wants his reader to see that a faith which cannot be *justified* (proved genuine by its fruits) *before men* is counterfeit, not real—it is mere profession and therefore worthless. It is in this context that James' statement appears concerning the need of works in relation to justification. "You see that a man is justified by works and not by faith alone" (2:24). He is speaking of a *Christian being justified before men by his works,* whereas Paul in Romans 3:28 is speaking of a *sinner being justified before God apart from his works.* Calvin expressed both ideas when he wrote "it is faith alone which justifies, but the faith which justifies can never be alone."[2] Paul is concerned with the former idea in Romans 3:28; James is stressing the latter in 2:24; neither is contradicting the other.

Packer, in dealing with the various Biblical uses of the word *justify,* states that "In James 2:21,24-25, its reference is to the proof of a man's acceptance with God which is given when his actions show that he has the kind of living, working faith to which God imputes righteousness.

"James' statement that Christians, like Abraham, are justified by works (vs. 24) is thus not contrary to Paul's insistence that Christians,

---

[1] See the Outline on 3:9—5:21 and especially Note 1, pp. 24,25, Note 2, pp. 29-33, and Note 3, pp. 41-44.

[2] Quoted by Bishop H. C. G. Moule, *The Epistle of Paul the Apostle to the Romans,* p. 137.

like Abraham, are justified by faith (Rom. 3:28; 4:1-5), but is comple-
mentary to it.   James himself quotes Gen. 15:6 for exactly the same
purpose as Paul does—to show that it was faith which secured Abraham's
acceptance as righteous (vs. 23; cf. Rom. 4:3 ff., Gal. 3:6ff).   The justification which concerns James is not the believer's original acceptance
by God, but the subsequent vindication of his profession of faith by his
life.   It is in terminology, not thought, that James differs from Paul."[3]

BIBLIOGRAPHY ON JUSTIFICATION

Berkhof, L. *Systematic Theology.* Grand Rapids: Wm. B. Eerdmans Publishing Co.,
    1949, pp. 510-526.

Berkouwer, G. C. *Faith and Justification.* Grand Rapids: Wm. B. Eerdmans Publish-
    ing Co., 1954, 207 pages.

Buchanan, James. *The Doctrine of Justification.* Grand Rapids: Baker Book House,
    1955, 514 pages.

Calvin, John. *Institutes of the Christian Religion.* Grand Rapids: Wm. B. Eerd-
    mans Publishing Co., 1953, Book III, Chs. 11-18.

Cunningham, William. *Historical Theology.* London: The Banner of Truth Trust,
    1960, Vol. II, pp. 1-120.

Hodge, Charles. *Systematic Theology.* Grand Rapids: Wm. B. Eerdmans Publish-
    ing Co., 1952, Vol. III, pp. 114-212.

Morris, Leon. *The Apostolic Preaching of the Cross.* Grand Rapids: Wm. B. Eerd-
    mans Publishing Co., 1956, pp. 224-274.

Owen, John. *The Doctrine of Justification by Faith.* Evansville, Indiana: Sovereign
    Grace Publishers, 1959, 457 pages.

Packer, James I. "Just, Justify, Justification," *Baker's Dictionary of Theology.*
    Grand Rapids: Baker Book House, 1960, pp. 303-308.

Packer, James I. "Justification," *The New Bible Dictionary.* Grand Rapids: Wm.
    B. Eerdmans Publishing Co., 1962, pp. 683-686.

---

[3] J. I. Packer, "Just, Justify, Justification," *Baker's Dictionary of Theology*, p. 304.

APPENDIX B

DOES ROMANS 7:14-25 DESCRIBE PAUL'S EXPERIENCE BEFORE OR AFTER HIS CONVERSION?

The answer one gives to the question as to whether Paul, in Romans 7:14-25, is writing of his experience *before* or *after* his conversion, is of vital significance. If this were Paul's pre-Christian experience, then the passage would have no bearing on the nature of the Christian life, but would simply be a description of a lost man's struggle with sin. On the other hand, if it is an account of Paul's struggle with indwelling sin as a saved person, then the passage has far reaching implications in relation to the doctrine of sanctification. Those who hold to some form of "perfectionism" as well as many of the advocates of the "victorious" or "higher life" movement find it hard, if not impossible, to harmonize such testimony with their own views of sanctification. But others see in these words not only a description of the apostle's personal Christian experience with inward corruption but also an accurate description of every saint's struggle with indwelling sin.[1]

Which view of Romans 7:14-25 is correct? Is Paul telling of his past experience as a lost man who tried to keep God's law but failed? Or is he describing his present experience as a saved man, a believer struggling with indwelling sin? The purpose of this appendix is to show that Paul is writing of *his experience as a mature Christian*. The state described in these verses was the state of Paul's heart when he wrote the Roman letter. It is a description of the great apostle's struggle with his carnal nature—a struggle with the sin which remained in him after regeneration. The following arguments are given in support of this position.

1. The tenses of the verbs show that Paul is writing of his *present* experience as a believer.

In vss. 7-13 Paul tells how, as an unsaved man, he had been unable to keep God's law. The law, in accomplishing its intended purpose, had revealed to him the fact that he was spiritually dead and thus lost.

---

[1] This view of sanctification was the position held by the Reformers: Luther, Calvin, Beza, etc. The *Westminster Confession of Faith* states it thus: "This sanctification is throughout in the whole man, yet imperfect in this life: there abide still some remnants of corruption in every part: whence ariseth a continual and irreconcilable war; the flesh lusteth against the Spirit, and the Spirit against the flesh." Hodge, in his *Systematic Theology*, Vol. III, Chapter XVIII on "Sanctification" (pp. 213-258) has a very good treatment of the subject. In dealing with "perfectionism" he points out that "The doctrine of Lutherans and Reformed, the two great branches of the Protestant Church, is, that sanctification is never perfected in this life; that sin is not in any case entirely subdued; so that the most advanced believer has need as long as he continues in the flesh, daily to pray for the forgiveness of sins" (p. 245). See also L. Berkhof, *Systematic Theology*, Ch. X, "Sanctification."

Throughout these verses (7-13) he writes in the *past tense.* "I should not have known," vs. 7; "sin . . . wrought in me," vs. 8; "I was once alive . . . I died," vs. 9; "sin . . . killed me," vs. 11; "Did that which is good, then, bring death to me? . . . It was sin working death in me . . . ," vs. 13.

In vss. 14-25 Paul abruptly changes to the *present tense.* He begins to describe his present struggle with sin and uses the present tense throughout the remainder of the chapter. "I am carnal," vs. 14; "I do not understand my own actions . . . I do . . . I do," vs. 15; "I do . . . I agree," vs. 16; "it is no longer I that do it," vs. 17; "I can will . . . but I cannot do it," vs. 18, etc. Note verses 19, 20, 21, 22, and 23. In vs. 24 he cries out, "Wretched man that *I am!* (present tense) who will (future tense) deliver me." And in vs. 25 he concludes, "So then, I of myself serve the law of God with my mind, but with my flesh I serve the law of sin."

2.   The fact that Paul acknowledges Jesus Christ as his Lord and deliverer shows that he was writing of his experience as a Christian. "Who will deliver *me* from this body of death? Thanks be to God through Jesus Christ *our Lord!"* (vss. 24, 25). The apostle informs us in Romans 10:9,10 that all who believe in and confess Jesus as the risen Lord are saved. In I Corinthians 12:3 he states that "no one can say 'Jesus is Lord' except by the Holy Spirit." Inasmuch as Paul confesses Jesus Christ as *his* Lord in vs. 25, it is clear that he is describing his experience as a Christian, *not* as an unbelieving Jew.

3.   Paul makes statements in 7:23,25 concerning his attitude toward God's law that, according to his own teaching, could be made only by a *saved* person.

The apostle in describing his experience says, "I delight in the law of God, in my inmost self," vs. 22; "I of myself serve the law of God with my mind," vs. 25. Yet Paul teaches that the unsaved man's mind does not and cannot submit to God's law. In Romans 8:7,8 he states that "the mind that is set on the flesh is hostile to God; it does not submit to God's law, indeed it cannot; and those who are in the flesh cannot please God." It is certain that he is referring to the unregenerate or unsaved man when he uses the phrase "in the flesh" in 8:8, for concerning the saints (believers) to whom he is writing he says, "But *you* are *not in the flesh* . . . if the Spirit of God really dwells in you. And anyone who does not have the Spirit of Christ does not belong to him," 8:9. Since *Paul served the law of God with his mind* (7:25) and since *the unregenerate cannot do this* (8:7,8) it is certain that Paul was writing of his experience as a saved man.

4.   The structure of Paul's argument from chapters one through eight supports this view. As Hodge states, Paul's "great object in the first eight chapters, is to show that the whole work of the sinner's salvation, his justification and sanctification, are not of the law, but of grace; that

legal obedience can never secure the one, nor legal efforts the other."[2] In the first five chapters Paul proves that justification is by faith, not by works of the law. In chapter six, he shows that justification by faith does not lead to sin but to obedience. In the latter part of this chapter and the first part of chapter seven, he explains that the believer is free from the law and is now under grace—that while he was under law (before his conversion) he brought forth fruit for death, but being under grace, he now brings forth fruit for God. The question then arises: "Is the law sin?" (7:7). In 7:7-13 Paul explains that it is not the law's fault that a sinner cannot be *justified* by keeping its commands; the fault lies in the lost man himself, in his sinful nature. The law, by revealing sin, brings the knowledge of death (this is its function), but it cannot bring salvation (only Christ can save). But this does not make the law sin, the law is holy and just and good, the sin is in man's heart! In 7:14-25 he shows that the law is equally powerless to sanctify the believer. Just as it cannot free the lost man from sin's guilt neither can the law free the saved man from sin's power. But the Christian does not look upon the law as sin because it cannot sanctify him. On the contrary he delights in the law of God in his inmost self, he serves it with his mind! He bemoans the fact that sin still dwells within him and longs for and is assured of deliverance from its power, through Jesus Christ his Lord. In chapter eight, Paul shows that even though the believer is plagued with sin and afflictions while in this world, he is nevertheless secure in Christ, for through His death he has been freed from the law and thereby delivered from condemnation.

Thus it is clear from the structure and movement of his argument that Paul's purpose is to demonstrate the inability of God's holy law either to *save* or to *sanctify;* this he does by appealing to his own experience with the law, first as a lost person (7:7-13) and then as a Christian (7:14-25). (See the Outline on 7:7-25 and Note 6, p. 60f. on Indwelling Sin.)

5. This view of the passage (that the struggle with sin described here is the experience of a saved person) is in harmony with the teaching of the rest of the Scriptures. Paul, in writing to the saints at Galatia, states, "But I say, walk by the Spirit, and do not gratify the desires of the flesh. For the desires of the flesh are against the Spirit, and the desires of the Spirit are against the flesh; for these are opposed to each other, to prevent you from doing what you would," (Gal. 5:16,17). John declares that "If we say we have no sin, we deceive ourselves, and the truth is not in us," (I John 1:8). The presence of indwelling sin was confessed by Job (Job 40:4, 42:5,6) and by Isaiah (Isa. 6:5). David,

---

[2] Charles Hodge, *Commentary on the Epistle to the Romans*, p. 244.

a man after God's own heart, testified to the power of sin in his life (Psa. 32 and 51). See Philippians 3:12 and I Peter 2:11. Note also Eccles. 7:20; I Kings 8:46; Proverbs 20:9, and James 3:2. [3]

In light of the above facts, that Paul writes in the first person, present tense, that he acknowledges Jesus Christ as his Lord and looks to Him for deliverance, that he delights in and serves the Law of God with his mind, it is certain that he is writing of his experience as a saved person. It is clear from the teaching of the rest of the Bible that the natural man could not do nor experience these things.

This interpretation of the passage is also supported by the context (i.e., the structure and movement of Paul's argument in chapters 1-8) and by the analogy of faith (i.e., it is in harmony with what the rest of the Bible teaches concerning the renewed man's struggle with sin).

In defense of this interpretation, see the following commentaries on Romans: Hodge, pp. 239-247; Haldane, pp. 302-310; Moule, pp. 129-131 and Appendix E, pp. 263,264; Murray, Vol. 1, pp. 256-259; Calvin, pp. 259, ff.; and Shedd, pp. 189-194.

BIBLIOGRAPHY ON SANCTIFICATION

The following books, dealing with the Biblical doctrine of holiness and the work of the Spirit in the believer's sanctification, are recommended for further study in this important field.

Berkouwer, G. C. *Faith and Sanctification* (tr. by John Vriend).   Grand Rapids: Wm. B. Eerdmans Publishing Co., 1952, 193 pages.

---

[3] Further confirmation that believers are plagued with indwelling sin throughout life can be found in the writings of the most eminent of the Lord's servants: men such as Luther, Bradford, Rutherford, Berkeley, Edwards, Brainerd, Toplady, Doddridge, Romaine, Newton, Spurgeon, to name but a few. Arthur W. Pink, in a tract on "The Christian in Romans Seven" (published by the Bible Truth Depot, Swengel, Pennsylvania), gives several excellent excerpts from the writings of some of these men in which they testify to the presence of indwelling sin in their hearts. The following quotation from Spurgeon, from Pink's tract will serve as an example. "There are some professing Christians who can speak of themselves in terms of admiration; but, from my inmost heart, I loathe such speeches more and more every day that I live. Those who talk in such a boastful fashion must be constituted very differently from me. While they are congratulating themselves, I have to lie humbly at the foot of Christ's Cross, and marvel that I am saved at all, for I know that I am saved. I have to wonder that I do not believe Christ more, and equally wonder that I am privileged to believe in Him at all—to wonder that I do not love Him more, and equally to wonder that I love Him at all—to wonder that I am not holier, and equally to wonder that I have any desire to be holy at all considering what a polluted, debased, depraved nature I find still within my soul, notwithstanding all that Divine grace has done in me. If God were ever to allow the fountains of the great deeps of depravity to break up in the best man that lives, he would make as bad a devil as the Devil himself is. I care nothing for what these boasters say concerning their own perfections; I feel sure that they do not know themselves, or they could not talk as they often do. There is tinder enough in the saint who is nearest to heaven to kindle another hell if God should but permit a spark to fall upon it. In the very best of men, there is an infernal and well-nigh infinite depth of depravity. Some Christians never seem to find this out. I almost wish that they might not do so, for it is a painful discovery for any one to make; but it has the beneficial effect of making us cease from trusting in ourselves, and causing us to glory only in the Lord." pp. 13,14.

Bonar, Horatius. *God's Way of Holiness.* Chicago: Moody Press, n.d., 112 pages, (paperback).

Kuyper, Abraham. *The Practice of Godliness.* Grand Rapids: Wm. B. Eerdmans Publishing Co., 1948, 121 pages.

Kuyper, Abraham. *The Work of the Holy Spirit.* Grand Rapids: Wm. B. Eerdmans Publishing Co., 1941, 664 pages.

Owen, John. *Indwelling Sin,* published with two other of Owen's treatises under the title, *Temptation and Sin.* Jenkintown, Pa.: Sovereign Grace Publishers, distributed by Zondervan Publishing House, Grand Rapids, 1958, 322 pages.

Owen, John. *The Holy Svirit.* Grand Rapids: Kregel Publications, 1954, 356 pages.

Ryle, J. C. *Holiness.* Westwood, New Jersey: Fleming H. Revell Company, n.d., 333 pages.

Smeaton, George. *The Doctrine of the Holy Spirit.* London: The Banner of Truth Trust, 1958, 372 pages.

Warfield, B. B. *Perfectionism.* Philadelphia: The Presbyterian and Reformed Publishing Company, 1958, 464 pages.

APPENDIX C

THE MEANING OF "FOREKNEW" IN ROMANS 8:29

"For those whom he foreknew he also predestined to be conformed to the image of his Son, in order that he might be the first-born among many brethren. And those whom he predestined he also called; and those whom he called he also justified; and those whom he justified he also glorified." Romans 8:29,30

Broadly speaking there have been two general views as to the meaning and use of the word "foreknew" in Romans 8:29. One class of commentators (the Arminians) maintain that Paul is saying that God predestined to salvation those whom He *foreknew* would respond to His offer of grace (i.e., those whom He saw would of their own free will repent of their sins and believe the gospel). Godet, in commenting on Romans 8:29, asks the question: "In what respect did God thus *foreknow* them?" and answers that they were "foreknown as sure to fulfill the conditions of salvation, viz. *faith;* so: foreknown as His *by faith.*"[1] The word "foreknew" is thus understood by the Arminians to mean that God knew beforehand which sinners would believe, etc., and on the basis of this knowledge He predestined them unto salvation.

The other class of commentators (the Calvinists) reject the above view on two grounds. First, because the Arminians' interpretation is not in keeping with the meaning of Paul's language and second, because it is out of harmony with the system of doctrine taught in the rest of the Scriptures. Calvinists contend that the passage teaches that God set His heart upon (i.e., foreknew) certain individuals; these He predestined or marked out to be saved. Notice that the text does *not* say that God *knew* SOMETHING ABOUT *particular individuals* (that they would do this or that), but it states that God *knew the individuals* THEMSELVES —those whom He *knew* He predestined to be made like Christ. The word "foreknew" as used here is thus understood to be equivalent to "foreloved"—those who were the objects of God's love, He marked out for salvation.

The questions raised by the two opposing interpretations are these: Did God look down through time and see that certain individuals would believe and thus predestine them unto salvation on the basis of this foreseen faith? Or did God set His heart on certain individuals and because of His love for them predestine that they should be called and given faith in Christ by the Holy Spirit and thus be saved? In other words, is the individual's faith the *cause* or the *result* of God's predestination?

---

[1] Frederic Godet, *Commentary on the Epistle to the Romans*, p. 325. Italics are his.

A.   The meaning of "foreknew" in Romans 8:29

God has always possessed perfect knowledge of all creatures and of all events. There has never been a time when anything past, present, or future was not fully known to Him. But it is not His knowledge of future events (of what people would do, etc.) which is referred to in Romans 8:29,30, for Paul clearly states that those whom He *foreknew* He predestined, He called, He justified, etc. Since all men are *not* predestined, called, and justified, it follows that all men were *not foreknown* by God in the sense spoken of in verse 29.

It is for this reason that Arminians are forced to add some qualifying notion. They read into the passage some idea not contained in the language itself such as those whom He foreknew *would believe etc.*, He predestined, called, and justified. But according to the Biblical usage of the words "know," "knew," and "foreknew" there is not the least need to make such an addition, and since it is unnecessary, it is improper. When the Bible speaks of God knowing particular individuals, it often means that He has special regard for them, that they are the objects of His affection and concern. For example in Amos 3:2, God, speaking to Israel says, "You only have I known of all the families of the earth; therefore I will punish you for all your iniquities." The Lord knew *about* all the families of the earth, but He knew Israel in a special way. They were His chosen people whom He had set His heart upon. See Deuteronomy 7:7,8; 10:15. Because Israel was His in a special sense He chastised them, cf. Hebrews 12:5,6. God, speaking to Jeremiah, said, "Before I formed you in the womb, I knew you," (Jeremiah 1:5). The meaning here is not that God knew *about* Jeremiah but that He had special regard for the prophet before He formed him in his mother's womb. Jesus also used the word "knew" in the sense of personal, intimate awareness. "On that day many will say to me, 'Lord, Lord, did we not prophesy in your name, and cast out demons in your name, and do many mighty works in your name?' And then will I declare to them, 'I never knew you; depart from me, you evildoers' " (Matt. 7:22,23). Our Lord cannot be understood here as saying, I knew nothing about you, for it is quite evident that He knew all too much about them—their evil character and evil works; hence, His meaning must be, I never knew you intimately nor personally, I never regarded you as the objects of my favor or love. Paul uses the word in the same way in I Corinthians 8:3, "But if one loves God, one is *known* by him," and also II Timothy 2:19, "the Lord knows those who are His." The Lord knows *about* all men but He only *knows* those "who love Him, who are called according to His purpose" (Rom. 8:28)—*those who are His!*

Murray's argument in favor of this meaning of "foreknew" is very good. "It should be observed that the text says '*whom* he foreknew'; *whom* is the object of the verb and there is no qualifying addition. This, of itself, shows that, unless there is some other compelling reason, the expression 'whom he foreknew' contains within itself the differentiation which is presupposed. If the apostle had in mind some 'qualifying adjunct' it would have been simple to supply it. Since he adds none we are forced to inquire if the actual terms he uses can express the differentiation implied. The usage of Scripture provides an affirmative answer. Although the term 'foreknew' is used seldom in the New Testament, it is altogether indefensible to ignore the meaning so frequently given to the word 'know' in the usage of Scripture; 'foreknow' merely adds the thought of 'beforehand' to the word 'know'. Many times in Scripture 'know' has a pregnant meaning which goes beyond that of mere cognition. It is used in a sense practically synonymous with 'love', to set regard upon, to know with peculiar interest, delight, affection, and action (cf. Gen. 18:19; Exod. 2:25; Psalm 1:6; 144:3; Jer. 1:5; Amos 3:2; Hosea 13:5; Matt. 7:23; I Cor. 8:3; Gal. 4:9; II Tim. 2:19; I John 3:1). There is no reason why this import of the word 'know' should not be applied to 'foreknow' in this passage, as also in 11:2 where it also occurs in the same kind of construction and where the thought of election is patently present (cf. 11:5,6). When this import is appreciated, then there is no reason for adding any qualifying notion and 'whom he foreknew' is seen to contain within itself the differentiating element required. It means 'whom he set regard upon' or 'whom he knew from eternity with distinguishing affection and delight' and is virtually equivalent to 'whom he foreloved'. This interpretation, furthermore, is in agreement with the efficient and determining action which is so conspicuous in every other link of the chain—it is God who predestinates, it is God who calls, it is God who justifies, and it is he who glorifies. Foresight of faith would be out of accord with the determinative action which is predicated of God in these other instances and would constitute a weakening of the total emphasis at the point where we should least expect it . . . . It is not the foresight of difference but the foreknowledge that makes difference to exist, not a foresight that recognizes existence but the foreknowledge that determines existence. It is a sovereign distinguishing love."[2]

Hodge observes that "as *to know* is often *to approve* and *love*, it may express the idea of peculiar affection in this case; or it may mean to *select* or *determine upon* . . . . The usage of the word is favourable to either modification of this general idea *of preferring*. 'The people which he foreknew,' i.e., loved or selected, Rom. 11:2; 'Who verily was foreordained (Gr. *foreknown*), i.e., *fixed upon, chosen* before the foundation of the world,' I Peter 1:20; II Tim. 2:19; John 10:14,15; see also Acts 2:23; I Peter 1:2. The idea, therefore, obviously is, that those whom God peculiarly loved, and by thus loving, distinguished or selected from the rest of mankind; or to express both ideas in one word, those whom *he elected* he predestined, etc."[3]

---

[2] John Murray, *The Epistle to the Romans*, Vol. I, pp. 316-318. Italics are his.

[3] Charles Hodge, *Commentary on the Epistle to the Romans*, pp. 283, 284. Italics are his.

Although God knew *about* all men before the world began, He did not *know* all men in the sense that the Bible sometimes uses the word "know," i.e., with intimate personal awareness and love. It is in this latter sense that God foreKNEW those whom He predestined, called, and justified, as outlined in Romans 8:29, 30!

B.   Romans 8:29 does not refer to the foresight of faith, good works, etc.

As was pointed out above, it is unnecessary and therefore indefensible to add any qualifying notion such as faith to the verb foreknew in Romans 8:29. The Arminians make this addition, not because the language requires it, but because their theological system requires it— they do it to escape the doctrines of unconditional predestination and election. They *read* the notion of foreseen faith *into* the verse and then appeal to it in an effort to prove that predestination was based on foreseen events. Thus particular individuals are said to be saved, *not* because *God willed* that they should be saved (for He willed the salvation of everyone) *but* because *they themselves willed* to be saved. Hence salvation is made to depend ultimately on the individual's will, not on the sovereign will of Almighty God—faith is understood to be man's gift to God, not God's gift to man.

Haldane, comparing Scripture with Scripture, clearly shows that the foreknowledge mentioned in Romans 8:29 cannot have reference to foreseen faith, good works, or the sinner's response to God's call. "Faith cannot be the cause of foreknowledge, because foreknowledge is before predestination, and faith is the effect of predestination. 'As many as were ordained to eternal life believed,' Acts 13:48. Neither can it be meant of the foreknowledge of good works, because these are the effects of predestination. 'We are His workmanship, created in Christ Jesus unto good works; which God hath before ordained (or before prepared) that we should walk in them;' Eph. 2:10. Neither can it be meant of foreknowledge of our concurrence with the external call, because our effectual calling depends not upon that concurrence, but upon God's purpose and grace, given us in Christ Jesus before the world began, 2 Tim. 1:9. By this foreknowledge, then, is meant, as has been observed, the love of God towards those whom he predestinates to be saved through Jesus Christ. All the called of God are foreknown by Him,—that is, they are the objects of His eternal love, and their calling comes from this free love. 'I have loved thee with an everlasting love; therefore with loving-kindness I have drawn thee,' Jer. 31:3."[4]

Murray, in rejecting the view that "foreknew" in Romans 8:29 refers to the foresight of faith, is certainly correct in stating that "It needs to be emphasized that the rejection of this interpretation is not dictated by a predestinarian interest. Even if it were granted that 'foreknew'

---

[4] Robert Haldane, *Exposition of the Epistle to the Romans*, p. 397.

means the foresight of faith, the biblical doctrine of sovereign election is not thereby eliminated or disproven. For it is certainly true that God foresees faith; he foresees all that comes to pass. The question would then simply be: whence proceeds this faith which God foresees? And the only biblical answer is that the faith which God foresees is the faith he himself creates (cf. John 3:3-8; 6:44, 45, 65; Eph. 2:8; Phil. 1:29; II Pet. 1:2). Hence his eternal foresight of faith is preconditioned by his decree to generate this faith in those whom he foresees as believing, and we are thrown back upon the differentiation which proceeds from God's own eternal and sovereign election to faith and its consequents. The interest, therefore, is simply one of interpretation as it should be applied to this passage. On exegetical grounds we shall have to reject the view that 'foreknew' refers to the foresight of faith."[5]

C. Various ways in which the Greek word "foreknew" (proegno) has been rendered in modern English translations of the New Testament

The root Greek word (proegno) literally translated foreknew and foreknowledge occurs seven times in the Greek New Testament. Twice it refers to previous knowledge on the part of *man:* In Acts 26:5 to the Jews' previous knowledge of Paul, and in II Peter 3:17 to the Christians' previous knowledge (being forewarned) of scoffers who would come in the last days. Five times it refers to *God's* foreknowledge: Three of these times it is used as a verb, Romans 8:29; 11:2; and I Peter 1:2, and twice as a noun, Acts 2:23 and I Peter 1:20. The following quotations show how various modern translations have attempted to convey in English the Biblical connotations of the word when used in reference to *God's* foreknowledge. In each quotation the English word or phrase which corresponds to the Greek word "foreknew" is CAPITALIZED so that the reader may see at a glance how the translators have rendered it. These various renderings certainly show, in the opinion of these translators, that when used in reference to God's foreknowledge in the New Testament, the word connotes more than simple knowledge of future events.[6]

Moffatt's Translation

Rom. 8:29   "For he decreed of old that those whom he PREDESTINED should share the likeness of his Son . . ."

Rom. 11:2   "God has not repudiated his People, his PREDESTINED People!"

---

[5] Murray, *Romans*, Vol. I, p. 316.

[6] See the article on "Foreknow" in the *International Standard Bible Encyclopaedia*, Vol. II, pp. 1128-1131 and *Baker's Dictionary of Theology*, p. 225. See also W. Cunningham, *Historical Theology*, Vol. II, pp. 441-449. Cf. the article on "Predestination" by J. I. Packer in *The New Bible Dictionary*, pp. 1024-1026.

I Pet. 1:2   "whom God the Father has PREDESTINED and chosen, . . ."

I Pet. 1:20   "He was PREDESTINED before the foundation of the world . . ."

Acts 2:23   "this Jesus, betrayed in the PREDESTINED COURSE of God's deliberate purpose, . . ."

Goodspeed's Translation

Rom. 8:29   "For those whom he HAD MARKED OUT FROM THE FIRST he predestined to be made like his Son, . . ."

Rom. 11:2   "God has not repudiated his people, which he HAD MARKED OUT FROM THE FIRST."

I Pet. 1:2   "whom God the Father has chosen and PREDESTINED . . ."

I Pet. 1:20   "who was PREDESTINED for this before the foundation of the world, . . ."

Acts 2:23   "But you, by the fixed purpose and INTENTION of God, handed him over to wicked men, . . ."

Wuest, An Expanded Translation of the New Testament

Rom. 8:29   "Because, those whom He FOREORDAINED He also marked out beforehand . . ."

Rom. 11:2   "God did not repudiate His people whom He FOREORDAINED."

I Pet. 1:2   "chosen-out ones, this choice having been determined by the FOREORDINATION of God the Father . . ."

I Pet. 1:20   "who indeed was FOREORDAINED before the foundation of the universe was laid, . . ."

Acts 2:23   "this One, having been delivered up by the counsel of God which [in the council held by the Trinity] had decided upon His destiny, even by the FOREORDINATION of God WHICH IS THAT ACT FIXING HIS DESTINY, . . ."

Phillips' New Testament

Rom. 11:2   "It is unthinkable that God should have repudiated his own people, the people WHOSE DESTINY HE HIMSELF AP- POINTED."

I Pet. 1:2   "whom God the Father KNEW and chose long ago to be made holy by his Spirit, . . ."

I Pet. 1:20   "It is true that God CHOSE him to fulfill his part before the world was founded, . . ."

The Amplified New Testament

Rom. 8:29   "For those whom He FOREKNEW—OF WHOM HE WAS AWARE . . ."

Rom. 11:2   "No, God has not rejected *and* disowned His people [whose destiny] He had MARKED OUT *and* APPOINTED *and* FOREKNOWN FROM THE BEGINNING."

Williams' New Testament

Rom. 8:29   "For those ON WHOM HE SET HIS HEART BEFOREHAND He marked off as His own to be made like His Son, . . ." Williams gives the following footnote: "Lit., *foreknew* but in Septuagint used as translated."

Rom. 11:2   "No, God has not disowned His people, ON WHOM HE SET HIS HEART BEFOREHAND."

I Pet. 1:20   "who was FOREORDAINED . . ."

The New English Bible

Rom. 8:29   "For God KNEW HIS OWN BEFORE EVEN THEY WERE, and also ordained that they should be shaped to the likeness of his Son, . . ."

Rom. 11:2   "No! God has not rejected the people which he ACKNOWLEDGED OF OLD AS HIS OWN."

I Pet. 1:2   "chosen of old IN THE PURPOSE of God the Father, . . ."

I Pet. 1:20   "He was PREDESTINED before the foundation of the world, . . ."

Acts 2:23   "When he had been given to you, by the deliberate will and PLAN of God, you used heathen men to crucify and kill him."

D. Conclusion

As was stated at the outset, Calvinists reject the Arminian interpretation of Romans 8:29 on two grounds, (1) because it is not in keeping with the meaning of Paul's language, and (2) because it is out of harmony with the system of doctrine taught in the rest of the Scriptures. This Appendix has been devoted to demonstrating the validity of the first objection. Appendix D, which follows, on Romans and the Five Points of Calvinism, deals with the latter objection.

APPENDIX D

ROMANS AND THE "FIVE POINTS" OF CALVINISM

A Personal Word of Explanation to the Reader

It is assumed that you have worked your way through Paul's letter and have now come to the last section of this study. You may be wondering why an appendix dealing with the "Five Points of Calvinism" would be added to an outline of Romans. What connection, if any, exists between the two and what justification can there be for such an addition?

In your study of Romans you have come face to face with some of the most sobering (and to those who are saved, comforting) doctrines that have ever been revealed by God to man. Among other things, you were confronted with the apostle's teaching concerning the sinner's complete inability to save himself (Chs. 1-3), justification by faith alone, based on the substitutionary work of Christ, who, as the "last Adam" acted as the representative of *His* people (Chs. 3-5), the eternal security of those who have been justified through faith (Ch. 8), and God's sovereign election of particular sinners unto salvation—"He has mercy upon whomever He wills, and He hardens the heart of whomever He wills" (Chs. 9, 11). Some of these doctrines may have been new to you; perhaps some were even perplexing. This would be the case for many Christians in our day should they be exposed to these ideas. No doubt, to some, such views would appear not only new but unthinkable. But such an attitude reveals an unfamiliarity with the Scriptures, for these doctrines are emphasized repeatedly throughout the Bible.

There have been times, in the history of the Church, when these truths were openly proclaimed from the pulpit and readily received by multitudes who acknowledged the Christian faith. During such periods these doctrines were regarded as the very foundation of the Gospel—and rightly so! This was the case during the great Protestant Reformation of the 16th century in Germany, France, Holland, etc. As early as the beginning of the 17th century, these doctrines were formulated into a five point system known as "Calvinism." This system of theology has been proclaimed and defended by many outstanding theologians and preachers of both the past and present.

Spurgeon was absolutely correct when, a century ago, he declared that, "It is no novelty, then, that I am preaching; no new doctrine. I love to proclaim these strong old doctrines, that are called by nickname Calvinism, but which are surely and verily the revealed truth of God as it is in Christ Jesus. By this truth I make a pilgrimage into [the] past, and as I go, I see father after father, confessor after confessor, martyr after martyr, standing up to shake hands with me . . . . taking these things to be the standard of my faith, I see the land of the ancients peopled with my brethren; I behold multitudes who confess the same as I do, and acknowledge that this is the religion of God's own church."[1]   In defense of this system of theology, Spurgeon wrote, "I have my own private opinion that there is no such thing as preaching Christ and Him crucified, unless we preach what nowadays is called Calvinism.   It is a nickname to call it Calvinism; Calvinism is the gospel, and nothing else. I do not believe we can preach the gospel, if we do not preach justification by faith, without works; nor unless we preach the sovereignty of God in His dispensation of grace; nor unless we exalt the electing, unchangeable, eternal, immutable, conquering love of Jehovah; nor do I think we can preach the gospel, unless we base it upon the special and particular redemption of His elect and chosen people which Christ wrought out upon the cross; nor can I comprehend a gospel which lets saints fall away after they are called, . . ."[2]   Though a century has passed since Spurgeon made these declarations, the truth has not changed, nor will it!

But the truth can be, and often is, lost to a given locality or a particular generation.   So it is to a great degree in our day.   For this reason, we have added the material which follows with a sincere desire to help clarify the Biblical message of salvation by grace.

Before entering into the discussion of the "five points" let us make clear our threefold purpose.   First, we want to show that the doctrines (listed above) which you encountered in your study of Romans form the heart of that system of theology known to history as Calvinism. Since it is assumed that you are familiar with the contents of Romans, the pages which follow will be devoted entirely to the study of Calvinism; it will be left for you to make the correlation between the doctrines which were set forth by Paul in the Roman letter and the doctrines which, many centuries later, were formulated into the Calvinistic system of theology.   Second, we wish to show that these doctrines are logically interrelated and that when they are viewed together as a system, they explain and support one another in a most remarkable fashion.   Third, and most important! we want to demonstrate that these doctrines which make up *Calvinism* are taught not only in *Romans* but *throughout the Bible!*

The material which follows is divided into two parts.   Part I deals with the origin of the five points and gives an analysis of the contents of the system.   In order to show how and why the five point structure of Calvinism was developed, it will be necessary to deal with the Arminian system of theology.   As the study progresses, it will become increasingly evident that there is no middle ground between these two systems; either

---

[1] C. H. Spurgeon, "Election," Bible Truth Depot, Swengel, Pa., 23 pages.   Also included in *Spurgeon's Sermons on Sovereignty*, Baptist Examiner Book Shop, Ashland, Kentucky.

[2] *C. H. Spurgeon's Autobiography*, Vol. I, p. 172.

one is a Calvinist or he is an Arminian—he cannot be both, for the two systems are mutually exclusive of each other.

Part II is devoted to a Biblical defense of the five points. Each point is briefly introduced and related to the overall system; then some of the more prominent verses in which it is supported are quoted in full. It is important that you carefully study Part I first and clearly understand the issues at stake before moving into the Biblical proof of the system presented in Part II.

PART ONE

A BRIEF SURVEY OF THE ORIGIN AND CONTENTS OF THE "FIVE POINTS" OF CALVINISM

I.   The Origin of the "Five Points"

To understand how and why the system of theology known to history as Calvinism came to bear this name and to be formulated into five points, one must understand the theological conflict which occurred in Holland during the first quarter of the seventeenth century.

A.   The Protest of the Arminian Party

In 1610, just one year after the death of James Arminius (a Dutch seminary professor) *five articles of faith* based on his teachings were drawn up by his followers. The Arminians, as his followers came to be called, presented these five doctrines to the State of Holland in the form of a "Remonstrance" (i.e., a protest). The Arminian party insisted that the Belgic Confession of Faith and the Heidelberg Catechism (the official expression of the doctrinal position of the Churches of Holland) be changed to conform to the doctrinal views contained in the Remonstrance. The Arminians objected to those doctrines upheld in both the Catechism and the Confession relating to divine sovereignty, human inability, unconditional election or predestination, particular redemption, irresistible grace, and the perseverance of the saints. It was in connection with these matters that they wanted the official standards of the Church of Holland revised.

B.   The "Five Points" of Arminianism

Roger Nicole summarizes the five articles contained in the Remonstrance as follows: "I. God elects or reproves on the basis of foreseen faith or unbelief. II. Christ died for all men and for every man, although only believers are saved. III. Man is so depraved that divine grace is necessary unto faith or any good deed. IV. This grace may be resisted. V. Whether all who are truly regenerate will certainly persevere in the faith is a point which needs further investigation."[3]

The last article was later altered so as to definitely teach the possibility of the truly regenerate believer's losing his faith and thus losing his salvation. Arminians however have not been in agreement on this point—some have held that all who are regenerated by the Spirit of God are eternally secure and can never perish.

---

[3] Roger Nicole, "Arminianism," *Baker's Dictionary of Theology*, p. 64.

C. The Philosophical Basis of Arminianism

J. I. Packer, in analyzing the system of thought embodied in the Remonstrance, observes, "The theology which it contained (known to history as Arminianism) stemmed from two philosophical principles: first, that divine sovereignty is not compatible with human freedom, nor therefore with human responsibility; second, that ability limits obligation . . . . From these principles, the Arminians drew two deductions: first, that since the Bible regards faith as a free and responsible act, it cannot be caused by God, but is exercised independently of Him; second, that since the Bible regards faith as obligatory on the part of all who hear the gospel, ability to believe must be universal. Hence, they maintained, Scripture must be interpreted as teaching the following positions: (1.) Man is never so completely corrupted by sin that he cannot savingly believe the gospel when it is put before him, nor (2.) is he ever so completely controlled by God that he cannot reject it. (3.) God's election of those who shall be saved is prompted by His foreseeing that they will of their own accord believe. (4.) Christ's death did not ensure the salvation of anyone, for it did not secure the gift of faith to anyone (there is no such gift); what it did was rather to create a possibility of salvation for everyone if they believe. (5.) It rests with believers to keep themselves in a state of grace by keeping up their faith; those who fail here fall away and are lost. Thus, Arminianism made man's salvation depend ultimately on man himself, saving faith being viewed throughout as man's own work and, because his own, not God's in him."[4]

D. The Rejection of Arminianism by the Synod of Dort and the Formation of the Five Points of Calvinism

A national Synod was called to meet in Dort in 1618 for the purpose of examining the views of Arminius in the light of Scripture. The Great Synod was convened by the States-General of Holland on November 13, 1618. There were 84 members and 18 secular commissioners. Included were 27 delegates from Germany, the Palatinate, Switzerland and England. There were 154 sessions held during the seven months that the Synod met to consider these matters, the last of which was on May 9, 1619.

"The Synod," Warburton writes, "had given a very close examination to the 'five points' which had been advanced by the Remonstrants, and had compared the teaching advanced in them with the testimony of Scripture. Failing to reconcile that teaching with the Word of God, which they had definitely declared could alone be accepted by them as the rule of faith, they had unanimously rejected them. They felt, however, that a mere rejection was not sufficient. It remained for them

---

[4]James I. Packer, "Introductory Essay," John Owen, *The Death of Death in the Death of Christ*, pp. 3, 4.

142

to set forth the true Calvinistic teaching in relationship to those matters which had been called into question. This they proceeded to do, embodying the Calvinistic position in five chapters which have ever since been known as 'the five points of Calvinism.' "[5]   The name *Calvinism* was derived from the great French reformer, John Calvin (1509-1564), who had done so much in expounding and defending these views.

No doubt it will seem strange to many in our day that the Synod of Dort rejected as heretical the five doctrines advanced by the Arminians, for these doctrines have gained wide acceptance in the modern Church. In fact, they are seldom questioned in our generation. But the vast majority of the Protestant theologians of that day took a much different view of the matter. They maintained that the Bible set forth a system of doctrine quite different from that advocated by the Arminian party. Salvation was viewed by the members of the Synod as *a work of grace from beginning to end;* in no sense did they believe that the sinner saved himself or contributed to his salvation. Adam's fall had completely ruined the race. All men were by nature spiritually dead and their wills were in bondage to sin and Satan. The ability to believe the gospel was itself a gift from God, bestowed only upon those whom He had chosen to be the objects of His unmerited favor. It was not man, but God, who determined which sinners would be shown mercy and saved. This, in essence, is what the members of the Synod of Dort understood the Bible to teach.

In the chart which follows, the five points of Arminianism (rejected by the Synod) and the five points of Calvinism (set forth by the Synod) are given, side by side, so that it might be readily seen wherein and to what extent these two systems of doctrine differ.

---

[5] Ben A. Warburton, *Calvinism*, p. 61. Although there were five Calvinistic Articles, there were only four chapters. This was because the third and fourth Articles were combined into one chapter. Consequently, the third chapter is always designated as Chapter III-IV.

II. The Five Points of Arminianism Contrasted with the Five Points of Calvinism

THE "FIVE POINTS" OF ARMINIANISM	THE "FIVE POINTS" OF CALVINISM
1. *Free Will or Human Ability*	1. *Total Inability or Total Depravity*
Although human nature was seriously affected by the fall, man has not been left in a state of total spiritual helplessness. God graciously enables every sinner to repent and believe, but He does so in such a manner as not to interfere with man's freedom. Each sinner possesses a free will, and his eternal destiny depends on how he uses it. Man's freedom consists of his ability to choose good over evil in spiritual matters; his will is not enslaved to his sinful nature. The sinner has the power to either cooperate with God's S p i r i t and be regenerated or resist God's grace and perish. The lost sinner needs the Spirit's assistance, but he d o e s not have to be regenerated by the Spirit before he can believe, for faith is man's act and precedes the new birth. Faith is the sinner's gift to God; it is man's contribution to salvation.	Because of the fall, man is unable of himself to savingly believe the gospel. The sinner is dead, blind, and deaf to the things of God; his heart is deceitful a n d desperately corrupt. His will is not free, it is in bondage to his evil nature, therefore, he will not—indeed he cannot—choose good over evil in the spiritual r e a l m. Consequently, it takes much more than the Spirit's assistance to bring a s i n n e r to Christ—it takes regeneration by which the Spirit makes the sinner alive and gives him a new nature. Faith is not something man contributes to salvation but is itself a part of God's gift of salvation—it is God's gift to the sinner, not the sinner's gift to God.
2. *Conditional Election*	2. *Unconditional Election*
God's choice of certain individuals unto salvation before the foundation of the w o r l d was based upon His foreseeing that they would respond to His call. He selected only t h o s e	God's choice of certain individuals unto salvation before the foundation of the w o r l d rested solely in His own sovereign will. His choice of particular sinners was not based on

whom He knew would of themselves freely believe the gospel. Election therefore was determined by or conditioned upon what man would do. The faith which God foresaw and upon which He based His choice was not given to the sinner by God (it was not created by the regenerating power of the Holy Spirit) but r e s u l t e d solely from man's will. It was left entirely up to man as to who would believe and therefore as to who would be elected unto salvation. God c h o s e those whom He knew would, of their own free will, choose Christ. Thus the sinner's c h o i c e of Christ, not God's choice of the sinner, is the ultimate cause of salvation.

any foreseen response or obedience on their part, such as faith, repentance, etc. On the contrary, God gives faith and repentance to each individual whom He selected. These acts are the result, not the cause of God's choice. Election therefore was not determined by or conditioned upon any virtuous quality or act foreseen in man. Those whom God sovereignly elected He brings through the power of the Spirit to a willing acceptance of C h r i s t. Thus God's choice of the sinner, not the sinner's choice of Christ, is the ultimate cause of salvation.

3. *Universal Redemption or General Atonement*

C h r i s t' s redeeming work made it possible for everyone to be saved but did not actually secure the salvation of anyone. Although Christ died for all men and for every man, only those who believe in Him are saved. His death enabled God to pardon sinners on the condition that they believe, but it did not actually put away anyone's sins. Christ's redemption becomes effective only if man chooses to accept it.

3. *Particular Redemption or Limited Atonement*

C h r i s t' s redeeming work was intended to save the elect only and actually secured salvation for them. His death was a substitutionary endurance of the penalty of sin in the place of certain specified sinners. In addition to putting away the sins of His people, Christ's redemption secured everything necessary for their salvation, including faith which unites them to Him. The gift of faith is infallibly a p p l i e d by the Spirit to all for whom Christ died, t h e r e b y guaranteeing their salvation.

145

4. *The Holy Spirit Can Be Effectually Resisted*

The Spirit calls inwardly all those who are called outwardly by the gospel invitation; He does all that He can to bring every sinner to salvation. But inasmuch as man is free, he can successfully r e s i s t the Spirit's call. The Spirit cannot regenerate the sinner until he believes; faith (which is man's contribution) precedes a n d makes possible the new birth. Thus, man's free will limits the Spirit in the application of Christ's s a v i n g work. The Holy Spirit can only draw to Christ those who allow Him to have His way with them. Until the s i n n e r responds, the Spirit cannot give life. God's grace, therefore, is not invincible; it can be, and often is, resisted and thwarted by man.

4. *The Efficacious Call of the Spirit or Irresistible Grace*

In addition to the outward general call to salvation which is made to everyone who hears the gospel, the Holy Spirit extends to the elect a special inward call that i n e v i t a b l y brings them to salvation. The external call (which is made to all without distinction) can be, and often is, rejected; whereas the i n t e r n a l call (which is made only to the elect) cannot be rejected; it always results in conversion. By means of this special call the Spirit irresistibly draws s i n n e r s to Christ. He is not limited in His work of applying salvation by man's will, nor is He dependent upon man's cooperation for success. The S p i r i t graciously causes the elect sinner to cooperate, to believe, to repent, to come freely and willingly to Christ. God's grace, therefore, is invincible; it never fails to result in the salvation of those to whom it is extended.

5. *Falling from Grace*

Those who believe and are truly saved can lose their salvation by failing to keep up their faith, etc.

All Arminians have not been agreed on this p o i n t; some have held that believers are eternally secure in Christ— that once a sinner is regenerated, he can never be lost.

5. *Perseverance of the Saints*

All who were chosen by God, redeemed by Christ, and given faith by the Spirit are eternally s a v e d. They are kept in faith by the p o w e r of Almighty God and thus persevere to the end.

According to Arminianism:	According to Calvinism:
Salvation is accomplished through the combined efforts of *God* (who takes the initiative) and *man* (who must respond)—man's response being the determining factor. God has provided salvation for everyone, but His provision becomes effective only for those who, of their own free will, "choose" to cooperate with Him and accept His offer of grace. At the crucial point, man's will plays a decisive role; thus *man*, not God, determines who will be the recipients of the gift of salvation.	Salvation is accomplished by the almighty power of the Triune God. The Father chose a people, the Son died for them, the Holy Spirit makes Christ's death effective by bringing the elect to faith and repentance, thereby causing them to willingly obey the gospel. The entire process (election, redemption, regeneration) is the work of God and is by grace alone. Thus *God*, not man, determines who will be the recipients of the gift of salvation.
REJECTED by the Synod of Dort	**REAFFIRMED** by the Synod of Dort
This was the system of thought contained in the "Remonstrance" (though the "five points" were not originally arranged in this order). It was submitted by the Arminians to the Church of Holland in 1610 for adoption but was rejected by the Synod of Dort in 1619 on the ground that it was unscriptural.	This system of theology was reaffirmed by the Synod of Dort in 1619 as the doctrine of salvation contained in the Holy Scriptures. The system was at that time formulated into "five points" (in answer to the five points submitted by the Arminians) and has ever since been known as "the five points of Calvinism."

III.   The Basic Concepts of Each System Are Much Older Than the Synod of Dort

A.   The Controversy between Pelagius and Augustine

Neither John Calvin nor James Arminius originated the basic concepts which undergird the two systems that bear their names. The fundamental principles of each system can be traced back many centuries prior to the time when these two men lived. For example, the basic doctrines of the Calvinistic position had been vigorously defended by Augustine against Pelagius during the fifth century. Cunningham writes, "As there was nothing new in substance in the Calvinism of Calvin, so there was nothing new in the Arminianism of Arminius; . . . . The doctrines of Arminius can be traced back as far as the time of Clemens Alexandrinus, and seem to have been held by many of the fathers of the third and fourth centuries, having been diffused in the church through the corrupting influence of pagan philosophy. Pelagius and his followers, in the fifth century, were as decidedly opposed to Calvinism as Arminius was, though they deviated much further from sound doctrine than he did."[6]

Pelagius denied that human nature had been corrupted by sin. He maintained that the only ill effects which the race had suffered as the result of Adam's transgression was the bad example which he had set for mankind. According to Pelagius, every infant comes into the world in the same condition as Adam was before the fall. His leading principle was that *man's will is absolutely free.* Hence every one has the power, within himself, to believe the gospel as well as to perfectly keep the law of God.

Augustine, on the other hand, maintained that human nature had been so completely corrupted by Adam's fall that no one, in himself, has the ability to obey either the law or the gospel. Divine grace is essential if sinners are to believe and be saved, and this grace is extended only to those whom God predestined to eternal life before the foundation of the world. The act of faith, therefore, results, not from the sinner's free will (as Pelagius taught) but from God's free grace which is bestowed on the elect only.

B.   Semi-Pelagianism, the Forerunner of Arminianism

Smeaton, in showing how Semi-Pelagianism (the forerunner of Arminianism) originated, states that "Augustin's unanswerable polemic had so fully discredited Pelagianism in the field of argument, that it could no longer be made plausible to the Christian mind. It collapsed. But a new system soon presented itself, teaching that *man with his own natural powers is able to take the first step toward his conversion,* and that this obtains or merits the Spirit's assistance. Cassian . . . was the founder of this middle way, which came to be called SEMI-PELAGIAN-ISM, because it occupied intermediate ground between Pelagianism and Augustinianism, and took in elements from both. He acknowledged that Adam's sin extended to his posterity, and that human nature was corrupted by original sin. But, on the other hand, he held a system of universal grace for all men alike, making the final decision in the case of every individual dependent on the exercise of free-will." Speaking of those who followed Cassian, Smeaton continues, "they held that the first movement of the will in the assent of faith must be ascribed to the natural powers of the human mind. This was their primary error. Their maxim was: '*it is mine to be willing* to believe, and it is the part of God's grace to assist.' They asserted the sufficiency of Christ's grace for all, and that every one, according to his own will, obeyed or rejected the invitation, while God equally wished and equally aided all men to be saved . . . . The entire system thus formed is a half-way house containing elements

_____
[6] William Cunningham, *Historical Theology,* Vol. II, p. 374.

of error and elements of truth, and not at all differing from the Arminianism which, after the resuscitation of the doctrines of grace by the Reformers, diffused itself in the very same way through the different Churches."[7]

C. Calvinism, the Theology of the Reformation

The leaders of the Protestant Reformation of the sixteenth century rejected Pelagianism and Semi-Pelagianism on the ground that both systems were unscriptural. Like Augustine, the Reformers held to the doctrines of the sovereignty of God, the total depravity of man, and of unconditional election. As Boettner shows, they stood together in their view of predestination. "It was taught not only by Calvin, but by Luther, Zwingli, Melancthon (although Melancthon later retreated toward the Semi-Pelagian position), by Bullinger, Bucer, and all of the outstanding leaders in the Reformation. While differing on some other points they agreed on this doctrine of Predestination and taught it with emphasis. Luther's chief work, 'The Bondage of the Will,' shows that he went into the doctrine as heartily as did Calvin himself."[8]

Packer states that "all the leading Protestant theologians of the first epoch of the Reformation, stood on precisely the same ground here. On other points, they had their differences; but in asserting the helplessness of man in sin, and the sovereignty of God in grace, they were entirely at one. To all of them, these doctrines were the very life-blood of the Christian faith . . . . To the Reformers, the crucial question was not simply, whether God justifies believers without works of law. It was the broader question, whether sinners are wholly helpless in their sin, and whether God is to be thought of as saving them by free, unconditional, invincible grace, not only justifying them for Christ's sake when they come to faith, but also raising them from the death of sin by His quickening Spirit in order to bring them to faith. Here was the crucial issue: whether God is the author, not merely of justification, but also of faith; whether, in the last analysis, Christianity is a religion of utter reliance on God for salvation and all things necessary to it, or of self-reliance and self-effort."[9]

---

[7] George Smeaton, *The Doctrine of the Holy Spirit*, pp. 300, 301. Italics and capitalizations are his. Semi-Pelagianism was repudiated by the Synod of Orange in 529 A. D., just as Arminianism was repudiated by the Synod of Dort almost eleven hundred years later.

[8] Loraine Boettner, *The Reformed Doctrine of Predestination*, p. 1.

[9] James I. Packer and O. R. Johnston, "Historical and Theological Introduction," Martin Luther, *Bondage of the Will*, pp. 58, 59. In speaking of the English Reformation, Buis shows that "the advocates of that Reformation were definitely Calvinistic." To substantiate this he quotes the following from Fisher, " 'The Anglican Church agreed with the Protestant Churches on the continent on the subject of predestination. On this subject, for a long period, the Protestants generally were united in opinion.' 'The leaders of the English Reformation, from the time when the death of Henry VIII placed them firmly upon Protestant ground, profess the doctrine of absolute as distinguished from conditional predestination.' " Harry Buis, *Historic Protestantism and Predestination*, p. 87.

Thus it is evident that the five points of Calvinism, drawn up by the Synod of Dort in 1619, was by no means a new system of theology. On the contrary, as Dr. Wyllie asserts of the Synod, "It met at a great crisis and it was called to review, re-examine and authenticate over again, in the second generation since the rise of the Reformation, that body of truth and system of doctrine which that great movement had published to the world."[10]

IV. The Difference between Calvinism and Arminianism

The issues involved in this historic controversy are indeed grave, for they vitally affect the Christian's concept of God, of sin, and of salvation. Packer, in contrasting these two systems, is certainly correct in asserting that "The difference between them is not primarily one of emphasis, but of content. One proclaims a God Who saves; the other speaks of a God Who enables man to save himself. One view [Calvinism] presents the three great acts of the Holy Trinity for the recovering of lost mankind—election by the Father, redemption by the Son, calling by the Spirit—as directed towards the same persons, and as securing their salvation infallibly. The other view [Arminianism] gives each act a different reference (the objects of redemption being all mankind, of calling, those who hear the gospel, and of election, those hearers who respond), and denies that any man's salvation is secured by any of them. The two theologies thus conceive the plan of salvation in quite different terms. One makes salvation depend on the work of God, the other on a work of man; one regards faith as part of God's gift of salvation, the other as man's own contribution to salvation; one gives all the glory of saving believers to God, the other divides the praise between God, Who, so to speak, built the machinery of salvation, and man, who by believing operated it. Plainly, these differences are important, and the permanent value of the 'five points,' as a summary of Calvinism, is that they make clear the points at which, and the extent to which, these two conceptions are at variance."[11]

V. The *One Point* Which the "Five Points" of Calvinism Are Concerned to Establish

While recognizing the permanent value of the five points as a summary of Calvinism, Packer warns against simply equating Calvinism with the five points. He gives several excellent reasons why such an equation is incorrect, one of which we quote: ". . . the very act of setting

---

[10] Quoted by Warburton, *Calvinism*, p. 58. Smeaton says of the work of the Synod of Dort that "it may be questioned whether anything more valuable as an ecclesiastical testimony for the doctrines of sovereign, special, efficacious grace was ever prepared on this important theme since the days of the apostles." George Smeaton, *The Doctrine of the Holy Spirit*, p. 320.

[11] Packer, "Introductory Essay," (above, fn. 4), pp. 4,5.

out Calvinistic soteriology [the doctrine of salvation] in the form of five distinct points (a number due, as we saw, merely to the fact that there were five Arminian points for the Synod of Dort to answer) tends to obscure the organic character of Calvinistic thought on this subject. For the five points, though separately stated, are really inseparable. They hang together; you cannot reject one without rejecting them all, at least in the sense in which the Synod meant them. For to Calvinism there is really only *one* point to be made in the field of soteriology: the point that *God saves sinners*. *God*—the Triune Jehovah, Father, Son and Spirit; three Persons working together in sovereign wisdom, power and love to achieve the salvation of a chosen people, the Father electing, the Son fulfilling the Father's will by redeeming, the Spirit executing the purpose of Father and Son by renewing. *Saves*—does everything, first to last, that is involved in bringing man from death in sin to life in glory: plans, achieves and communicates redemption, calls and keeps, justifies, sanctifies, glorifies. *Sinners*—men as God finds them, guilty, vile, helpless, powerless, unable to lift a finger to do God's will or better their spiritual lot. *God saves sinners*—and the force of this confession may not be weakened by disrupting the unity of the work of the Trinity, or by dividing the achievement of salvation between God and man and making the decisive part man's own, or by soft-pedalling the sinner's inability so as to allow him to share the praise of his salvation with his Saviour. This is the one point of Calvinistic soteriology which the 'five points' are concerned to establish and Arminianism in all its forms to deny: namely, that sinners do not save themselves in any sense at all, but that salvation, first and last, whole and entire, past, present and future, is of the Lord, to whom be glory for ever; amen."[12]

This brings to completion Part One of our survey. No attempt whatsoever has been made in this section to prove the truthfulness of the Calvinistic doctrines. Our sole purpose has been to give a brief history of the system and to explain its contents. We are now ready to consider its Biblical support.

---

[12] Packer, "Introductory Essay," (above, fn. 4), p. 6. Italics are his.

151

PART TWO

BIBLICAL SUPPORT FOR THE "FIVE POINTS" OF CALVINISM

Introductory Remarks

The question of supreme importance is not how the system under consideration came to be formulated into five points, or why it was named Calvinism, but rather *is it supported by Scripture?* The final court of appeal for determining the validity of any theological system is the inspired, authoritative Word of God. If Calvinism can be verified by clear and explicit declarations of Scripture, then it must be received by Christians; if not, it must be rejected. For this reason, Biblical passages are given below in support of the five points.

After each point has been introduced, some of the more important verses in which it is taught are quoted. All quotations are from the *Revised Standard Version* of the Bible. In each case, the italics within the verses are ours. Apart from the remarks contained in the headings under which the verses are given, there are no explanatory comments as to their meaning. This procedure was necessary because of the limited design of this introductory survey.

Although the "five points" are dealt with below under separate headings, and texts are classified in support of each of them individually, they must not be evaluated on a purely individual basis. For these five doctrines are not presented in the Bible as separate and independent units of truth. On the contrary, in the Biblical message they are woven into one harmonious, interrelated system in which God's plan for recovering lost sinners is marvelously displayed. In fact, these doctrines are so inseparably connected that no one of them can be fully appreciated unless it is properly related to, and viewed in light of the other four; for *they mutually explain and support one another.* To judge these doctrines individually without relating each to the others would be like attempting to evaluate one of Rembrandt's paintings by looking at only one color at a time and never viewing the work as a whole. Do not, therefore, merely judge the Biblical evidence for each point separately, but rather consider carefully the collective value of the evidence when these five doctrines are viewed together as a system. When thus properly correlated, they form a fivefold cord of unbreakable strength.

I. TOTAL DEPRAVITY OR TOTAL INABILITY

The view one takes concerning salvation will be determined, to a large extent, by the view one takes concerning sin and its effects on human nature. It is not surprising, therefore, that the first article dealt with in the Calvinistic system is the Biblical doctrine of total inability or total depravity.

When Calvinists speak of man as being totally depraved, they mean that man's nature is corrupt, perverse, and sinful throughout. The adjective "total" does not mean that each sinner is as totally or completely corrupt in his actions and thoughts as it is possible for him to be. Instead, the word "total" is used to indicate that the *whole* of man's being has been affected by sin. The corruption extends to *every part* of man, his body and soul; sin has affected all (the totality) of man's faculties—his mind, his will, etc.

As a result of this inborn corruption, the natural man is totally unable to do anything spiritually good; thus Calvinists speak of man's "total inability." The inability intended by this terminology is *spiritual inability;* it means that the sinner is so spiritually bankrupt that *he can do nothing pertaining to his salvation.* It is quite evident that many unsaved people, when judged by man's standards, do possess admirable qualities and do perform virtuous acts. But in the spiritual realm, when judged by God's standards, the unsaved sinner is incapable of good. The natural man is enslaved to sin; he is a child of Satan, rebellious toward God, blind to truth, corrupt, and unable to save himself or to prepare himself for salvation. In short, the unregenerate man is DEAD IN SIN, and his WILL IS ENSLAVED to his evil nature.

Man did not come from the hands of his Creator in this depraved, corrupt condition. God made Adam upright; there was no evil whatsoever in his nature. Originally, Adam's will was free from the dominion of sin; he was under no natural compulsion to choose evil, but through his fall he brought spiritual death upon himself and all his posterity. He thereby plunged himself and the entire race into spiritual ruin and lost for himself and his descendants the ability to make right choices in the spiritual realm. His descendants are still free to choose—every man makes choices throughout life—but inasmuch as Adam's offspring are born with sinful natures, they do not have the ABILITY to choose spiritual good over evil. Consequently, man's will is no longer free (i.e., free from the dominion of sin) as Adam's will was free before the fall. Instead, man's will, as the result of inherited depravity, is in bondage to his sinful nature.

The Westminster Confession of Faith gives a clear, concise statement of this doctrine. "Man, by his fall into a state of sin, hath wholly lost all ability of will to any spiritual good accompanying salvation; so as a natural man, being altogether averse from good, and dead in sin, is not able, by his own strength, to convert himself, or to prepare himself thereunto."[13]

A. As the result of Adam's transgression, men are born in sin and by nature are spiritually dead; therefore, if they are to become God's children and enter His kingdom, they must be born anew of the Spirit.

---

[13] Chapter IX, Section 3.

1. When Adam was placed in the garden of Eden, he was warned
    not to eat the fruit of the tree of knowledge of good and evil
    on the threat of immediate *spiritual* death.

    Genesis 2:16,17: And the Lord God commanded the man, say-
        ing, "You may freely eat of every tree of the garden; but
        of the tree of the knowledge of good and evil you shall
        not eat, for in the day that you eat of it you shall *die*."

2. Adam disobeyed and ate of the forbidden fruit (Genesis 3:1-7);
    consequently, he brought spiritual death upon himself and upon
    the race.

    Romans 5:12: Therefore as sin came into the world through
        one man [Adam, see vs. 14] and *death* through sin, and
        so death spread to all men because all men sinned.

    Ephesians 2:1-3: And you he *made alive,* when you were *dead*
        through the trespasses and sins in which you once walked,
        following the course of this world, following the prince of
        the power of the air, the spirit that is now at work in
        the sons of disobedience. Among these we all once lived
        in the passions of our flesh, following the desires of body
        and mind, and so we were *by nature* children of wrath, like
        the rest of mankind.

    Colossians 2:13: And you, who were *dead* in trespasses and the
        uncircumcision of your flesh, *God made alive* together with
        him, having forgiven us all our trespasses.

3. David confessed that he, as well as all other men, was born in
    sin.

    Psalm 51:5: Behold, I was brought forth in iniquity, and in
        sin did my mother conceive me.

    Psalm 58:3: The wicked go astray from the womb, they err
        from their birth, speaking lies.

4. Because men are born in sin and are by nature spiritually dead,
    Jesus taught that men must be born anew if they are to enter
    God's kingdom.

    John 3:5-7: Jesus answered, "Truly, truly, I say to you,
        unless one is born of water and the Spirit, he cannot *enter*
        the kingdom of God. That which is born of the flesh is
        flesh, and that which is born of the Spirit is spirit. Do
        not marvel that I said to you, '*You must be born anew*.' "
        Compare John 1:12,13.

B. As the result of the fall, men are blind and deaf to spiritual truth. Their minds are darkened by sin; their hearts are corrupt and evil.

Genesis 6:5: The Lord saw that the wickedness of man was great in the earth, and that *every imagination of the thoughts of his heart was only evil continually.*

Genesis 8:21: . . . the imagination of man's heart is *evil* from his youth . . .

Ecclesiastes 9:3: . . . the *hearts* of men are *full of evil,* and madness is in their hearts while they live . . .

Jeremiah 17:9: The *heart* is *deceitful above all things,* and *desperately corrupt;* who can understand it?

Mark 7:21-23: "For from within, *out of the heart of man,* come evil thoughts, fornication, theft, murder, adultery, coveting, wickedness, deceit, licentiousness, envy, slander, pride, foolishness. All these evil things come from within, and they defile a man."

John 3:19: And this is the judgment, that the light has come into the world, and *men loved darkness* rather than light, because their deeds were evil.

Romans 8:7,8: For the *mind* that is set on the flesh is hostile to God; *it* does not submit to God's law, indeed it *cannot;* and those who are in the flesh *cannot please God.*

I Corinthians 2:14: The unspiritual man does not receive the gifts of the Spirit of God, for they are folly to him, and *he is not able to understand them* because they are spiritually discerned.

Ephesians 4:17-19: Now this I affirm and testify in the Lord, that you must no longer live as the Gentiles do, in the futility of their minds; they are *darkened in their understanding,* alienated from the life of God because of the ignorance that is in them, *due to their hardness of heart;* they have become callous and have given themselves up to licentiousness, greedy to practice every kind of uncleanness.

Ephesians 5:8: For once you were *darkness,* but now you are light in the Lord . . .

Titus 1:15: To the pure all things are pure, but to the corrupt and unbelieving nothing is pure; *their very minds and consciences are corrupted.*

C. Before sinners are born into God's kingdom through the regenerating power of the Spirit, they are children of the devil and under his control; they are slaves to sin.

John 8:44: You are of *your father the devil*, and *your will* is to do your father's desires.

Ephesians 2:1,2: And you he made alive, when you were dead through the trespasses and sins in which you once walked, following the course of this world, *following the prince of the power of the air*, the spirit that is now at work in the sons of disobedience.

II Timothy 2:25,26: God may perhaps grant that they will repent and come to know the truth, and they may escape from *the snare of the devil*, after being *captured by him to do his will.*

I John 3:10: By this it may be seen who are the children of God, and who are the *children of the devil:* whoever does not do right is not of God, nor he who does not love his brother.

I John 5:19: We know that we are of God, and the whole world is *in the power of the evil one.*

John 8:34: Jesus answered them, "Truly, truly, I say to you, every one who commits sin is *a slave to sin.*"

Romans 6:20: When you were *slaves of sin*, you were free in regard to righteousness.

Titus 3:3: For we ourselves were once foolish, disobedient, led astray, *slaves* to various passions and pleasures, passing our days in malice and envy, hated by men and hating one another.

D. The reign of sin is universal; all men are under its power; consequently, none is righteous—not even one!

II Chronicles 6:36: . . . for there is *no man* who does not sin . . . Compare I Kings 8:46.

Job 15:14-16: What is man, that he can be clean? Or he that is born of a woman, that he can be righteous? Behold, God puts no trust in his holy ones, and the heavens are not clean in his sight; how much less one who is abominable and corrupt, a man who drinks iniquity like water!

Psalm 130:3: If thou, O Lord, shouldst mark iniquities, Lord, *who could stand?*

Psalm 143:2: Enter not into judgment with thy servant; for no *man living* is righteous before thee.

Proverbs 20:9: *Who* can say, "I have made my heart clean; I am pure from my sin"?

Ecclesiastes 7:20: Surely there is *not a righteous man on earth* who does good and never sins.

Ecclesiastes 7:29: Behold, this alone I found, that God made man upright, but they have sought out many devices.

Isaiah 53:6: All we like sheep have gone astray; we have turned every one to his own way. . .

Isaiah 64:6: We have all become like one who is unclean, and all our righteous deeds are like a polluted garment. We all fade like a leaf, and our iniquities, like the wind, take us away.

Romans 3:9-12: What then? Are we Jews any better off? No, not at all; for I have already charged that *all men,* both Jews and Greeks, *are under the power of sin,* as it is written; "None is righteous, no, not one; no one understands, no one seeks for God. All have turned aside, together they have gone wrong; *no one does good, not even one."*

James 3:2,8: For we all make many mistakes, and if any one makes no mistakes in what he says he is a perfect man, able to bridle the whole body also . . . . but no human being can tame the tongue—a restless evil, full of deadly poison.

I John 1:8,10: If we say we have no sin, we deceive ourselves, and the truth is not in us . . . . If we say we have not sinned, we make him a liar, and his word is not in us.

E. Men left in their dead state are unable of themselves to repent, to believe the gospel, or to come to Christ. They have no power within themselves to change their natures or to prepare themselves for salvation.

Job 14:4: Who can bring a clean thing out of an unclean? There is not one.

Jeremiah 13:23: Can the Ethiopian change his skin or the leopard his spots? Then also you can do good who are accustomed to do evil.

Matthew 7:16-18: You will know them by their fruits. Are grapes gathered from thorns, or figs from thistles? So, every sound tree bears good fruit, but the bad tree bears evil fruit. A sound tree cannot bear evil fruit, *nor can a bad tree bear good fruit.*

Matthew 12:33: "Either make the tree good, and its fruit good; or make the tree bad, and its fruit bad; for the tree is known by its fruit."

John 6:44: *No one can come to me unless* the Father who sent me *draws him;* and I will raise him up at the last day.

John 6:65: And he said, "This is why I told you that *no one can come to me unless it is granted him* by the Father."

Romans 11:35,36: "Or *who has given a gift to him* that he might be repaid?" For *from him* and through him and to him *are all things.* To him be glory forever. Amen.

I Corinthians 2:14: The *unspiritual man* does not receive the gifts of the Spirit of God, for they are folly to him, and *he is not able to understand them* because they are spiritually discerned.

I Corinthians 4:7: For who sees *anything different in you?* What have you that you did not receive? If then you received it, *why do you boast as if it were not a gift?*

II Corinthians 3:5: Not that we are *sufficient of ourselves* to claim anything as coming from us; our sufficiency is *from God.*

For further Biblical confirmation that men are unable of themselves to do anything toward gaining salvation, see the Scriptures given below under Point IV on Efficacious Grace. Note especially those verses which state that GOD *gives* faith, *grants* repentance, *creates* a new heart within the sinner, and other similar expressions.

II. UNCONDITIONAL ELECTION

Because of Adam's transgression, his descendants enter the world as guilty, lost sinners. As fallen creatures, they have no desire to have fellowship with the Creator. He is holy, just, and good, whereas they are sinful, perverse, and corrupt. Left to their own choices, they inevitably follow the god of this world and do the will of their father, the devil. Consequently, men have cut themselves off from the Lord of heaven and have forfeited all rights to His love and favor. It would have been perfectly just for God to have left all men in their sin and misery and to have shown mercy to none. God was under no obligation whatsoever to provide salvation for anyone. It is in this context that the Bible sets forth the doctrine of election.

The doctrine of election declares that God, before the foundation of the world, chose certain individuals from among the fallen members of Adam's race to be the objects of His undeserved favor. These, and these only, He purposed to save. God could have chosen to save all men (for He had the power and authority to do so) or He could have chosen to save none (for He was under no obligation to show mercy to any)—but He did neither. Instead He chose to save some and to exclude others. His eternal choice of particular sinners unto salvation was not based upon any foreseen act or response on the part of those selected, but was based solely on His own good pleasure and sovereign will. Thus election was not determined by, or conditioned upon, anything that men would do, but resulted entirely from God's self-determined purpose.

Those who were not chosen to salvation were passed by and left to their own evil devices and choices. It is not within the creature's jurisdiction to call into question the justice of the Creator for not choosing every one to salvation. It is enough to know that the Judge of the earth has done right. It should, however, be kept in mind that if God had not graciously *chosen* a people for Himself and sovereignly determined to *provide* salvation for them and *apply* it to them, none would be saved. The fact that He did this for some, to the exclusion of others, is in no way unfair to the latter group, unless of course one maintains that God was under obligation to provide salvation for sinners—a position which the Bible utterly rejects.

The doctrine of election should be viewed not only against the backdrop of human depravity and guilt, but it should also be studied in connection with the *eternal covenant* or agreement made between the members of the Godhead. For it was in the execution of this covenant that the *Father* chose out of the world of lost sinners a definite number of individuals and gave them to the Son to be His people. The *Son*, under the terms of this compact, agreed to do all that was necessary to save those "chosen" and "given" to Him by the Father. The *Spirit's* part in the execution of this covenant was to apply to the elect the salvation secured for them by the Son.

Election, therefore, is but *one* aspect (though an important aspect) of the saving purpose of the Triune God, and thus must not be viewed *as* salvation. For the act of election *itself* saved no one; what it did was to mark out certain individuals for salvation. Consequently, the doctrine of election must not be divorced from the doctrines of human guilt, redemption, and regeneration or else it will be distorted and misrepresented. In other words, if it is to be kept in its proper Biblical balance and correctly understood, *the Father's act of election* must be related to the *redeeming work of the Son* who gave Himself to save the elect and to the *renewing work of the Spirit* who brings the elect to faith in Christ!

A.   General statements showing that God has an elect people, that He predestined them to salvation, and thus to eternal life.

Deuteronomy 10:14,15: Behold, to the Lord your God belong heaven and the heaven of heavens, the earth with all that is in it; yet *the Lord set his heart in love* upon your fathers and *chose* their descendants after them, you above all peoples, as at this day.

Psalm 33:12: Blessed is the nation whose God is the Lord, the people whom he has *chosen* as his heritage!

Psalm 65:4: Blessed is he whom thou dost *choose* and bring near, to dwell in thy courts! We shall be satisfied with the goodness of thy house, thy holy temple!

Psalm 106:5: . . . that I may see the prosperity of thy *chosen ones*, that I may rejoice in the gladness of thy nation, that I may glory with thy heritage.

Haggai 2:23: "On that day, says the Lord of hosts, I will take you, O Zerubbabel my servant, the son of Shealtiel, says the Lord, and make you like a signet ring; for I have *chosen* you, says the Lord of hosts."

Matthew 11:27: ". . . no one knows the Father except the Son and any one to whom the Son *chooses* to reveal him."

Matthew 22:14: "For many are called, but few are *chosen.*"

Matthew 24:22,24,31: And if those days had not been shortened, no human being would be saved; but for the sake of the *elect* those days will be shortened . . . . For false Christs and false prophets will arise and show great signs and wonders, so as to lead astray, if possible, even *the elect* . . . . and he will send out his angels with a loud trumpet call, and they will gather *his elect* from the four winds, from one end of heaven to the other.

Luke 18:7: And will not God vindicate *his elect,* who cry to him day and night?

Romans 8:28-30: We know that in everything God works for good with those who love him, who are *called according to his purpose.* For those whom he foreknew he also *predestined* to be conformed to the image of his Son, in order that he might be the first-born among many brethren. And those whom he predestined he also called; and those whom he called he also justified; and those whom he justified he also glorified.

Romans 8:33: Who shall bring any charge against *God's elect?*

Romans 11:28: As regards the gospel they are enemies of God, for your sake; but as regards *election* they are beloved for the sake of their forefathers.

Colossians 3:12: Put on then, as *God's chosen ones,* holy and beloved, compassion, kindness, . . .

I Thessalonians 5:9: For God has not *destined* us for wrath, *but to obtain salvation* through our Lord Jesus Christ.

Titus 1:1: Paul, a servant of God and an apostle of Jesus Christ, to further the faith of *God's elect* and their knowledge of the truth which accords with godliness . . .

I Peter 1:1,2: To the exiles of the dispersion . . . *chosen* and *destined* by God the Father and sanctified by the Spirit for obedience to Jesus Christ and for sprinkling with his blood . . .

I Peter 2:8,9: . . . for they stumble because they disobey the word, as they were *destined* to do. But you are a *chosen* race, a royal priesthood, a holy nation, God's own people, that you may declare the wonderful deeds of him who *called* you out of darkness into his marvelous light.

Revelation 17:14: "They will make war on the Lamb, and the Lamb will conquer them, for he is Lord of lords and King of kings, and those with him are *called* and *chosen* and faithful."

B. Before the foundation of the world, God chose particular individuals unto salvation. His selection was *not based upon any foreseen response or act* performed by those chosen. Faith and good works are the *result,* not the *cause* of God's choice.

1. God did the choosing.

Mark 13:20: And if the Lord had not shortened the days, no human being would be saved; but for the sake of *the elect, whom he chose,* he shortened the days.

See also I Thessalonians 1:4 and II Thessalonians 2:13 quoted below.

2. God's choice was made before the foundation of the world.

Ephesians 1:4: Even as he *chose* us in him *before the foundation of the world,* that we should be holy and blameless before him.

See II Thessalonians 2:13; II Timothy 1:9; Revelation 13:8 and Revelation 17:8 quoted below.

3. God chose particular individuals unto salvation—their names were written in the book of life before the foundation of the world.

Revelation 13:8: And all who dwell on earth will worship it, every one whose *name* has not been *written before the foundation of the world* in the book of life of the Lamb that was slain.

Revelation 17:8: ". . . and the dwellers on earth whose *names* have not been *written* in the book of life *from the foundation of the world,* will marvel to behold the beast, because it was and is not and is to come."

4. God's choice was not based upon any forseen merit residing in those whom He chose, nor was it based on any foreseen good works performed by them.

    Romans 9:11-13: Though they were *not yet born and had done nothing either good or bad,* in order that God's purpose of *election* might continue, *not because of works* but because of his *call,* she was told, "The elder will serve the younger." As it is written, "Jacob I loved, but Esau I hated."

    Romans 9:16: So it depends *not upon man's will or exertion,* but upon *God's mercy.*

    Romans 10:20: ". . . I have been found by those who did not seek me; I have shown myself to those who did not ask for me."

    I Corinthians 1:27-29: *God chose* what is *foolish* in the world to shame the wise, *God chose* what is *weak* in the world to shame the strong, *God chose* what is *low and despised* in the world, even things that are not, to bring to nothing things that are, *so that no human being might boast in the presence of God.*

    II Timothy 1:9: . . . who saved us and called us with a holy calling, not in virtue of *our works* but in virtue of *his own purpose* and the *grace* which he gave us in Christ Jesus *ages ago.*

5. Good works are the result, not the ground, of predestination.

    Ephesians 1:12: We who first hoped in Christ have been *destined* and *appointed* to live for the praise of his glory.

    Ephesians 2:10: For we are his workmanship, created in Christ Jesus *for good works,* which *God prepared beforehand,* that we should walk in them.

    John 15:16: You did not choose me, but *I chose you* and *appointed you* that you should go and bear fruit and that your fruit should abide; so that whatever you ask the Father in my name, he may give it to you.

6. God's choice was not based upon foreseen faith. Faith is the result and therefore the evidence of God's election, not the cause or ground of His choice.

    Acts 13:48: And when the Gentiles heard this, they were glad and glorified the word of God; and as many as were *ordained* to eternal life *believed.*

    Acts 18:27: . . . he greatly helped those who *through grace had believed.*

Philippians 1:29: For it has been *granted* to you that for the sake of Christ you should not only *believe* in him but also suffer for his sake.

Philippians 2:12,13: Therefore, my beloved, as you have always obeyed, so now, not only as in my presence but much more in my absence, work out your own salvation with fear and trembling; *for God is at work in you, both to will and to work for his good pleasure.*

I Thessalonians 1:4,5: For *we know*, brethren beloved by God, that *he has chosen you; for our gospel came to you* not only in word, but also *in power* and *in the Holy Spirit* and *with full conviction.*

II Thessalonians 2:13,14: ... *God chose you from the beginning to be saved, through* sanctification by the Spirit and *belief in the truth.* To this he called you through our gospel, so that you may obtain the glory of our Lord Jesus Christ.

James 2:5: ... Has not *God chosen* those who are poor in the world *to be rich in faith* and *heirs of the kingdom* which he has promised to those who love him?

See the Appendix on The Meaning of "Foreknew" in Romans 8:29. See also those verses quoted below under Point IV on Efficacious Grace, which teach that faith and repentance are the gifts of God and are wrought in the soul by the regenerating power of the Holy Spirit.

7. It is by faith and good works that one confirms his calling and election.

II Peter 1:5-11: For this very reason make every effort to supplement your faith with virtue, and virtue with knowledge, and knowledge with self-control, and self-control with steadfastness, and steadfastness with godliness, and godliness with brotherly affection, and brotherly affection with love. For if these things are yours and abound, they keep you from being ineffective or unfruitful in the knowledge of our Lord Jesus Christ. For whoever lacks these things is blind and shortsighted and has forgotten that he was cleansed from his old sins. Therefore, brethren, be the more zealous *to confirm your call and election,* for if you do this you will never fall; so there will be richly provided for you an entrance into the eternal kingdom of our Lord and Savior Jesus Christ.

C. Election is not salvation but is *unto* salvation.   Just as the president-elect does not become the president of the United States *until* he is inaugurated, those chosen unto salvation are not saved *until* they are regenerated by the Spirit and justified by faith in Christ.

Romans 11:7: What then? Israel failed to obtain what it sought. *The elect obtained it,* but the rest were hardened.

II Timothy 2:10:   Therefore I endure everything for the sake of *the elect,* that they also *may obtain the salvation* which in Christ Jesus goes with eternal glory.

See Acts 13:48; I Thessalonians 1:4 and II Thessalonians 2:13, 14 quoted above.   Compare Ephesians 1:4 with Romans 16:7. In Ephesians 1:4 Paul shows that men were *chosen* "in Christ" before the world began.   From Romans 16:7 it is clear that men are not *actually* "in Christ" until their conversion.

D. Election was based on the sovereign, distinguishing mercy of Almighty God.   It was not man's will but God's will that determined which sinners would be shown mercy and saved.

Exodus 33:19: ". . . I will be gracious to whom I will be gracious, and will show mercy on whom I will show mercy."

Deuteronomy 7:6,7: "For you are a people holy to the Lord your God; the Lord your God has chosen you to be a people for his own possession, out of all the peoples that are on the face of the earth.   It was not because you were more in number than any other people that the Lord set his love upon you and chose you, for you were the fewest of all peoples."

Matthew 20:15: " 'Am I not allowed to do what I choose with what belongs to me?' . . ."

Romans 9:10-24:   And not only so, but also when Rebecca had conceived children by one man, our forefather Isaac, though they were not yet born and had done nothing either good or bad, in order that God's purpose of election might continue, not because of works but because of his call, she was told, "the elder will serve the younger."   As it is written, "Jacob I loved, but Esau I hated."   What shall we say then?   Is there injustice on God's part?   By no means!   For he says to Moses, *"I will have mercy on whom I have mercy and I will have compassion on whom I have compassion."*   So it depends not upon man's will or exertion, *but upon God's mercy.*   For the Scripture says to Pharaoh, "I have raised you up for the very purpose of showing my power in you, so that my name may be proclaimed in all the earth."   So then he has mercy *upon whomever he wills,* and he hardens the heart of whomever he wills. You will say to me then, "Why does he still find fault? For who can resist his will?" But, who are you, a man, to answer back to God? Will what is molded say to its molder, "Why have you made me thus?" *Has the potter no right over the clay,* to make out of the same lump one *vessel for beauty* and another for menial use? What if God, desiring to show his wrath and to make known his power, has endured with much patience the vessels of wrath made for destruction, in order to make known the riches of his glory for the *vessels of mercy, which he has prepared beforehand for glory,* even us whom he has called, not from the Jews only but also from the Gentiles?

Romans 11:4-6: But what is God's reply to him? "I have kept for myself seven thousand men who have not bowed the knee to Baal." So too at the present time there is a remnant, *chosen by grace.* But if it is by grace, it is no longer on the basis of works; otherwise grace would no longer be grace. Compare I Kings 19:10, 18.

Romans 11:33-36: O the depth of the riches and wisdom and knowledge of God! How unsearchable are his judgments and how inscrutable his ways! "For who has known the mind of the Lord, or who has been his counselor?" "Or who has given a gift to him that he might be repaid?" For from him and through him and to him are all things. To him be glory for ever. Amen.

Ephesians 1:5: He destined us in love to be his sons through Jesus Christ, according to the purpose of his will.

E. The doctrine of election is but a part of the much broader Biblical doctrine of God's absolute sovereignty. The Scriptures not only teach that God predestined certain individuals unto eternal life, but that all events, both small and great, come about as the result of God's eternal decree. The Lord God rules over heaven and earth with absolute control; nothing comes to pass apart from His eternal purpose.

I Chronicles 29:10-12: Therefore David blessed the Lord in the presence of all the assembly; and David said: "Blessed art thou, O Lord, the God of Israel our father, for ever and ever. Thine, O Lord, is the greatness, and the power, and the glory, and the victory, and the majesty; for all that is in the heavens and in the earth is thine; thine is the kingdom, O Lord, and thou art exalted as head above all. Both riches and honor come from thee, and thou rulest over all. In thy hand are power and might; and in thy hand it is to make great and to give strength to all."

Job 42:1,2: Then Job answered the Lord: "I know that thou canst do all things, and that no purpose of thine can be thwarted."

Psalm 115:3: Our God is in the heavens; he does whatever he pleases.

Psalm 135:6: Whatever the Lord pleases he does, in heaven and on earth, in the seas and all deeps.

Isaiah 14:24,27: The Lord of hosts has sworn: "As I have planned, so shall it be, and as I have purposed, so shall it stand . . . . For the Lord of hosts has purposed, and who will annul it? His hand is stretched out, and who will turn it back?"

Isaiah 46:9-11: "Remember the former things of old; for I am God, and there is no other; I am God, and there is none like me, declaring the end from the beginning and from ancient times things not yet done, saying, 'My counsel shall stand, and I will accomplish all my purpose, calling a bird of prey from the east, the man of my counsel from a far country. I have spoken, and I will bring it to pass; I have purposed, and I will do it.' "

Isaiah 55:11: "So shall my word be that goes forth from my mouth; it shall not return to me empty, but it shall accomplish that which I purpose, and prosper in the things for which I sent it."

Jeremiah 32:17: " 'Ah Lord God! It is thou who hast made the heavens and the earth by thy great power and by thy outstretched arm! Nothing is too hard for thee.' "

Daniel 4:35: All the inhabitants of the earth are accounted as nothing; and he does according to his will in the host of heaven and among the inhabitants of the earth; and none can stay his hand or say to him, "What doest thou?"

Matthew 19:26: ". . . with God all things are possible."

III. PARTICULAR REDEMPTION OR LIMITED ATONEMENT

As was observed above, election itself saved no one; it only marked out particular sinners for salvation. Those *chosen* by the Father and given to the Son had to be *redeemed* if they were to be saved. In order to secure their redemption, Jesus Christ came into the world and took upon Himself human nature so that He might identify Himself with His people and act as their legal representative or substitute. Christ, acting on behalf of His people, perfectly kept God's law and thereby worked out a perfect righteousness which is imputed or credited to them the moment they are brought to faith in Him. Through what He did, they are constituted righteous before God. They are also freed from all

166

guilt and condemnation as the result of what Christ suffered for them. Through His substitutionary sacrifice He endured the penalty of their sins and thus removed their guilt forever. Consequently, when His people are joined to Him by faith, they are credited with perfect righteousness and are freed from all guilt and condemnation. They are saved, not because of what they themselves have done or will do, but solely on the ground of Christ's redeeming work.

Historical or main line Calvinism has consistently maintained that Christ's redeeming work was definite in *design* and *accomplishment*—that it was intended to render complete satisfaction for certain specified sinners and that it actually secured salvation for these individuals and for no one else. The salvation which Christ earned for His people includes everything involved in bringing them into a right relationship with God, including the gifts of faith and repentance. Christ did not die simply to make it possible for God to pardon sinners. Neither does God leave it up to sinners as to whether or not Christ's work will be effective. On the contrary, all for whom Christ sacrificed Himself will be saved infallibly. Redemption, therefore, was designed to bring to pass God's purpose of election.

All Calvinists agree that Christ's obedience and suffering were of infinite value, and that if God had so willed, the satisfaction rendered by Christ would have saved every member of the human race. It would have required no more obedience, nor any greater suffering for Christ to have secured salvation for every man, woman, and child who ever lived than it did for Him to secure salvation for the elect only. But He came into the world to represent and save only those given to Him by the Father. Thus Christ's saving work was limited in that it was designed to save some and not others, but it was not limited in value for it was of infinite worth and would have secured salvation for everyone if this had been God's intention.

The Arminians also place a limitation on the atoning work of Christ, but one of a much different nature. They hold that Christ's saving work was designed to make possible the salvation of all men on the condition that they believe, but that Christ's death *in itself* did not actually secure or guarantee salvation for anyone.

Since all men will not be saved as the result of Christ's redeeming work, a limitation must be admitted. Either the atonement was limited in that it was *designed to secure* salvation for certain sinners but not for others, or it was limited in that it was not intended to secure salvation for any, but was *designed only to make it possible* for God to pardon sinners on the condition that they believe. In other words, one must limit its design either in *extent* (it was not intended for all) or *effectiveness* (it did not secure salvation for any). As Boettner so aptly observes, for the Calvinist, the atonement "is like a narrow bridge which goes all the way across the stream; for the Arminian it is like a great wide bridge that goes only half-way across."[14]

A. The Scriptures describe the end intended and accomplished by Christ's work as the full salvation (actual reconciliation, justification, and sanctification) of His people.

1. The Scriptures state that Christ came, not to enable men to save themselves, but to *save* sinners.

Matthew 1:21: ". . . she will bear a son, and you shall call his name Jesus, for he will *save his people* from their sins."

Luke 19:10: "For the Son of man came to seek and to *save* that which was lost."

II Corinthians 5:21: For our sake he [God] made him [Christ] to be sin who knew no sin, so that in him *we might become* the righteousness of God.

Galatians 1:3,4: Grace to you and peace from God the Father and our Lord Jesus Christ, *who gave himself* for our sins *to deliver us* from the present evil age, according to the will of our God and Father.

I Timothy 1:15: The saying is sure and worthy of full acceptance, that Christ Jesus came into the world to *save* sinners. And I am the foremost of sinners.

Titus 2:14: . . . who *gave himself* for us to *redeem us* from all iniquity and to purify for himself a people of his own who are zealous for good deeds.

---

[14] Boettner, *Predestination*, p. 153. Spurgeon's comments, as to whether it is the Calvinists or the Arminians who limit the atonement, are to the point. "We are often told that we limit the atonement of Christ, because we say that Christ has not made a satisfaction for all men, or all men would be saved. Now, our reply to this is, that, on the other hand, our opponents limit it: we do not. The Arminians say, Christ died for all men. Ask them what they mean by it. Did Christ die so as to secure the salvation of all men? They say, 'No, certainly not.' We ask them the next question—Did Christ die so as to secure the salvation of any man in particular? They answer 'No.' They are obliged to admit this, if they are consistent. They say, 'No. Christ has died that any man may be saved if'—and then follow certain conditions of salvation. Now, who is it that limits the death of Christ? Why, you. You say that Christ did not die so as infallibly to secure the salvation of anybody. We beg your pardon, when you say we limit Christ's death; we say, 'No, my dear sir, it is you that do it.' We say Christ so died that he infallibly secured the salvation of a multitude that no man can number, who through Christ's death not only may be saved, but are saved and cannot by any possibility run the hazard of being anything but saved. You are welcome to your atonement; you may keep it. We will never renounce ours for the sake of it." Quoted from Packer, "Introductory Essay," (above, fn. 4), p. 14.

I Peter 3:18: For *Christ* also *died* for sins once for all, the righteous for the unrighteous, *that he might bring us to God*, being put to death in the flesh but made alive in the spirit.

2. The Scriptures declare that, as the result of what Christ did and suffered, His people are reconciled to God, justified, and given the Holy Spirit who regenerates and sanctifies them. All these blessings were secured by Christ Himself for His people.

a. Christ, by His redeeming work, secured *reconciliation* for His people.

Romans 5:10: For if while we were enemies we were *reconciled* to God *by the death of his Son*, much more, now that we are reconciled, shall we be saved by his life.

II Corinthians 5:18,19: All this is from God, who through Christ *reconciled* us to himself and gave us the ministry of reconciliation; that is, God was in Christ reconciling the world to himself, not counting their trespasses against them, and entrusting to us the message of reconciliation.

Ephesians 2:15,16: ... by abolishing in his flesh the law of commandments and ordinances, that he might create in himself one new man in place of the two, so making peace, and *might reconcile us* both to God in one body through the cross, thereby bringing the hostility to an end.

Colossians 1:21,22: And you, who once were estranged and hostile in mind, doing evil deeds, *he has now reconciled* in his body of flesh by his death, *in order to* present you holy and blameless and irreproachable before him.

b. Christ secured the righteousness and pardon needed by His people for their *justification*.

Romans 3:24,25: ... they are *justified* by his grace as a gift, *through the redemption which is in Christ Jesus*, whom God put forward as an expiation by his blood, to be received by faith. This was to show God's righteousness, because in his divine forbearance he had passed over former sins.

Romans 5:8,9: But God shows his love for us in that *while we were yet sinners Christ died for us*. Since, therefore, we are now *justified by his blood*, much more shall we be saved by him from the wrath of God.

I Corinthians 1:30: He is the source of your life in Christ Jesus, whom God made our wisdom, our *righteousness* and sanctification and redemption.

Galatians 3:13: Christ *redeemed us* from the curse of the law, having become a curse for us . . .

Colossians 1:13,14: He has delivered us from the dominion of darkness and transferred us to the kingdom of his beloved Son, in whom *we have redemption*, the forgiveness of sins.

Hebrews 9:12: . . . he entered once for all into the Holy Place, *taking* not the blood of goats and calves but *his own blood, thus securing an eternal redemption.*

I Peter 2:24: He himself *bore our sins* in his body on the tree, that we might die to sin and live to righteousness. By his wounds you have been healed.

c. Christ secured the gift of the Spirit which includes *regeneration* and *sanctification* and all that is involved in them.

Ephesians 1:3,4: Blessed be the God and Father of our Lord Jesus Christ, who has blessed us in Christ *with every spiritual blessing* in the heavenly places, even as he chose us in him before the foundation of the world, that we should be holy and blameless before him.

Philippians 1:29: For it has been *granted to you* that for the sake of Christ you should not only *believe* in him but also suffer for his sake.

Acts 5:31: "God exalted him at his right hand as Leader and Savior, *to give repentance* to Israel and forgiveness of sins."

Titus 2:14: . . . who gave himself for us to *redeem us* from all iniquity and *to purify* for himself a people of his own who are zealous for good deeds.

Titus 3:5,6: . . . he saved us, not because of deeds done by us in righteousness, but in virtue of his own mercy, by the washing of *regeneration* and *renewal* in the Holy Spirit, which he poured out upon us richly *through* Jesus Christ our Savior.

Ephesians 5:25,26: Husbands, love your wives, as Christ loved the church and gave himself up for her, that he might *sanctify* her, having cleansed her by the washing of water with the word.

I Corinthians 1:30: He is the source of your life in Christ Jesus, whom God made our wisdom, our righteousness and *sanctification* and redemption.

Hebrews 9:14: ... how much more shall the *blood of Christ*, who through the eternal Spirit offered himself without blemish to God, *purify* your conscience from dead works to serve the living God.

Hebrews 13:12: So Jesus also *suffered* outside the gate *in order to sanctify* the people through his own blood.

I John 1:7: ... but if we walk in the light, as he is in the light, we have fellowship with one another, and the *blood of Jesus* his Son *cleanses* us from all sin.

B. Passages which represent the Lord Jesus Christ, in all that He did and suffered for His people, as fulfilling the terms of a gracious compact or arrangement which He had entered into with His heavenly Father before the foundation of the world.

1. Jesus was sent into the world by the Father to save the people which the Father had given to Him. Those given to Him by the Father come to Him (see and believe in Him) and none of them shall be lost.

John 6:35-40: Jesus said to them, "I am the bread of life; he who comes to me shall not hunger, and he who believes in me shall never thirst. But I said to you that you have seen me and yet do not believe. *All that the Father gives me will come to me;* and him who comes to me I will not cast out. For I have come down from heaven, not to do my own will, but *the will of him who sent me;* and this is the will of him who sent me, *that I should lose nothing of all that he has given me,* but raise it up at the last day. For this is the will of my Father, that every one who sees the Son and believes in him should have eternal life; and I will raise him up at the last day."

2. Jesus, as the good shepherd, lays down His life for His sheep. All who are "His sheep" are brought by Him into the fold and are made to hear His voice and follow Him. Notice that the Father had given the sheep to Christ!

John 10:11,14-18: "I am the good shepherd. The good shepherd lays down his life for *the sheep* .... I am the good shepherd; *I know my own* and my own know me, as the Father knows me and I know the Father; and I lay down my life for *the sheep.* And I have *other sheep,* that are not of this fold; *I must bring them also,* and they *will* heed my voice.

So there shall be one flock, one shepherd. For this reason
the Father loves me, because I lay down my life, that I
may take it again. No one takes it from me, but I lay
it down of my own accord. I have power to lay it down,
and I have power to take it again; *this charge I have received from my Father."*

John 10:24-29: [The unbelieving Jews demanded of Him] "If
you are the Christ, tell us plainly." Jesus answered them,
"I told you, and you do not believe. The works that I do
in my Father's name, they bear witness to me; but you
do not believe, *because you do not belong to my sheep. My
sheep hear my voice,* and *I know them,* and *they* follow me;
and *I give them eternal life,* and *they* shall never perish, and
no one shall snatch *them* out of my hand. My *Father, who
has given them to me,* is greater than all, and no one is able
to snatch *them* out of the Father's hand."

3.   Jesus, in His high priestly prayer, prays not for the world but
for those given to Him by the Father. In fulfillment of the
Father's charge Jesus had accomplished the work the Father
had sent Him to do—to make God known to His people and to
give them eternal life.

John 17:1-11, 20, 24-26: When Jesus had spoken these words,
he lifted up his eyes to heaven and said, "Father, the hour
has come; glorify thy Son that the Son may glorify thee,
*since thou hast given him power over all flesh, so that he
might give eternal life to all whom thou hast given him.*
And this is eternal life, that they know thee the only true
God, and *Jesus Christ whom thou hast sent.* I glorified
thee on earth, having *accomplished the work which thou
gavest me to do;* and now, Father, glorify thou me in thy
own presence with the glory which I had with thee *before
the world was made.*

"I have *manifested thy name to the men whom thou gavest
me out of the world;* thine they were, and thou gavest them
to me, and they have kept thy word. Now they know that
everything that thou hast given me is from thee; for I have
given them the words which thou gavest me, and they
have received them and know in truth that I came from
thee; and they have believed that thou didst send me. I
am praying for them; *I am not praying for the world but
for those whom thou hast given me,* for they are thine;
all mine are thine, and thine are mine, and I am glorified
in them. And now I am no more in the world, but they
are in the world, and I am coming to thee. Holy Father,

keep them in thy name *which thou hast given me,* that they may be one, even as we are one . . . . I do not pray for these only, but *also for those who are to believe in me* through their word, . . . Father, I desire that they also, *whom thou hast given me,* may be with me where I am, to behold my glory which thou hast given me in thy love for me *before the foundation of the world.* O righteous Father, the world has not known thee, but I have known thee; and *these know that thou hast sent me.* I made known to them thy name, and I will make it known, that the love with which thou hast loved me may be in them, and I in them."

4. Paul declares that all of the "spiritual blessings" which the saints inherit such as sonship, redemption, the forgiveness of sin, etc., result from their being "in Christ," and he traces these blessings back to their ultimate source in the eternal counsel of God—to that great blessing of their having been chosen in Christ before the foundation of the world and destined to be God's sons through Him.

Ephesians 1:3-12: Blessed be the God and Father of our Lord Jesus Christ, *who has blessed us* in Christ *with every spiritual blessing* in the heavenly places, *even as he chose us in him before the foundation of the world,* that we should be holy and blameless before him. He *destined us* in love *to be his sons through Jesus Christ, according to the purpose of his will,* to the praise of his glorious grace which he freely bestowed on us in the Beloved. In him we have *redemption* through his blood, *the forgiveness of our trespasses,* according to the riches of his grace which he lavished upon us. For he has made known to us in all wisdom and insight the mystery of his will, according to his purpose which he set forth in Christ as a plan for the fullness of time, to unite all things in him, things in heaven and things on earth.

In him, *according to the purpose of him who accomplishes all things according to the counsel of his will,* we who first hoped in Christ have been destined and appointed to live for the praise of his glory.

5. The parallel which Paul draws between the condemning work of Adam and the saving work of Jesus Christ the "second man," the "last Adam," can best be explained on the principle that both stood in covenant relation to "tneir people" (Adam stood as the federal head of the race, and Christ stood as the federal head of the elect). As Adam involved his people in death and

condemnation by his sin, even so Christ brought justification and life to His people through His righteousness.

> Romans 5:12,17-19: Therefore as sin came into the world through one man [Adam] and death through sin, and so death spread to all men because all men sinned . . . . If, because of one man's trespass, death reigned through that one man, much more will those who receive the abundance of grace and the free gift of righteousness reign in life through the one man Jesus Christ.   Then as one man's trespass led to condemnation for all men, so *one man's act of righteousness leads to acquittal and life for all men.*   For as by one man's disobedience many were made sinners, so *by one man's obedience many will be made righteous.*

C. Some passages speak of Christ's dying for "all" men and of His death as saving the "world," yet others speak of His death as being definite in design and of His dying for particular people and securing salvation for them.

   1. There are two classes of texts that speak of Christ's saving work in *general terms:*   (a) Those containing the word "world"— e.g., John 1:9,29; 3:16,17; 4:42; II Corinthians 5:19; I John 2:1,2; 4:14 and (b) Those containing the word "all"—e.g., Romans 5:18; II Corinthians 5:14,15; I Timothy 2:4-6; Hebrews 2:9; II Peter 3:9.

   One reason for the use of these expressions was to correct the false notion that salvation was for the Jews alone.   Such phrases as "the world," "all men," "all nations," and "every creature" were used by the New Testament writers to emphatically correct this mistake.   These expressions are intended to show that Christ died for all men without *distinction* (i.e., He died for Jews and Gentiles alike) but they are not intended to indicate that Christ died for all men without *exception* (i.e., He did not die for the purpose of saving each and every lost sinner).

   2. There are other passages which speak of His saving work in *definite terms* and show that it was intended to infallibly save a particular people, namely those given to Him by the Father.

   Matthew 1:21: ". . . for he will save *his people* from their sins."

   Matthew 20:28: ". . . the Son of man came not to be served but to serve, and to give his life as *a ransom for many.*"

   Matthew 26:28: ". . . for this is my blood of the covenant, which is poured out *for many* for the forgiveness of sins."

John 10:11: "I am the good shepherd. The good shepherd lays down his life for *the sheep*."

John 11:50-53: ". . . you do not understand that it is expedient for you that one man should die for *the people*, and not that the whole nation should perish." He did not say this of his own accord, but being high priest that year he prophesied that Jesus should die for the nation, and not for the nation only, but to gather into one *the children of God who are scattered abroad*. So from that day on they took counsel how to put him to death.

Acts 20:28: Take heed to yourselves and to all the flock, in which the Holy Spirit has made you guardians, to feed *the church* of the Lord *which he obtained for himself with his own blood*.

Ephesians 5:25-27: Husbands, love your wives, *as Christ loved the church* and *gave himself up for her,* that he might sanctify *her*, having cleansed *her* by the washing of water with the word, that *the church* might be presented before him in splendor, without spot or wrinkle or any such thing, that *she* might be holy and without blemish.

Romans 8:32-34: He who did not spare his own Son but gave him up *for us all*, will he not also *give* us all things with him? Who shall bring any charge against *God's elect?* It is God who justifies; who is to condemn?

Hebrews 2:17; 3:1: Therefore he had to be made like his brethren in every respect, so that he might become a merciful and faithful high priest in the service of God, to make expiation *for the sins of the people* . . . . Therefore, holy brethren, *who share in a heavenly call,* consider Jesus, the apostle and high priest of our confession.

Hebrews 9:15: Therefore he is the mediator of a new covenant, so that *those who are called* may receive the promised eternal inheritance, since a death has occurred which *redeems them* from the transgressions under the first covenant.

Hebrews 9:28: . . . Christ, having been offered once to bear the sins of *many* . . .

Revelation 5:9: . . . and they sang a new song, saying, "Worthy art thou to take the scroll and to open its seals, for thou wast slain and by thy blood didst *ransom men* for God *from every tribe and tongue and people and nation* . . ."

Review also the verses quoted above under B, 1, 2, 3.

175

IV. THE EFFICACIOUS CALL OF THE SPIRIT OR IRRESISTIBLE GRACE

Each member of the Trinity—the Father, the Son, and the Holy Spirit—participates in and contributes to the salvation of sinners. As was shown above, the Father, before the foundation of the world, marked out those who were to be saved and gave them to the Son to be His people. At the appointed time the Son came into the world and secured their redemption. But these two great acts—election and redemption—do not complete the work of salvation, because included in God's plan for recovering lost sinners is the renewing work of the Holy Spirit by which the benefits of Christ's obedience and death are applied to the elect. It is with this phase of salvation (its application by the Spirit) that the doctrine of Irresistible or Efficacious Grace is concerned. Simply stated, this doctrine asserts that the Holy Spirit never fails to bring to salvation those sinners whom He personally calls to Christ. He inevitably applies salvation to every sinner whom He intends to save, and it is His intention to save all the elect.

The *gospel invitation extends a call* to salvation to every one who hears its message. It invites all men without distinction to drink freely of the water of life and live. It promises salvation to all who repent and believe. But this outward general call, extended to the elect and non-elect alike, will not bring sinners to Christ. Why? Because men are by nature dead in sin and are under its power. They are of themselves unable and unwilling to forsake their evil ways and to turn to Christ for mercy. Consequently, the unregenerate will not respond to the gospel call to repentance and faith. No amount of external threatenings or promises will cause blind, deaf, dead, rebellious sinners to bow before Christ as Lord and to look to Him alone for salvation. Such an act of faith and submission is contrary to the lost man's nature.

Therefore, the *Holy Spirit,* in order to bring God's elect to salvation, extends to them *a special inward call* in addition to the outward call contained in the gospel message. Through this special call the Holy Spirit performs a work of grace within the sinner which inevitably brings him to faith in Christ. The inward change wrought in the elect sinner enables him to understand and believe spiritual truth; in the spiritual realm he is given the seeing eye and the hearing ear. The Spirit creates within him a new heart or a new nature. This is accomplished through regeneration or the new birth by which the sinner is made a child of God and is given spiritual life. His will is renewed through this process so that the sinner spontaneously comes to Christ of his own free choice. Because he is given a new nature so that he loves righteousness, and because his mind is enlightened so that he understands and believes the Biblical gospel, the renewed sinner freely and willingly turns to Christ as Lord and Saviour.

176

Thus the once dead sinner is drawn to Christ by the inward supernatural call of the Spirit who through regeneration makes him alive and creates within him faith and repentance.

Although the general outward call of the gospel can be, and often is, rejected, the special inward call of the Spirit never fails to result in the conversion of those to whom it is made. This special call is not made to all sinners but is issued to the elect only! The Spirit is in no way dependent upon their help or cooperation for success in His work of bringing them to Christ. It is for this reason that Calvinists speak of the Spirit's call and of God's grace in saving sinners as being "efficacious," "invincible," or "irresistible." For the grace which the Holy Spirit extends to the elect cannot be thwarted or refused, it never fails to bring them to true faith in Christ!

The doctrine of Irresistible or Efficacious Grace is set forth in the Westminster Confession of Faith in the following words. "All those whom God hath predestinated unto life, and those only, he is pleased, in his appointed and accepted time, effectually to call, by his word and Spirit, out of that state of sin and death in which they are by nature, to grace and salvation by Jesus Christ; enlightening their minds spiritually and savingly to understand the things of God; taking away their heart of stone, and giving unto them an heart of flesh; renewing their wills, and by his almighty power determining them to that which is good, and effectually drawing them to Jesus Christ; yet so as they come most freely, being made willing by his grace."[15]

A. General statements showing that salvation is the work of the Spirit as well as that of the Father and the Son.

   Romans 8:14: For all who are led by the Spirit of God are sons of God.

   I Corinthians 2:10-14: For the Spirit searches everything, even the depths of God. For what person knows a man's thoughts except the spirit of the man which is in him? So also no one comprehends the thoughts of God except the Spirit of God. Now we have received not the spirit of the world, but the Spirit which is from God, that we might understand the gifts bestowed on us by God. And we impart this in words not taught by human wisdom but taught by the Spirit, interpreting spiritual truths to those who possess the Spirit.

   I Corinthians 6:11: But you were washed, you were sanctified, you were justified in the name of the Lord Jesus Christ and in the Spirit of our God.

---

[15] Chapter X, Section 1.

I Corinthians 12:3: Therefore I want you to understand that no one speaking by the Spirit of God ever says "Jesus be cursed!" and no one can say "Jesus is Lord" except by the Holy Spirit.

II Corinthians 3:6: . . . the written code kills, but the Spirit gives life.

II Corinthians 3:17,18: Now the Lord is the Spirit, and where the Spirit of the Lord is, there is freedom. And we all, with unveiled face, beholding the glory of the Lord, are being changed into his likeness from one degree of glory to another; for this comes from the Lord who is the Spirit.

I Peter 1:2: . . . chosen and destined by God the Father and sanctified by the Spirit for obedience to Jesus Christ and for sprinkling with his blood . . .

B. Through regeneration or the new birth sinners are given spiritual life and made God's children. The Bible describes this process as a spiritual resurrection, a creation, the giving of a new heart, etc. The inward change, which is thus wrought through the Holy Spirit, results from God's power and grace, and in no way is He dependent upon man's help for success in this work.

1. Sinners, through regeneration, are brought into God's kingdom and are made His children. The *author* of this "second" birth is the Holy Spirit; the *instrument* which He uses is the word of God.

John 1:12,13: But to all who received him, who believed in his name, he gave power to become children of God; *who were born,* not of blood nor of the will of the flesh nor of the will of man, but *of God.*

John 3:3-8: Jesus answered him, "Truly, truly, I say to you, unless one is *born anew,* he cannot *see* the kingdom of God." Nicodemus said to him, "How can a man be born when he is old? Can he enter a second time into his mother's womb and be born?" Jesus answered, "Truly, truly, I say to you, unless one is born of water and the Spirit, he cannot *enter* the kingdom of God. That which is born of the flesh is flesh, and that which is *born of the Spirit* is spirit. Do not marvel that I said to you, 'You must be born anew.' The wind blows where it wills, and you hear the sound of it, but you do not know whence it comes or whither it goes; so it is with every one who is born of the Spirit."

Titus 3:5: . . . he saved us, not because of deeds done by us in righteousness, but in virtue of his own mercy, by the washing of *regeneration* and *renewal in the Holy Spirit.*

I Peter 1:3: Blessed be the God and Father of our Lord Jesus Christ! By his great mercy we have been *born anew* to a living hope through the resurrection of Jesus Christ from the dead.

I Peter 1:23: You have been *born anew*, not of perishable seed but of imperishable, through the living and abiding *word of God*.

I John 5:4: For whatever is *born of God* overcomes the world; and this is the victory that overcomes the world, our faith.

2. Through the Spirit's work the dead sinner is given a new heart (nature) and made to walk in God's law. In Christ he becomes a new creation.

Deuteronomy 30:6: And the Lord your God will *circumcise your heart* and the heart of your offspring, so that you will love the Lord your God with all your heart and with all your soul, that you may live.

Ezekiel 36:26,27: A *new heart* I will give you, and a *new spirit* I will put within you; and I will take out of your flesh the heart of stone and give you a heart of flesh. And I will put my spirit within you, and cause you to walk in my statutes and be careful to observe my ordinances. Compare Ezekiel 11:19.

Galatians 6:15: For neither circumcision counts for anything, nor uncircumcision, but *a new creation*.

Ephesians 2:10: For we are his workmanship, *created* in Christ Jesus for good works, which God prepared beforehand, that we should walk in them.

II Corinthians 5:17,18: Therefore, if any one is in Christ, he *is a new creation;* the old has passed away, behold, the new has come. All this is from God, who through Christ reconciled us to himself and gave us the ministry of reconciliation.

3. The Holy Spirit raises the sinner from his state of spiritual death and makes him alive.

John 5:21: For as the Father raises the dead and gives them life, so also the Son *gives life* to whom he will.

Ephesians 2:1,5: And you *he made alive*, when you were dead through the trespasses and sins . . . . even when we were dead through our trespasses, [God] made us *alive* together with Christ . . .

Colossians 2:13: And you, who were dead in trespasses and the uncircumcision of your flesh, *God made alive* together with him, having forgiven us all our trespasses.

C. God makes known to His chosen ones the secrets of the kingdom through the inward personal revelation given by the Spirit.

Matthew 11:25-27: At that time Jesus declared, "I thank thee, Father, Lord of heaven and earth, that thou hast hidden these things from the wise and understanding and revealed them to babes; yea, Father, for such was thy gracious will. All things have been delivered to me by my Father; and no one knows the Son except the Father, and no one *knows the Father* except the Son and any one to whom the Son *chooses to reveal him.*"

Luke 10:21: In that same hour he rejoiced in the Holy Spirit and said, "I thank thee, Father, Lord of heaven and earth, that thou hast hidden these things from the wise and understanding and *revealed* them to babes; yea, Father, for such was thy gracious will."

Matthew 13:10,11,16: Then the disciples came and said to him, "Why do you speak to them in parables?" And he answered them, "To you it has been *given to know the secrets* of the kingdom of heaven, but to them it has not been given . . . . But blessed are your eyes, for they *see*, and your ears, for they *hear*."

Luke 8:10: "To you it has been *given to know* the secrets of the kingdom of God; but for others they are in parables, so that seeing they may not see, and hearing they may not understand."

Matthew 16:15-17: He said to them, "But who do you say that I am?" Simon Peter replied, "You are the Christ, the Son of the living God." And Jesus answered him, "Blessed are you, Simon Bar-Jona! For flesh and blood has not *revealed* this to you, but *my Father* who is in heaven."

John 6:37,44,45,64,65: "All that the Father *gives me will come to me;* and him who comes to me I will not cast out . . . . No one can come to me unless the Father who sent me *draws* him; and I will raise him up at the last day. It is written in the prophets, 'And they shall all be *taught* by God.' Every one who has *heard* and *learned from the Father* comes to me . . . . But there are some of you that do not believe." For Jesus knew from the first who those were that did not believe, and who it was that should betray him. And he said, "This is why I told you that no one can come to me unless it is *granted* him *by the Father.*"

I Corinthians 2:14: The unspiritual man does not receive the gifts of the Spirit of God, for they are folly to him, and he is not able to understand them because they are *spiritually discerned.*

Ephesians 1:17,18: ... that the God of our Lord Jesus Christ, the Father of glory, may *give* you a *spirit of wisdom and of revelation* in the knowledge of him, having *the eyes of your hearts enlightened,* that you may *know* what is the hope to which he has called you, ...

See also John 10:3-6, 16, 26-29.

D. *Faith* and *repentance* are *divine gifts* and are wrought in the soul through the regenerating work of the Holy Spirit.

Acts 5:31: "God exalted him at his right hand as Leader and Savior, to *give repentance* to Israel and forgiveness of sins."

Acts 11:18: When they heard this they were silenced. And they glorified God, saying, "Then to the Gentiles also God has *granted repentance* unto life."

Acts 13:48: And when the Gentiles heard this, they were glad and glorified the word of God; and as many as were *ordained* to eternal life *believed.*

Acts 16:14: One who heard us was a woman named Lydia, from the city of Thyatira, a seller of purple goods, who was a worshipper of God. *The Lord opened her heart* to *give heed* to what was said by Paul.

Acts 18:27: And when he wished to cross to Achaia, the brethren encouraged him, and wrote to the disciples to receive him. When he arrived, he greatly helped those who *through grace had believed.*

Ephesians 2:8,9: For by grace you have been saved through faith; and this is not your own doing, *it is the gift of God*—not because of works, lest any man should boast.

Philippians 1:29: For it has been *granted to you* that for the sake of Christ you should not only *believe* in him but also suffer for his sake.

II Timothy 2:25,26: ... God may perhaps *grant* that they will *repent* and come to *know* the truth, and they may escape from the snare of the devil, after being captured by him to do his will.

E. The gospel invitation extends a general outward call to salvation to all who hear the message. In addition to this external call, the Holy

Spirit extends a special inward call to the elect only. The general call of the gospel can be, and often is, rejected, but the special call of the Spirit cannot be rejected; it always results in the conversion of those to whom it is made.

Romans 1:6,7: . . . including yourselves who are *called* to belong to Jesus Christ; To all God's beloved in Rome, who are *called* to be saints . . .

Romans 8:30: And those whom he predestined he also *called;* and those whom he *called* he also justified; and those whom he justified he also glorified.

Romans 9:23,24: . . . in order to make known the riches of his glory for the vessels of mercy, which he has prepared beforehand for glory, even us whom he has *called,* not from the Jews only but also from the Gentiles?

I Corinthians 1:1,2,9,23-31: Paul, *called* by the will of God to be an apostle of Christ Jesus, and our brother Sosthenes, To the church of God which is at Corinth, to those sanctified in Christ Jesus, *called* to be saints . . . . God is faithful, by whom you were *called* into the fellowship of his Son, Jesus Christ our Lord . . . . but we preach Christ crucified, a stumbling block to Jews and folly to Gentiles, but to those who are *called,* both Jews and Greeks, Christ the power of God and the wisdom of God. For the foolishness of God is wiser than men, and the weakness of God is stronger than men.

For consider your *call,* brethren; not many of you were wise according to worldly standards, not many were powerful, not many were of noble birth; but God chose what is foolish in the world to shame the wise, God chose what is weak in the world to shame the strong, God chose what is low and despised in the world, even things that are not to bring to nothing things that are, so that no human being might boast in the presence of God. He is the source of your life in Christ Jesus, whom God made our wisdom, our righteousness and sanctification and redemption; therefore, as it is written, "Let him who boasts, boast of the Lord."

Galatians 1:15,16: But when he who had set me apart before I was born, and had *called* me through his grace, was pleased to reveal his Son to me, in order that I might preach him among the Gentiles, I did not confer with flesh and blood.

Ephesians 4:4: There is one body and one spirit, just as you were *called* to the one hope that belongs to your call.

II Timothy 1:9: ... who saved us and *called* us with a holy calling, not in virtue of our works but in virtue of his own purpose and the grace which he gave us in Christ Jesus ages ago.

Hebrews 9:15: Therefore he is the mediator of a new covenant, so that those who are *called* may receive the promised eternal inheritance ...

Jude 1: To those who are *called,* beloved in God the Father and kept for Jesus Christ.

I Peter 1:15: ... but as he who *called* you is holy, be holy yourselves in all your conduct.

I Peter 2:9: But you are a chosen race, a royal priesthood, a holy nation, God's own people, that you may declare the wonderful deeds of him who *called* you out of darkness into his marvelous light.

I Peter 5:10: And after you have suffered a little while, the God of all grace, who has *called* you to his eternal glory in Christ, will himself restore, establish, and strengthen you.

II Peter 1:3: His divine power has granted to us all things that pertain to life and godliness, through the knowledge of him who *called* us to his own glory and excellence.

Revelation 17:14: "... they will make war on the Lamb, and the Lamb will conquer them, for he is Lord of lords and King of kings, and those with him are *called* and chosen and faithful."

F. The application of salvation is all of grace and is accomplished solely through the almighty power of God.

Isaiah 55:11: " ... so shall my word be that goes forth from my mouth; it shall not return to me empty, but it shall *accomplish* that which *I purpose,* and prosper in the thing for which I sent it."

John 3:27: John answered, "No one can receive anything except what is *given* him from heaven."

John 17:2: " ... since thou hast given him power over all flesh, so that he might *give* eternal life to all whom thou hast given him."

Romans 9:16: So it depends not upon man's will or exertion, but upon *God's mercy.*

I Corinthians 3:6,7: I planted, Apollos watered, but *God gave the growth.* So neither he who plants nor he who waters is anything, but only God who *gives* the growth.

I Corinthians 4:7: For who sees anything different in you? What have you that you did not *receive?* If then you received it, why do you boast as if it were not a *gift?*

Philippians 2:12,13: Therefore, my beloved, as you have always obeyed, so now, not only as in my presence but much more in my absence, work out your own salvation with fear and trembling; for *God is at work in you,* both to *will* and to *work* for his good pleasure.

James 1:18: *Of his own will* he brought us forth by the word of truth that we should be a kind of first fruits of his creatures.

I John 5:20: And we know that the Son of God has come and has *given us understanding,* to *know* him who is true; and we are in him who is true, in his Son Jesus Christ. This is the true God and eternal life.

V. THE PERSEVERANCE OF THE SAINTS OR THE SECURITY OF BELIEVERS

The elect are not only redeemed by Christ and renewed by the Spirit; they are also *kept* in faith by the almighty power of God. All those who are spiritually united to Christ through regeneration are eternally secure in Him. Nothing can separate them from the eternal and unchangeable love of God. They have been predestined unto eternal glory and are therefore assured of heaven.

The doctrine of the perseverance of the saints does not maintain that all who *profess* the Christian faith are certain of heaven. It is *saints*—those who are set apart by the Spirit—who *persevere* to the end. It is *believers*—those who are given true, living faith in Christ—who are *secure* and safe in Him. Many who profess to believe fall away, but they do not fall from grace for they were never in grace. True believers do fall into temptations, and they do commit grievous sins, but these sins do not cause them to lose their salvation or separate them from Christ.

The Westminster Confession of Faith gives the following statement of this doctrine: "They whom God hath accepted in his Beloved, effectually called and sanctified by his Spirit, can neither totally nor finally fall away from the state of grace: but shall certainly persevere therein to the end, and be eternally saved."[16]

Boettner is certainly correct in asserting that "This doctrine does not stand alone but is a necessary part of the Calvinistic system of theology. The doctrines of Election and Efficacious Grace logically imply the certain salvation of those who receive these blessings. If God

---

[16] Chapter XIX, Section 1.

has chosen men absolutely and unconditionally to eternal life, and if His Spirit effectively applies to them the benefits of redemption, the inescapable conclusion is that these persons shall be saved."[17]

The following verses show that God's people are given *eternal life* the moment they believe. They are *kept by God's power* through faith and *nothing can separate them from His love*. They have been *sealed* with the Holy Spirit who has been given as the *guarantee* of their salvation, and they are thus assured of an eternal inheritance.

Isaiah 43:1-3: But now thus says the Lord, he who created you, O Jacob, he who formed you, O Israel: "Fear not, for I have redeemed you: I have called you by name, you are mine. When you pass through the waters I will be with you; and through the rivers, they shall not overwhelm you; when you walk through fire you shall not be burned, and the flame shall not consume you. For I am the Lord your God, the Holy One of Israel, your Savior."

Isaiah 54:10: "For the mountains may depart and the hills be removed, but my steadfast love shall not depart from you, and my covenant of peace shall not be removed, says the Lord, who has compassion on you."

Jeremiah 32:40: "I will make with them an everlasting covenant, that I will not turn away from doing good to them; and I will put the fear of me in their hearts, that they may not turn from me."

Matthew 18:12-14: "What do you think? If a man has a hundred sheep, and one of them has gone astray, does he not leave the ninety-nine on the hills and go in search of the one that went astray? And if he finds it, truly, I say to you, he rejoices over it more than over the ninety-nine that never went astray. So it is not the will of my Father who is in heaven that *one* of these little ones *should perish*."

John 3:16: For God so loved the world that he gave his only Son, that whoever believes in him *should not perish* but have *eternal life*.

John 3:36: He who believes in the Son *has eternal life* . . .

John 5:24: "Truly, truly, I say to you, he who hears my word and believes him who sent me *has eternal life;* he does *not come into judgment,* but *has passed from death to life*."

John 6:35-40: Jesus said to them, "I am the bread of life; he who comes to me shall *not hunger,* and he who believes in me shall *never thirst*. But I said to you that you have seen me and yet do not believe. All that the Father gives me will come to me; and *him who comes to me I will not cast out*. For I have come down from heaven, not to do my own will, but the will of him who sent me; and this is the will

---

[17] Boettner, *Predestination*, p. 182.

of him who sent me, that I should *lose nothing* of all that he has given me, but raise it up at the last day. For this is the will of my Father, that every one who sees the Son and believes in him should have eternal life; and I will raise him up at the last day."

John 6:47: "Truly, truly, I say to you, he who believes *has eternal life.*"

John 10:27-30: "My sheep hear my voice, and I know them, and they follow me; and I give them *eternal life,* and *they shall never perish,* and *no one shall snatch them out of my hand.* My Father, who has given them to me, is greater than all, and no one is able to snatch them out of the Father's hand. I and the Father are one."

John 17:11,12,15: "And now I am no more in the world, but they are in the world, and I am coming to thee. Holy Father, *keep them* in thy name which thou hast given me, that they may be one, even as we are one. While I was with them, I *kept them* in thy name which thou hast given me; I have guarded them, and *none of them is lost* but the son of perdition, that the scripture might be fulfilled . . . . I do not pray that thou shouldst take them out of the world, but that thou shouldst *keep them from the evil one.*"

Romans 5:8-10: But God shows his love for us in that while we were yet sinners Christ died for us. Since, therefore, we are *now justified* by his blood, *much more shall we be saved* by him *from the wrath of God.* For if while we were enemies we were reconciled to God by the death of his Son, much more, now that we are reconciled, shall we be *saved by his life.*

Romans 8:1: There is therefore now *no condemnation* for those who are in Christ Jesus.

Romans 8:29,30: For those whom he *foreknew* he also *predestined* to be conformed to the image of his Son, in order that he might be the first-born among many brethren. And those whom he predestined he also *called;* and those whom he called he also *justified;* and those whom he justified he also *glorified.*

Romans 8:35-39: Who shall separate us from the love of Christ? Shall tribulation, or distress, or persecution, or famine, or nakedness, or peril, or sword? As it is written, "For thy sake we are being killed all the day long; we are regarded as sheep to be slaughtered." No, in all these things we are *more than conquerors through him* who loved us. For I am sure that neither death, nor life, nor angels, nor principalities, nor things present, nor things to come, nor powers, nor height, nor depth, *nor anything else in all creation, will be able to separate us from the love of God in Christ Jesus our Lord.*

I Corinthians 1:7-9: . . . so that you are not lacking in any spiritual gift, as you wait for the revealing of our Lord Jesus Christ; who will *sustain you to the end, guiltless* in the day of our Lord Jesus Christ. *God is faithful,* by whom you were called into the fellowship of his Son, Jesus Christ our Lord.

I Corinthians 10:13: No temptation has overtaken you that is not common to man. God is faithful, and he will not let you be tempted *beyond your strength,* but with the temptation will also provide the way of escape, that you may be *able* to endure it.

II Corinthians 4:14,17: . . . knowing that he who raised the Lord Jesus will *raise us* also with Jesus and bring us with you into his presence . . . . For this slight momentary affliction is preparing us for an eternal weight of glory beyond all comparison.

Ephesians 1:5,13,14: He destined us in love to be his sons through Jesus Christ, according to the purpose of his will, . . . In him you also, who have heard the word of truth, the gospel of your salvation, and have believed in him, were *sealed* with the promised Holy Spirit, which is *the guarantee of our inheritance* until we acquire possession of it, to the praise of his glory.

Ephesians 4:30: And do not grieve the Holy Spirit of God, in whom you were *sealed* for the day of redemption.

Colossians 3:3,4: For you have died, and your life is hid with Christ in God. When Christ who is our life appears, then you also *will appear* with him *in glory.*

I Thessalonians 5:23,24: May the God of peace himself sanctify you wholly; and may your spirit and soul and body be *kept sound* and *blameless* at the coming of our Lord Jesus Christ. He who calls you is *faithful,* and *he will do it.*

II Timothy 4:18: The Lord will rescue me from every evil and save me for his heavenly kingdom. To him be the glory for ever and ever. Amen.

Hebrews 9:12,15: . . . he entered once for all into the Holy Place, taking not the blood of goats and calves but his own blood, thus *securing an eternal redemption* . . . . Therefore he is the mediator of a new covenant, so that those who are called may *receive* the *promised eternal inheritance,* since a death has occurred which redeems them from the transgressions under the first covenant.

Hebrews 10:14: For by a single offering he has *perfected for all time* those who are *sanctified.*

Hebrews 12:28: Therefore let us be grateful for *receiving* a kingdom that *cannot be shaken,* and thus let us offer to God acceptable worship, with reverence and awe.

I Peter 1:3-5: Blessed be the God and Father of our Lord Jesus Christ! By his great mercy *we have been born anew* to a living hope through the resurrection of Jesus Christ from the dead, and to an inheritance which is imperishable, undefiled, and unfading, kept in heaven for you, who by *God's power* are *guarded* through faith for a salvation ready to be revealed in the last time.

I John 2:19,25: They went out from us, but they were not of us; for if they had been of us, they would have *continued with us;* but they went out, that it might be plain that they all are not of us . . . . And this is what he has *promised us, eternal life.*

I John 5:4,11-13, 20: For whatever is born of God *overcomes* the world; and this is the victory that overcomes the world, our faith . . . . And this is the testimony, that *God gave us eternal life,* and this life is in his Son. He who has the Son *has life;* he who has not the Son has not life. I write this to you who believe in the name of the Son of God, that you may know that you *have eternal life* . . . . And we know that the Son of God has come and has given us understanding, to know him who is true; and we are in him who is true, in his Son Jesus Christ. This is the true God and eternal life.

Jude 1: To those who are called, beloved in God the Father and *kept* for Jesus Christ.

Jude 24,25: Now to him who is able to *keep you from falling* and to present you without blemish before the presence of his glory with rejoicing, to the only God, our Savior through Jesus Christ our Lord, be glory, majesty, dominion, and authority, before all time and now and for ever. Amen.

This brings to completion the second phase of our survey. We have by no means exhausted the Biblical texts which support the "five points." We hope, however, that enough evidence has been presented to show that these doctrines are drawn directly from the Holy Scriptures.

A Personal Word of Conclusion

You have now completed this brief survey of the "five points." As was indicated at the outset, our goal has been threefold. First of all, we wanted to *identify* certain of the doctrines which you encountered in your study of Romans with those doctrines contained within the Calvinistic system of theology. To do this we included the material in Part I on the origin and contents of the five points. Second, we wanted to show the *interrelationship* that exists among these doctrines; for as was observed, each explains and supports the others so that together they form one harmonious system of thought. We attempted to develop this interrelationship by means of the separate introductions given to each of the five points in Part II. Third, and this is the most important! we wanted to *demonstrate* that these doctrines (dealt with in the five points) are taught not only in *Romans* but *throughout the Bible.* We did this in Part II by quoting the verses given under each of the five points.

Perhaps this has been your first formal introduction to Calvinism. Or it may be that you have previously come in contact with the system (or at least parts of it) but have never investigated the matter or given it much thought. Whatever the case may be, it is our hope that this survey will stimulate your interest and lead you into a serious study of the subject.

If you make such a study, you will find that "Calvinism is something much broader than the 'five points' indicate. Calvinism is a whole world-view, stemming from a clear vision of God as the whole world's Maker and King. Calvinism is the consistent endeavour to acknowledge the Creator as the Lord, working all things after the counsel of His will. Calvinism is a theocentric way of thinking about all life under the direction and control of God's own Word. Calvinism, in other words, is the theology of the Bible viewed from the perspective of the Bible—the God-centred outlook which sees the Creator as the source, and means, and end, of everything that is, both in nature and in grace. Calvinism is thus theism (belief in God as the ground of all things), religion (dependence on God as the giver of all things), and evangelicalism (trust in God through Christ for all things), all in their purest and most highly developed form. And Calvinism is a unified philosophy of history which sees the whole diversity of processes and events that take place in God's world as no more, and no less, than the outworking of His great preordained plan for His creatures and His church. The five points assert no more than that God is sovereign in saving the individual, but Calvinism, as such, is concerned with the much broader assertion that He is sovereign everywhere."[18]

If, in your investigation, you probe into the history and influence of Calvinism, you will discover that its doctrines have been incorporated into the majority of the great creeds of the Protestant churches; for example, the creeds or confessions of faith of the Presbyterian and Reformed Churches, the Established Church of England and her daughter the Episcopal Church of America, the free church of Holland, almost all of the churches of Scotland, and in the main the Baptist and Congregationalist Churches both in England and America are Calvinistic in contents.

Not only has Calvinism been incorporated into the creeds of the majority of the evangelical Protestant churches, it has also been championed

---

[18] Packer, "Introductory Essay," (above, fn. 4), p. 5.

by many of the churches' greatest theologians and preachers. A roll call of Calvinists would include such renowned leaders as Saint Augustine, John Wycliffe, Martin Luther, John Calvin, Ulrich Zwingli, Jerome Zanchius, Heinrich Bullinger, Martin Bucer, John Owen, George Whitefield, Augustus Toplady, John Bunyan, John Gill, John Newton, William Carey, Charles H. Spurgeon, Charles Hodge, William Cunningham, W. G. T. Shedd, A. H. Strong, B. B. Warfield, Abraham Kuyper, etc., etc.

It is not within the scope of an Appendix such as this to demonstrate the validity of such claims. However, the material in this Appendix has been published as a separate work in a paperback edition by The Presbyterian and Reformed Publishing Company of Philadelphia, Pa., under the title *The Five Points of Calvinism: Defined, Defended, Documented.* In this latter work we have added a selective bibliography which is designed to enable those interested in Calvinism to locate the major works written in English on this subject. We have *listed* and carefully *documented* (giving the author's full name, the title, the publisher's name and address, the date of publication, and number of pages) approximately 100 works dealing with Calvinistic theology. Included in this list are 60 individual books which are briefly introduced; we have indicated such things as the nature of their contents, their value, and their style. Many of the books reviewed have been written by the foremost theologians of both the past and present. They set forth and defend, explain and clarify, state and answer objections to, as well as show the influence and value of Calvinism. We have also included information on a number of systematic theologies, Confessions of Faith, booklets, and tracts.

SELECTIVE BIBLIOGRAPHY ON ROMANS

As was stated in the introduction, the *Interpretive Outline* is not a commentary in the usual sense of the word; for it does not deal with the interpretation of Romans verse by verse, nor does it discuss the conflicting views of the various interpretations which the letter has received. Instead, it was designed to aid the student to see the structure and argument of Romans and thus to understand its meaning.

For further help in the study of this important epistle, the following works are recommended. These do not exhaust the list of outstanding commentaries on Paul's letter, but were selected because of their accuracy, clarity, and usefulness. The selection was made to meet the needs of both the beginner and the advanced student of Romans. By acquiring these books, the reader will have the help necessary for solving almost any problem with which he may be faced in his study of this epistle.

Hodge, Charles, *Commentary on the Epistle to the Romans*. Grand Rapids: Wm. B. Eerdmans Publishing Company, first published 1835, rewritten 1864, reprinted 1955, 457 pages.

We agree wholeheartedly with the words of Wilbur Smith, "When one is studying the Epistle to the Romans, no matter what commentary he has on his shelf, if Hodge is there he will soon learn to turn to it first." *Profitable Bible Study*, p. 174. We consider this the best work available on Romans. Hodge gives an introductory analysis to each section, and then he comments upon each verse contained within that section. He concludes the section by listing the doctrines contained within it and then applies these principles to Christian living. He gives excellent summaries throughout his work which enable one to see the relation of the various parts to the whole. It is a superb example of accurate scholarship combined with a deep devotion to the Word of God.

Haldane, Robert, *Exposition of the Epistle to the Romans*. Jenkintown, Pa.: Sovereign Grace Publishers, first published 1835-1839, reprinted 1958, 660 pages.

Dr. Martyn Lloyd-Jones in his "Foreword" to the 1958 edition of this work states that "I always find it difficult to decide as to which is the better commentary on this Epistle, whether that of Charles Hodge or this by Haldane. While Hodge excels in accurate scholarship, there is greater warmth of spirit and more practical application in Haldane. In any case, both stand supreme as commentaries on this mighty Epistle."

Moule, Bishop H. C. G., *The Epistle of Paul the Apostle to the Romans*. London: Cambridge University Press (in the Cambridge Bible for Schools and Colleges series), first published 1879, reprinted 1903, 270 pages.

Moule's commentary, like Hodge's, is a tribute to sound scholarship. The work is concise and clear and is an invaluable help in the study of Romans. It is amazing how much information is included in so small a volume. It should be noted that Moule has also commented on Romans in *The Expositor's Bible;* the style however is very different from that which he employed in his commentary on Romans in the Cambridge Bible for Schools and Colleges series. The latter will prove much more helpful to the student, for in it Moule deals with the text, verse by verse, and gives critical justification for his interpretation, whereas in *The Expositor's Bible* he writes from the devotional point of view and gives a running exposition of the text without going into the technical justification for his conclusions.

Clark, Gordon H., "Romans," in *The Biblical Expositor*, ed., Carl F. H. Henry. Philadelphia: A. J. Holman Company, 1960, Vol. III, pp. 237-257.

Clark's is a short but excellent interpretive survey of the letter. It does not deal with the technical problems of the Greek text, nor does it state and refute the various interpretations which the author considers unsound as do the works of Hodge, Haldane and Moule. The brevity of this work (it only covers 21 pages) prohibits the consideration of such questions. However, through his masterful comprehension and clear exposition, Clark goes directly to the heart of the apostle's argument and presents what he believes to be Paul's meaning in a concise and positive manner.

Many other works of merit could be included in a list such as this, but we have purposely limited our recommendation to those works which we believe will prove to be the *most* helpful and therefore which should receive priority. However, as the student becomes familiar with Romans and the controversies that have arisen over the interpretation of this letter, he will want to include in his study other works. Below we have listed a number of commentaries which will prove helpful to varying degrees.

Arnold, Albert N., & Ford, D. B., "Commentary on the Epistle to the Romans," *An American Commentary on the New Testament.* Philadelphia: The American Baptist Publication Society, Vol. IV, 328 pages.

Alford, Henry, "The Epistle of Paul the Apostle to the Romans," *The New Testament for English Readers.* London: Rivingtons, 1865, Vol. III, 134 pages. Alford's four volume work has been recently reprinted in one volume by Moody Press, Chicago.

Brown, John, *Analytical Expositions of Romans.* Edinburgh: W. Oliphant & Co., 1857.

Calvin, John, *The Epistles of Paul to the Romans and Thessalonians*, tr. by R. Mackenzie, ed. by David W. Torrance and Thomas F. Torrance. Grand Rapids: Wm. B. Eerdmans Publishing Co., 1961, 433 pages.

Gill, John, "The Epistle of Paul the Apostle to the Romans," *An Exposition of the New Testament.* Atlanta: Turner Lassetter, 1954, 149 pages.

Hamilton, Floyd E., *The Epistle to the Romans.* Philadelphia: Presbyterian and Reformed Publishing Co., 1958, 235 pages.

Lange, J. P., "The Epistle of Paul to the Romans," *A Commentary on the Holy Scriptures.* New York: Charles Scribner & Co., 1871, Vol. V, 455 pages.

Liddon, H. P., *Explanatory Analysis of St. Paul's Epistle to the Romans.* Grand Rapids: Zondervan Publishing House, 1961, 309 pages.

Murray, John, *The Epistle to the Romans.* Grand Rapids: Wm. B. Eerdmans Publishing Co., 1959, Vol. I (Chs. I-VIII), 408 pages.

Sanday, Rev. W. & Headlam, Rev. A. C., "The Epistle to the Romans," *The International Critical Commentary.* New York: Charles Scribner's Sons, 1895, 450 pages.

SUBJECT AND AUTHOR INDEX

A

Abraham (See also Abrahamic Covenant, Jews, Land.),
Father of the Jews, 28, 94-101
Jews trusted in, for salvation, 18, 74-78
Justified by faith, 28, 33-35
God's promise to save his seed, 34, 74-78
Father of all believers, 33-35, 74-77, 92-93, 97-101
See Note No. 11, 94-101.

Abrahamic Covenant (See also Abraham, Mosaic Covenant, New Covenant.),
Twofold nature of, 95
Threefold physical promise of, 95-96
Threefold spiritual promise of, 95-97
Circumcision the sign of, 96
The Mosaic Covenant (Law) added to, 96
Full realization of, in Christ, 96-98
Jewish rejection not a failure of, 74-76
See Note No. 11, 94-101.

Adam, Created free from sin, 153
The natural head of the race, 42
Served as the representative of the race, 41-44
His first sin was imputed to the race, 37-44
Brought death and condemnation to all men, 37-44, 153-154
His fall corrupted human nature, 153
Law written on his heart, 20, 53, 55, 113
A type of Christ, 39-40
Christ, the last, 39, 42-44

Adoption (See also Believers.), 66, 67

Afflictions, Of believers, 66-68

All Men, Sense in which Christ died for, 42-44, 174

American Standard Version (See also Translations.), 3, see also fn., 26, 27, 38, 40

Amplified New Testament, The (See also Translations.), 3, 27, 40, 75, 84, 85-86, 97, 137

Apostle, 13, 54

Arminianism (See also Calvinism.),
Origin of, 141-143
Philosophical basis of, 142
Chart on the five points of, 144-147
Semi-Pelagianism, the forerunner of, 148
Diffused into the church through pagan philosophy, 147-148
Rejected by the Synod of Dort, 142-143, 147
Interpretation of foreknew in Romans 8:29, 131, 132, 134, 137
View of the atonement, 167, 168, 168 fn.

Arminius, James, 141, 142, 147, 148

Assurance (See Perseverance of the Saints.)

Atonement (See also Christ, Imputation, Justification, Faith, Calvinism, The Five Points of.),
Made by Christ, 26-27, 46-48, 51-52
Secured all the blessings of salvation, 167-171
Christ's part in the Eternal Covenant, 159, 171, 173
Arminian view of, 141, 142, 145, 167-168, 168 fn.
Calvinistic view of, 145, 166-168
Biblical defense of its limited design, 168-175

Augustine, Saint, 147, 148, 149, 190

Authority (See Bible.)

B

Baptism, 47, 48, 99

Belgic Confession, 141

Believers (See also Faith, Justification, Law.),
Abraham's seed, 33-34, 74-76, 95, 97-99
Died with Christ, 46-47
Dead to sin's guilt, 30, 32, 45-48
Under grace, not law, 49-50
Dead to the law, 51-52
Free from the law as a way of salvation, 49-52, 54-55
Under God's law as a rule of duty, 55
Love and desire to obey God's law, 56-59
Sin remains in, 57-62, 67, 126-130
Security of, 63-73, 184-188
Are in Christ (united to Him), 32, 52, 64, 65, 164, 167
Indwelt by the Holy Spirit, 66
Heirs with Christ, 66
Duties of, 55, 103-107
The weak and the strong, 108-112
See Note No. 12 on "Christian Liberty," 112-118.

Berkeley Version (See also Translations.), 3, 26, 40, 75

Berkhof, L., 126 fn.

Bible, Inspiration and authority of, 1 fn., 3
Interpretation of, 7, 115 fn.
The only rule for faith and practice, 113, 118, 152
Warning against opposing sound doctrine, 121-122

Bibliography, On Romans, 191-192
On Justification, 125
On Sanctification, 129-130

Boettner, Loraine, 149, 168, 184

193